South Asia Security Trends

South Asia Security Trends

Rahul K. Bhonsle
Brig. (Retd.)

PUBLISHERS & DISTRIBUTORS (P) LTD

Published by

ATLANTIC

PUBLISHERS & DISTRIBUTORS (P) LTD

B-2, Vishal Enclave, Opp. Rajouri Garden,
New Delhi-110027
Phones : 25413460, 25429987, 25466842

Sales Office
7/22, Ansari Road, Darya Ganj,
New Delhi-110002
Phones : 23273880, 23275880, 23280451
Fax : 91-11-23285873
web : www.atlanticbooks.com
e-mail : info@atlanticbooks.com

ISBN 978-81-269-0851-6

Printed in India
at Nice Printing Press, Delhi

Preface

"Can't live with each other, Can't live without each other."
Kant

South Asia primarily comprising of the states of Afghanistan (a recent addition), Bangladesh, Bhutan, India, Maldives, Nepal, Pakistan and Sri Lanka is emerging as the region of the future. The large population, wealth of resources, geographical significance astride the land as well as sea, lines of communications and burgeoning markets as well as employable manpower are some of the greatest strengths of this zone attracting global attention. The prospects for the teeming youth of the region are thus expanding.

The problem however lies in the gap between realisation of wealth of the future, ghosts of the past and the myriad trials of the present. People and governments are grappling with these challenges with great passion and attendant aggression that accompanies progress. Transformation places pressures on the margins as new forces attempt to breach traditional barriers of customs, traditions and societal structures and a recourse to violence appears the only path for the marginalized.

This paradox of promise and tribulations in South Asia was evident most significantly during the year 2006. The stock exchanges across the region soared (except Karachi), while India's booming economy demonstrated a steady northward trajectory pulling with it other markets as Bangladesh and Sri Lanka which had integrated under the South Asia Free

Trade Agreement (SAFTA). Perceptible observers, as noted columnist Khushwant Singh, remarked that 2006 was a good year and even went to the extent of describing it as the best since Independence.

Beneath these hopes of betterment lay many dreams gone sour as the region continued to grip with conflicts ranging from a broad spectrum of threats from the economic to human to transborder egress. The result has been that South Asian states have been swinging from crisis to crisis. For instance, as India came to grips with terrorism in Kashmir and espoused peace after almost two decades of violence, a wave of domestic terrorism in the form of heinous attacks in Mumbai and Malegaon and a spurt of Naxal incidents marred peace and threatened to upset the delicate communal harmony in the country. Pakistan discovered that it could be a target of terrorism which many believe was inbred, while Bangladesh fell victim to the rapacious onslaught of a greedy power seeking political class. Sri Lanka re-entered a fresh phase of fratricidal conflict as the Government as well as the LTTE openly declared the Cease Fire Agreement as null and void.

Nepal and Bhutan were two countries which demonstrated a turn for the better. Monarchy stepped down in Nepal, albeit due to coercion. In Bhutan in one of the most dramatic developments, King Jigme Singye Wangchuk handed over power to Crown Prince Jigme Namgyel Wangchuk who became the fifth Druk or Head of State on 14 December 2006. The handing over was preponed as the King had planned to relinquish the throne in 2008 with a simultaneous switch over to a parliamentary system of government. Perhaps more leaders in South Asia need to follow the example set by Jigme Wangchuk as they come to grips with the dichotomy of power and accountability in a permissive culture.

This book is an attempt to place the security events in South Asia in 2006 in perspective. The aim is not to provide instant history but to see beyond the media driven, hyphenated short-term view of happenings in the Subcontinent and portend the path ahead. Trend spotting especially of lurking dangers will hopefully provide the necessary motivation for adorning a sage path of cooperation, compromise and mutual assistance, for that is the way ahead for the multitudes of South Asia and not reliving memories of the past.

RAHUL K. BHONSLE

CONTENTS

INTRODUCTION

KEY TRENDS

- Afghanistan—Status quo will be a victory for NATO in 2007.
- Bangladesh—Unpredictable polity, shackles growth and economy.
- India—An overheated economy, militancy and terrorism continue to fetter the South Asian giant creating insecurities within.
- Nepal—Hope of order in the year ahead but caution will pay rich dividends.
- Pakistan—A state in peril as fundamentalism, terrorism and regionalism grips Islamabad. Will probably survive with proverbial luck and deft political maneuvering by the ruling junta.
- Sri Lanka—Fratricidal conflict continues as death wish grips the Government and the LTTE.

The South Asian region remained in the throes of small wars and insurgencies as states battled mostly with their own citizens in fratricidal conflict which defined the security flavour of the year from Kabul to New Delhi and Kathmandu to Colombo. In Afghanistan, NATO forces were trapped in their first bloody encounters after the Second World War as a resurgent Taliban struck back with vengeance in the southern belt of Kandahar and Helmand while Kabul continued to be under threat of suicide bombers. A hot summer is expected in Afghanistan particularly in the southern areas and along the Durand line as the Taliban are reportedly well entrenched in Waziristan. Pakistan faced a wave of terrorist attacks launched for the first time by the indigenous people, the most defining one being the crippling blow to national pride on the Punjab Regimental Centre at Dargai, a couple of hundred kilometers from Islamabad, which killed over 35 trainees. Balochistan continued to be on the boil with the killing of Akbar Bugti, which resulted in uniting the Marri-Mengal-Bugti tribal clans against the Pakistani regime.

In Sri Lanka, a virtual civil war, called by many analysts as Tamil Ealam IV erupted in the middle of the year and the deaths crossed over 3500, the highest after the cease fire was put into place in 2002. With hardening of stand by both sides, even the Norwegian peace mission is not hopeful of respite in the fratricidal conflict in the Island, where the LTTE losing its hold on the Eastern parts is increasingly belligerent. India steadfastly refused to take the plunge into Island politics, for how long remains to be seen.

Bangladesh remained in the midst of civil strife as elections were postponed and emergency declared in the beginning of 2007. The safe sanctuary provided to Indian terrorist groups of the North East had been a point of bitterness between the two countries apart from frequent exchange of fire between the border guards. Myanmar too is indulgent towards the militants of Manipur and Nagaland, primarily as the power of the state does not reach the remote Indo Myanmar border. Bhutan the idyllic kingdom was also rocked by unrest and blasts in its southern town of Phuntsholing with a restive Nepali refugee problem rocking the state. However an enlightened Monarch handed over power peacefully to his progeny and paved the way for elections in 2008. Nepal is one state which showed promise as a historic come down by the monarchy in the face of popular public support to the Maoists and the Seven Party Alliance will see elections supported by the United Nations in 2007.

India's tryst with terror continued, the vilest attack being on Suburban trains in the commercial capital, Mumbai in which 187 people lost their lives in July. The Naxal threat looms large in the underdeveloped tribal belt of Central India engulfing several states and affecting over 160 districts, while Kashmir and the North East continue to throw up challenges to the nation's security establishment. A coordinated multi pronged response with a resolve to stay the course alone will see some light in the year ahead.

Indo-Pakistan relations however appear to be heading towards a rapprochement of sorts. There is increasing realization in the Pakis i elite, that it cannot hold prosperity of an otherwise vibrant nation hostage to a lose-lose conflict with India. On the other hand the problems it faces in its Western areas be it Waziristan or Balochistan are likely to engage the attention providing a much needed diversion from the single point agenda of a conflict with India.

NATO forces are likely to face a resurgent and belligerent Taliban in Kabul and Kandahar. Reports already indicate that a large number of militants are being trained and given the safe sanctuaries available in Waziristan, much bloodshed can be expected. Negotiating with the Taliban as Pakistan has done will be playing with fire, a better approach would be to steadfastly support development, create visible improvements in the quality of life, extending the blanket of security and avoiding the collateral damage caused by aerial bombardment. Pakistan will also be singed by violence in Afghanistan as the peace in Waziristan remains temporary and the Baloch MMB (Mari-Mengal-Bugti) tribal combine will continue to challenge the state which has left them on the margins of development.

Sri Lanka by far will witness violence and the casualty levels are likely to increase substantially as the LTTE and the Government forces ironically believe they are engaged in one last war before return to peace. This, "last" war commenced in February and both parties are not likely to fulfill their commitment to a ceasefire which appears to be a far cry at present.

Each chapter covers the significant security trends in South Asian states in 2006 from Afghanistan, Bangladesh, India, Nepal, Pakistan to Sri Lanka. China though not a geographic part of South Asia is contiguous to the region has a major role to play, hence significant issues covering Beijing have also been covered in the book. The chapters indicate the key political and security developments in various states and an analysis has also been provided. This by no means is a chronological sequence of events but an attempt to understand the prominent trends in security in South Asia and project a possible path which may lead to solutions in the year ahead. The final chapter covers global trends in conflict impacting South Asia.

Every New Year rings in abundance, a new leaf, a hope to leave turbulence of the past behind and begin a new episode. No doubt there is much hope in the year ahead in South Asia, as the resurgent people of this vibrant region attempt to rise out of the welter of poverty, deprivation and human misery. The path to peace and security is ironically in the hands of the leaders of the states who need to forsake petty national interests for those of the region as a whole.

Afghanistan: History in Flashback?

1

"You will be brought down to your knees if Pakistan does not cooperate with you—Remember my words, if ISI is not with you and Pakistan is not with you, you will lose in Afghanistan."

Pakistan's President Pervez Musharraf on the BBC
On allegations of involvement of ISI with Taliban

"Twice I have had Harriers in support when c/s on the ground have been in heavy contact, on one occasion trying to break clean. A female harrier pilot 'couldn't identify the target', fired 2 phosphorous rockets that just missed our own compound so that we thought they were incoming RPGs (rocket-propelled grenades), and then strafed our perimeter missing the enemy by 200 meters."

Leaked E-mail of British Major in Afghanistan

KEY TRENDS—2006

Political

- Rising influence of Taliban in the South and East of the country.
- Perceived decline of power of the Karzai government restricted to Kabul and amongst key warlords. Regime perceived to be continuing in power with American support and subtle maneuvering of warlords. Regime considered reasonably stable, needing support of international community and Afghan elders.
- Perceived influence of Pakistan based Taliban in Afghan politics and through this body Pakistan intelligence agency—Inter Services Intelligence (ISI).

Militancy

- Rise of Taliban in the south and east.
- Emergence of suicide terrorism.
- Support bases for Taliban alleged in north and south Waziristan and northern Balochistan in Quetta.
- Increased number of strikes on the International Security Assistance Force (ISAF).
- Sporadic large scale attacks and occupation of areas temporarily by Taliban in the southern region.

Counter-Militancy

- NATO forces take over command of the ISAF.
- Organization of the Afghan Army and Police gains momentum. Effectiveness and influence however is restricted due to organizational and operational constraints.
- Increased use of air and helicopter strikes by NATO forces in the South creates tension between the security forces and the civil population.

Economy and Development

- Economic growth and development continues to languish.
- Development is not seen reaching grass roots. Weakens support of population to the Central Government in Kabul.
- Poppy cultivation shows an increase to 6,100 tons. Taliban capitalizes by thriving on clandestine drug economy. Some warlords also seen to benefit from higher poppy cultivation.

General

Afghanistan, the westernmost state of South Asia, saw a steep rise in violence during the year with the casualty toll estimated to be over 4000. Taliban that was said to be defeated and on the run in 2001 demonstrated phenomenal resilience by staging a comeback which, sources claimed, was due to backing by Pakistan. Tension between neighbors, Afghanistan and

Pakistan thus was high. This manifested into considerable animosities between the leadership. The key issues were support of Taliban by Pakistan and proposed construction of fencing by Islamabad on the Durand Line. Pakistan-Afghanistan border continued to be volatile. Sanctuary for Al Qaeda and Taliban remained areas of concern.[1]

NATO undertook major operational responsibility in Afghanistan after realignment and regrouping of forces during the year. This did not result in substantive operational effectiveness as the pace of Taliban resurgence continued. The organization of the Afghan National Army and Afghan National Police was a positive development though it would take long time to be operationally efficient. On the other hand, poppy cultivation touched a record high of 6,100 tons during 2006. Development in Afghanistan continues at a slow pace as security remains a key issue. This was highlighted by kidnapping and killing of an Indian engineer working for Bahrain Telecommunication Company in the beginning of the year. The restoration of stability and peace in Afghanistan is thus seen to be a long way ahead. Commitment of the international community will play a major role. Key security trends during the year have been covered herein.

POLITICAL DEVELOPMENTS IMPACTING SECURITY

General

The political trend in Afghanistan denotes relative stability, though Karzai's popularity seems to have taken a dip. He has the support of a majority of the Afghan leaders who constitute the jirga which supports the head of state in Afghanistan thus indicating limited potential threat to Karzai. He is however repeatedly accused of seeking support from tribal leaders and warlords with a dubious reputation of being a part of the crime and drug nexus. The Taliban has been attempting to make inroads into this support base, though at present their success is limited to lower strata of tribal leadership primarily in Southern Afghanistan. President Karzai understands the politics of Afghanistan and thus so far has succeeded in keeping the key leaders and elders happy by providing them a number of sops from time to time. He is quite impartial unlike the leadership in some other hot spots as Iraq and manages to keep the tribal hierarchy of all hues satiated. This is evident from examples such as nominating the powerful Uzbek warlord, Ahmed Rashid Dostum to the largely ceremonial post of Chief-of-Staff to the Commander-in-Chief of the Afghan Armed Forces.

The fall in popularity of the government due to large scale violence in the country and continued repressive measures by coalition troops however needs to be addressed urgently. Mr Karzai is seen by his detractors as an American prop. Reports also indicate that his personal security has been taken over by American Special Forces, a sure indication of lack of popular domestic support to the President. The image of President Karzai holding a joint press conference with US Secretary of State Condolezza Rice also did not go down well with the Afghan public and reflects insensitivity of American diplomats to niceties of protocol. Having the President of a country looking fetchingly at the global gendarme's diplomatic head was hardly enamoring for Karzai's image.[2]

President Karzai did assuage the population by expressing concern over large number of killings of fellow Afghans in coalition air strikes. He sought a new way to tackle terror by disarming terrorists, stopping resources of arms, money and equipment and reducing their level of motivation. While this assessment is correct in general, a dual policy would have to be adopted of simultaneously combating militants while continuing with development which can bring about lasting change. The focus on placing pressure on Pakistani leadership including President Musharraf during later part of the year perhaps arises from the need to curb support to the Taliban from Islamabad, either incidental or as a matter of deliberate policy.

Engaging the Taliban

Despite the mutual animosities, the Afghan Government did make attempts to engage the Taliban politically. However, Taliban spokesman Hanif rejected a common jirga till foreign troops were on the Afghan soil. This effort at reconciliation by Afghan and Pakistani leadership with the Taliban appears to be quite premature. Talks with militant groups are generally held when government forces have gained a clear upper hand. In this case there are no signs of a set back to Taliban, on the other hand the militancy is on a rising curve particularly in core area of southern Afghanistan and eastern areas of the country along the Durand Line. Taliban is seeking advantage of unpopularity of the Karzai government which has not been able to deliver promised governance at the grass roots. By exploiting this sentiment along with tribal affiliation the Taliban has grown from strength to strength. Thus Mullah Omar sees attempts for talks by the government as a weakness and an opportunity for grand standing. Thus recall of history of defeat of the British and Soviet forces, threat of suicide attacks in Europe, large number of trained suicide fighters ready to strike at will and opening of schools are all part of the political campaign of Taliban on an upward path.

Pakistan has been fostering an indigenous model of peace making based on the north Waziristan peace pact of September 2006 with local tribal leaders though some quarters allege the same to be with Taliban. This facilitated withdrawal of troops from the area as they were unable to suppress terrorists and suffered heavy casualties in Federally Administered Tribal Area (FATA). That area is now increasingly Talibinised and there is skepticism even in Pakistani government circles about the sagacity of this move.[3] Such a paradigm will not work in Afghanistan for the Taliban are not engaged in combat for a stake in the government but for total control over Kabul as well as Afghan society. Given the legacy of history of the state, such an eventuality is seen by the Taliban leadership as a distinct possibility. Thus till the Taliban clique of Mullahs led by Mullah Omar is neutralized, hopes of reconciliation will be limited.

The key issue would remain support of Taliban by Pakistan. Islamabad has been maintaining that the backing is by renegade elements and has no government approval. The ability of the Pakistan government to physically check support may appear limited as the writ of the state does not run in many western parts of the country along the Durand Line. On the other hand, there is considerable emotional and social empathy for Taliban in these areas and this has made the task of Islamabad difficult. Thus political stability in Afghanistan will come about only after the Taliban is sufficiently weakened to bring the leadership to a reconciliatory jirga. Till then the military option will predominate over the political. The danger lies in half measures being taken as was opted for by Pakistan in north Waziristan. This will only be a temporary reprieve for Karzai and the NATO (North Atlantic Treaty Organization) forces providing Mullah Omar space to once again rejuvenate forces.

THE BATTLE FOR CONTROL IN AFGHANISTAN IN 2006

General

The rise of the Taliban especially in southern Afghanistan areas of Kandahar, Helmand, Zabul and Uruzgan was evident as early as April 2006 even as the spring thaw raised temperatures. In a major clash on 14 April, 41 insurgents and 6 government troops were killed in Jalal Panjwai, Kandahar. Government troops used air support to cause heavy casualties to terrorists. In Kunar province a rocket exploded in Asadabad school on 12th April 2006, while on 23th April in Kandahar Taliban attacked a US construction company and 14 vehicles were torched on Uruzgan-Kandahar highway.[4] By June 2006 the emergence of a resurgent Taliban was acknowledged by the US commander in Afghanistan, Lt Gen Karl Eikenberry in his testimony to US lawmakers. The ability of the Taliban to establish new bases and direct operations against Alliance Forces was the most significant accretion to the force potential which thus provided a new dimension to the guerrilla war in Afghanistan.[5] A survey of attacks in 2005 and 2006 has been tabulated as per Table 1 below:[6]

Table 1: Survey of Attacks 2005 and 2006

Type of Attacks	2005	2006
Suicide	27	139
Roadside bombs	783	1677
Direct attacks by small arms, grenades and weapons	1558	4542

NATO took over operations in southern Afghanistan and deployed 6,000 troops in the south in end July replacing 3,000 coalition troops in Helmand, Kandahar, Uruzgan and Zabul. NATO strength in Afghanistan rose to 28,000. This was supplemented by the Afghan National Army, the quality and credibility of which remains questionable. NATO forces designated as International Security and Assistance Force (ISAF) were under British Command for nine months of the year with Lt General David Richards heading the force. Richards had the unenviable task of reining in a resurgent Taliban, impose government rule in the provinces and persuade local rulers to agree to being governed from Kabul.

Survey of Operations

During the peak campaigning season in the country from August 2006, the Taliban—NATO stand off in southern Afghanistan continued apace. An increase in attacks by NATO forces on Taliban hide-outs in Kandahar and Helmand was noticeable. The Panjweyi Valley in particular was the focus of operations with NATO forces successfully claiming to have killed a large number of Taliban using a combination of air and helicopter strikes with ground operations. There were deaths on both sides, with British and Canadian forces bearing the brunt, including death of 14 British soldiers in a helicopter crash which the Taliban falsely claimed to have been inflicted by its rockets. Reports indicate that the intensity of operations has been so heavy that the British helicopters did not have any respite during the period.[7]

However, civilian casualties in air strikes did not bode well for NATO as use of air power in counter militancy where guerrillas operate in a sea of population is always fraught with the risk of killing innocents. It also inures locals after some time and despite the lessons of Soviet fate in Afghanistan a decade and a half ago, the temptation to use air power has perhaps been too high for NATO experiencing intense counter insurgency combat for the first time. The proclivity for greater use of air power was also due to limited density of troops on the ground. Counter militancy operations are troop intensive. The recommended density is said to be 20 individuals per 4 square miles of territory as per noted guerrilla leader, T.E. Lawrence.[8] Against this norm, NATO deployment in Afghanistan is 28,000 troops. The USA has approximately 24,000 while the Afghan Army another 30,000. This makes a total strength of 82,000. This leaves large tracts of territory unsecured thereby providing inimical elements as the Taliban a free run.

Building up on intelligence and experience in combat in September, NATO troops undertook a large scale operation, code named Medusa to gain control of insurgency in Kandahar, the most violent of all provinces. However, despite heavy casualties, there was limited success. There was increased pressure on other NATO countries as Germany which is occupying the Provincial Reconstruction Team (PRT) in the relatively quiet northern provinces to send reinforcements to the south. Given the peculiar command and control of NATO in Afghanistan, deployment of national forces continued to be with the approval of the home government. Thus the brunt of the fighting was borne by the Canadian, British and Dutch forces in the south.

The resistance in southern Afghanistan initially surprised NATO commanders, which was a clear case of inability to assess the military situation before deployment of troops. After rapid occupation of Kabul, in 2001, there were limited efforts by the US forces to consolidate government control over southern Afghanistan which has been the stronghold of Taliban with Kandahar being the base. US forces on the other hand chose to hunt for Osama in the eastern areas adjoining Pakistan on the Durand Line. Taliban gained a respite and increased its presence in a large number of areas in the south particularly in Kandahar and Helmand. There were reports of their spread in other areas as well.

The death toll in Afghanistan till October had increased to 3,000 including 150 foreign soldiers. During that month a major operation was carried out by NATO forces in the Panjweyi Valley in Kandahar province, the heart of Taliban militancy on 25 and 26 October. Taliban claimed that NATO air strikes caused a large number of civilian casualties. The Taliban continued to attack Afghan government offices, aid organizations, vehicles and security posts. Tribal clashes were reported in Herat province which left almost 30 personnel dead. Kabul remained under constant threat of suicide attacks with the area of National Stadium and the Kabul—Jalalabad road being the key targets. Rocket attacks at night in Kandahar and other cities of the southern region were also common. The Taliban also mustered a large number of vehicles which were repainted in UN as well as Afghan Army colors for possible use in vehicle borne suicide attacks.

NATO forces planned to continue operations through the winter to eliminate the Taliban and set the stage for a final push in spring. The need for information operations and reconstruction was also appreciated. Conduct of strike operations in Waziristan and the North West Frontier Area was also discussed.[9] This option is fraught with political and military risks. Pakistan will not allow such an operation to take place on its territory. There have been frequent protests over alleged attacks by helicopters of US Armed Forces in Pakistani territory. Ground operations will thus not be acceptable. Air and helicopter attacks may be one option but there was risk of fratricide. On the other hand, militarily NATO does not have the troop strength or capability to conduct operations beyond Afghanistan where again it is thin on the ground. Thus continued dependence on Pakistan remains the answer. However with abdication of military responsibility over Waziristan and the writ of Pakistani government running low in North West Frontier Province, this area will continue to provide sanctuary to the Taliban.

With the onset of early winter there was some drop in level of operational activity and violence in November. The period was utilized for consolidation and taking stock of results achieved. Two key Taliban commanders were decapitated during December to include Mullah Mohammad Usman, commander of the Taliban militants in Ghazni who was arrested while Mohammad Osmani was killed in Helmand. NATO forces also used this period to turn over troops while Taliban recuperated from the serious losses it suffered throughout the region as well as in outlining strategy for the coming year.

The Taliban added the suicide attack, a relative novelty in Afghanistan to their operational repertoire. Mullah Omar proclaimed intention of attacks particularly on Kabul. These comprised of vehicle borne IEDs and suicide fighters. Thus Afghanistan saw a rise in suicide bombings during the year with more than 90 attacks reported in which over 100 people were killed in September and October while a year back no suicide attacks had been reported. In addition 17 suicide bombers were captured during the period. A large number of these personnel are reportedly trained in Pakistan. There are also reports of transfer of Improvised Explosive Device (IED) expertise from Iraq to Afghanistan.

US military intelligence reports indicated that a cell had been formed in Kabul specifically to target foreign troops. Hamir Mir, a Pakistani journalist, also indicated that 300 Taliban suicide bombers had entered Kabul and Jalalabad specifically to target Western forces during Ramadan. Mir is also reported to have stated that the Taliban have established governance in some parts in southern Afghanistan and the Afghan police are taking orders from them.[10]

The focus of victims shifted from local political leaders and groups to Western troops in the hope that this would put pressure for withdrawal by governments which are less committed to the cause of reestablishing order in Afghanistan. The aim of the terrorists was also to dispel the myth that Kabul is a secure place so that more nations are dissuaded from opening embassies and companies are prevented from establishing offices. Greater integration with the outside world will mean peace, which is not in keeping with the aims of the Taliban. The security forces had to exercise greater caution even during the winter months.

UK's Musa Qala Truce

While the Pakistan government had made peace with the Taliban in North Waziristan in September 2006, the British forces were alleged to have made a similar arrangement in Helmand region. A report in the *Times*, London by Michael Smith outlined details of the truce. It was reported to be a secret agreement with the elders in the area which proscribes the Taliban as well as the British forces from operating in Musa Qala, Sangin, Nowzad and Kajaki areas of Helmand province. British platoon posts in the area called as, "platoon houses" were said to be acting as, "magnets" for the Taliban which struck at regular intervals with mortars and rockets causing a number of civilian casualties as also disrupted routine life. It was reported that of the population of 2000 in Musa Qala, 400 had to be evacuated from the district center.

In deal-making in Lawrence of Arabia fashion, Brigadier Ed Butler, flew into Musa Qala protected only by his personal bodyguards and attended a shura of town elders to negotiate a withdrawal. The emphasis by both sides was on cessation of fighting and not ceasefire, which in the battle for moral ascendancy assumes importance as Afghans have an anathema for ceasefire. The British soldiers were replaced by Afghans in the town and the Taliban agreed not to launch attacks on the district center. It was reported that 9 British servicemen were killed in Musa Qala due to Taliban attacks on platoon houses.[11]

There was a lot of skepticism about the Musa Qala truce which is said to be an experiment by the British with the hope that locals will be able to keep the Taliban at bay. While there is no surety of this happening, as the Taliban with their ethnic affinity can force local elders to break their agreement, it is a better arrangement than pounding villages with air and helicopters which the British had been engaged in so far. The main concern is that these areas should not become sanctuaries for the Taliban and for this purpose certain surveillance arrangements were worked out with the locals rather than relying on their verbal assurances. The fragility of this arrangement has been evident as the Taliban are reported to have occupied Musa Qala in the post-winter season in 2007.

A Review of Operations

The large number of strikes on NATO forces who were being baptized under fire after decades of peace rattled many governments in Europe and there was resistance to build up from the current force of approximately 30,000. An accretion of 2,500 was planned which would be just a drop in the ocean as the Afghan Army will not be able to make up the shortfall. The level of professionalism desired to withstand militants was also lacking. The curious ethnic mix in the country as well as the Army is also acting as a stumbling block towards greater nationalization. A truly national Afghan Army and police are thus a long way off. Similarly, the country's socio-political culture and various unwritten civil codes as the Pushtunwali, make laws difficult to implement even for heinous crimes as murder. Reasons for poor performance of NATO is said to be due to limited strength on ground, lack of experience, support to Taliban by Pakistan, socio-political complexities of militancy and large quantum of funds made available to Taliban through control of poppy.

Resentment against American and Western troops in Afghanistan erupted with the killing of five people when an US Army vehicle crashed in a busy area in Kabul due to brake failure in May 2006. The resultant riots left 14 people dead. Instigation of these riots by anti-American elements cannot be ruled out. The need for alien troops to be extremely careful in interacting with locals was once again highlighted. A superior and supercilious attitude never pays, as the Indian Army with very wide experience in this field has realized over the years. While the intent of the political and military hierarchy may be noble, it many times translates on the ground into authoritative control and dominance over ethnically variant and economically weaker people. The we-they syndrome is most noticeable at the ground level and such incidents of violence can only be avoided if troops are psychologically attuned to be seen as working in the interests of the people rather than enforce law and order or even, "peace".

NATO use of air power will also prove counter-productive in the long run. It would be better to isolate small terrorist groups and neutralize them by small arms and mortars rather than air strikes. Air strikes are being exploited by Taliban claiming large scale civilian casualties. This may increase the degree of difficulty in neutralizing the Taliban in the short term but may pay in the longer run, for it is a battle for peace in Afghanistan and not killing as many Taliban as possible as NATO forces appear to be undertaking at present.

The Taliban was seen to grow from strength to strength. A good poppy crop at 6,100 tons provided them adequate money to fund their campaign. A stronghold in Waziristan was supplemented by presence in Quetta where the ISI is reported to have provided them safe houses. This enabled a wide arc of Taliban influence in pockets extending from the south west provinces of Nimroz, Helmand, Kandahar to the North East along the Durand line on the Pak-Afghan border.

The Taliban organized forces in large bands of over 70 to 150 and launched more or less conventional attacks, which also provided NATO forces opportunity to use superior fire power particularly air and helicopter. The key area of conflict has been Kandahar and Helmand where troops from Britain, The Netherlands and Canada have been deployed leading to the largest number of casualties to NATO in this area. Queen Elizabeth II in her Christmas message paid a tribute to valiant British soldiers in Iraq and Afghanistan, 42 of whom have lost their lives in Helmand. The British were also castigated for a truce made with the locals alleged by detractors as with the Taliban in Helmand's Musa Qala. The posts were withdrawn from the district centre as it had reportedly become a key target for Taliban attacks, in the process causing harassment and casualties to civilian population in the surrounding areas.[12]

The growth of Taliban and NATO experience in Afghanistan is being covered hereafter.

TALIBAN RESURGENCE

The Taliban is reported to have moral and military control over half of Afghanistan with the areas in the south and the east believed to be dominated by it, as per Afghanistan Independent Human Rights Commission. However, Stratfor.com believes that this may not be entirely true and the major influence is essentially in terms of ability to conduct disruptive activities rather than physical control to include governance. Other independent reports too do not indicate that the Taliban is carrying out effective governance in the area but has only local networks.[13] Taliban was quick to exploit control of poppy cultivation, ethnic and tribal loyalties and excesses committed by NATO forces particularly in terms of air strikes to win over the local populace. It was able to pay at least three to four times the sum paid by the Afghan government to the police and military to its fighters as reported in the *Security Trends,* November 2006 issue.

The reemergence of a Taliban threat thus engaged many Afghan watchers. A number of factors have led to this rise. While Pakistan reportedly attempted to step up vigilance in Waziristan, this did not have much impact on ground where remoteness of the area and its harsh terrain as well as a general culture of violence, lawlessness and fundamentalism provided the Taliban ideal space to fill the vacuum. The various treaties that the Pakistan government had with the Taliban in Waziristan, southern Waziristan in 2004 and northern Waziristan in September 2006 has been a subject of much debate. Even Pakistan government sources now admit that this truce is providing space to the Taliban to operate at will.[14] Some reports indicated that Taliban in Afghanistan comprised mainly of Pakistani and Afghani youth trained in the madarasas of north and south Waziristan. These terrorists are fighting a proxy war to subvert development in the country by Western countries, India and the Afghan government.[15]

Taliban also targeted Afghans who were assisting Western forces. They undertook classic activities of guerrilla groups such as burning schools and health centers which represent signs of progress. Taliban increasingly concentrated in small groups and attempted to raise the rebel flag in the southern and western districts of Afghanistan. The followers of former Prime Minister Gulbuddin Hekamatyar and his group, the Hizb-e-Islami is also said to have played a major role in this area though an attempt to form a coalition with Taliban was rejected by the Mullahs.

Mullah Omar, the Taliban chief, had warned of a bloody summer which was confirmed with the entire expanse of the area between Kabul and Kandahar–Zabul–Helmand on the boil. The level of violence in the areas which have been handed over by US forces to NATO in the south increased over a period which alarmed the Alliance as well as the UN.[16] What was significant is the intelligence failure that preceded the offensive by the Taliban. The Alliance as well as the Afghan Government appear to have limited information of the rise of the Taliban or in case they had, did not carry out in-depth analysis of possible manifestations.

The Taliban which had shunned the media in its previous avatar has been vocal in castigating the Karzai regime. Mullah Omar, Taliban commander, has proclaimed that President Karzai will have to face Islamic courts in the future for his alliance with the West. While these may be empty boasts, the danger of continued insurgency in Afghanistan necessitates a year of continuous engagement, military, political, and economic development for the world community.

OPERATIONAL DEPLOYMENTS—NATO AND US FORCES

NATO forces fought their first ground war in Afghanistan after their initiation in the air war in Kosovo in 1999. The measure of success by NATO in Afghanistan is evident as it has limited Taliban to hit and run operations and suicide strikes as opposed to military operations they were undertaking at the beginning of the year. This was also the first time that the USA has placed troops under NATO command. The battle has been won but the war is far from over as NATO forces are facing increased resistance from local population in the area of Kandahar partially due to massive helicopter and air bombardment causing very heavy damage to civil lives and property which the Taliban has been cashing on.

Redeployment of forces and review of operational responsibilities was undertaken in Afghanistan during the year. The strength of US forces was reduced by 2000 and troops were redeployed from the south to the eastern part along the Durand Line. NATO forces under British command took over South and Central Afghanistan. This redeployment was carried out when southern Afghanistan was in turmoil. NATO defence chiefs agreed to increase the strength by an accretion of 2,500 troops which was ratified by the governments at home. The total requirement however may be of a much larger contingent. NATO commitment in Afghanistan will increase with induction of an additional 2000 to 2500 troops in Afghanistan. This will take the strength up to over 30,000. US forces in Afghanistan also came under NATO control which facilitated unified coalition command in the country. NATO agreed to expand its military operations into eastern Afghanistan, even as it struggles to find troops to hold off a dogged Taliban-led insurgency in the volatile south.[17]

NATO forces undertook active operations particularly in the Kandahar area where the Taliban reestablished its hold in some of the traditional areas, such as the Panjweyi Valley. The success in elimination of large Taliban bands came to NATO with a heavy price. An adverse sentiment is gradually building up against Western forces due to excessive use of air and helicopter fire power which has seen the death of a number of civilians. The hearts and minds battle has thus received a serious setback.

The Helmand area which was a key area of operations has been pro-Taliban as the reach of the Afghan government has been limited. The aim of deployment in the area was to ensure that governance reaches the people. The British have been making efforts to rebuild houses destroyed in the campaign but this has apparently not satisfied the locals as there are reports that there has been large scale corruption in these deals. The British practice of deployment of troops in such areas in platoon strength rightly denoted as "magnets" invited Taliban reaction. Normal posts should be minimum a company as this has the requisite leadership, command and control, reserve as well as fire power to combat a larger threat. However, given the shortage of troops and due to pressure from the Afghan government, it is envisaged that the British were forced to deploy in penny packets. Deals with the moderate Taliban may be attempted by the US civil and political authorities on the lines of the North Waziristan pact made by Pakistan. While this may seem an honorable exit to the Western forces, it would be a problematic step for the Afghan government which has no scope for an exit.

General Richards, the joint commander, recognized the necessity to take Pakistan on board the efforts of the International Security Assistance Force (ISAF) to bring order into Afghanistan. He was seeking positive backing rather than confronting Musharraf with evidence of support by Pakistan intelligence agencies to the Taliban. Pakistan has powerful leverages in Afghanistan which are based on geographical proximity, tribal ties built over centuries and the large number of refugees which continue to be hosted in the country. Pakistan seems to have its own logic to the state of affairs in Afghanistan. One opinion goes that it seeks to keep it unstable so that it remains in the eye of the West, with substantial aid both military and civil flowing into the treasury. Pakistan has reportedly received $ 3.6 billion in aid over the past five years as per the US Congressional Research Service. Thus it is alleged that there has never been a serious effort on the part of Islamabad to support stability in Afghanistan.

NATO forces carried out systematic documentation of involvement of Inter Services Intelligence (ISI) of Pakistan in the rise of the Taliban in Afghanistan. An indication of this trend has been the large stocks of ammunition which were used in Operation Medusa in southern Afghanistan during the year, amounting to 400,000 rounds of small arms, 1,000 shells of mortar and 2,000 rocket propelled grenades. Ammunition dumps have also been noticed some of which were known to contain over a million rounds. This could not have been possible without the assistance of the ISI and Pakistan. Details of the entire operation planned by the ISI is likely to be exposed to include training camps, ammunition provided, weapons and the support infrastructure established for Mullah Omar in Quetta. Reports also indicate that approximately 1,500 Taliban fighters had been involved in Operation Medusa in the first fortnight of September.[18]

Quetta was reported to have been established as a base for Taliban where a number of safe houses had been set up by the ISI as indicated by Security-risks.com in August. The Baloch population was reported to be quite upset with the ingress of the Taliban in their area. To assuage the locals, Pakistani police carried out raids in some areas of Quetta though this was considered a sham exercise.

At least one British officer, Captain Leo Docherty resigned from the British Army protesting against the inept manner in which air power was being utilized in Afghanistan. As aide de camp to Colonel Charlie Knaggs in southern Afghanistan, Captain Leo would have been in the knowledge of planning and coordination of operations in the area. The officer protested intensive use of air power in the campaign saying that this would alienate the local population. Quite rightly so, as the Taliban is continually taking advantage of British air strikes and vitiating the population, alienating it against Coalition forces for their harsh methods. The officer protested the use of air power to solve problems which were more in the realms of politico-social security.[19]

The need for ensuring that aid and assistance reaches people in remote areas is paramount for the success of the NATO mission. Winter was the critical period as it indicated the level of determination of the Taliban in pursuing hit and run and suicide operations. Spring 2007 is even more ominous as it would denote to what extent the Taliban has rejuvenated and is able to adopt conventional mode of warfare.

NATO forces need to rotate troops and induct additional forces as well as aid agencies in Afghanistan so that the work of rebuilding the country starts in real earnest particularly in southern Afghanistan. The caveats imposed by many countries has greatly hampered full-scale employment and effective utilisation. Lt General Richards, the British commander, was frank in stating this to the media. It is reported by the *Economist* that when General Richards wanted to redeploy the NATO strategic reserve battalion from France in September at the critical phase of the operations in southern Afghanistan, the French government declined on the plea of a requirement in the Balkans.[20] NATO is also faced with a number of inter-operability problems as per the same report with lack of high altitude helicopters and compatible radio sets.

NATO's original commitment to Afghanistan was as a stabilization mission rather than a counter insurgency operation. However increasingly Southern Afghanistan is representing a war zone. Thus, NATO finds the mission changing from stabilization to peace making. More so, there is a need for a joint coordination with a large number of agencies operating in the area from different countries, with differing languages and varied agendas. Coordinating their functioning on the ground is essential to bring about stability.

The disagreements and pressures within the NATO alliance in waging the war in Afghanistan were also evident with the US ambassador castigating nations such as France, Germany, Italy, Spain and Turkey for their unwillingness to deploy troops in the more active southern region. Thus the pressure was mainly on British and Canadian troops. This considerably reduced flexibility of NATO as they find that at critical times they are short of troops. Fire power cannot make up this deficiency of what is commonly known as "boots on the ground". NATO shortfall in Afghanistan is said to be up to 15 per cent or 2500 troops as per NATO Supreme Allied Commander of Europe US Marine Corps Gen James Jones. In addition, there was a need for helicopters, transport aircraft and communication equipment. The shortfall was partly made up by the Polish contingent of 800 which arrived in January 2007. A dichotomy in common operational lexicon and concepts within the coalition was also evident with American policy of confrontation seen in direct opposition to European policy of engagement through consensus. The Americans want counter-terrorism and counter-insurgency operations to be given priority, while the Europeans prefer to call these stabilization and peacekeeping.[21]

The first Australian troops landed in Uruzgan in September. The area was relatively quiet and under control. This gave time to the soldiers from Down Under to settle down before they were engaged in active hostilities and peace building. The Australians are working in tandem with the Dutch contingent focusing on reconstruction. The commitment of a number of smaller but important European nations to peace and security in Afghanistan has been admirable. The Czech Armed Forces particularly distinguished themselves in major operations undertaken during the year including command of the vital task of defence of Kabul airport. The Czech Republic forces ensured smooth rotation of contingents and command of the Kabul air transport traffic, the lifeline to Afghanistan. Czech 601 Special Forces Group also distinguished in special operations in the highly sensitive Kandahar area during the year.[22] Such commitment of smaller nations to the NATO cause is thus admirable and needs emulation by major powers.

Public opinion in Britain, Canada and Italy has been increasingly against greater NATO commitment. Now that it has taken the plunge, NATO has to stick the course. The large number of western aid agencies involved in Afghanistan also requires presence of troops for security while fulfilling the task of nation-building. It will be a tough road ahead for the coalition with varied pressures, political and military, from different countries spread across two continents fighting a war on a third in the most challenging battlefield of the world and against the most battle hardened fighters. But the fruits of victory when it comes will firmly establish European nations in an advantageous position geopolitically.

TRENDS, PROBLEMS AND ISSUES IN AFGHANISTAN

Afghanistan has been a very difficult country to govern throughout its history. There are strong reasons to believe that a federal form is the best way of governance. An attempt to control the large number of tribes and sub-tribes who are fiercely independent have always failed, particularly in the south and the east. US and the NATO forces thus need to review their strategy in Afghanistan, adopt a more tribe-friendly approach, isolate the Taliban and bring benefits of presence of foreign donors and security evident to the indigenous people. This is a tall order. Dependence of the locals on poppy cultivation over the years is also difficult to reverse within a short period given that the area is dry, barren and has unusually cold winter.

Bloody battles are seen ahead in Afghanistan. History is not on the side of the Western alliance and with Pakistan either playing truant or unable to control the Pashtun tribal in its western border provinces of Waziristan and Balochistan, a carefully crafted strategy alone will reap dividends in the next three to four years. However, there are no indications of this happening as the problem is seen through a monocle perspective of preventing Taliban resurgence by mass extermination of concentrations and a search for the elusive, Osama.

The problems in Afghanistan are many. The troops available to the Government to bring the situation under control are extremely limited. An issue of concern is the likelihood of a correlation between suicide attacks and rural incidents of violence. A statement by Mullah Omar denotes that there may be some coordination in both these operations, which is dangerous. These could be coordinated by one of the Mullahs or covert leadership provided by the ISI. NATO forces are relatively inexperienced and hence are likely to face an uphill task as the support from the Afghan National Army is limited and of poor quality. It may be prudent to ensure a step-by-step approach extending operational reach in line with the ability to control an area effectively. Gradual extension will ensure that troops are operating within the reach of their own abilities. Effective use of air power without collateral damage will also pay rich dividends. Getting the rebel Taliban on board will be a major exercise in reconciliation which may receive some consideration.

With Taliban and feudal war lordism on the rise in this area, there is considerable speculation of the commitment and operational capabilities of NATO forces that provides them the ability to survive the brutal fighters. NATO is expecting to carry out more reconstruction work rather than anti-terrorist operations. Thus rebuilding schools, health centers, roads and so on will be the priority. However, there are reports that already over 250 schools have been destroyed by the Taliban.[23] Thus willy nilly, NATO forces will be drawn into combat situations where they will have to flush out terrorists from their hideouts. The troops thus need to be prepared for such missions, rather than being surprised by being engaged by the Taliban in a number of fire fights. The key issue in Afghanistan is getting Pakistan on board the US–NATO combine. This will cut off covert support to the feudal militias threatened by loss of control of the sizable narcotics pie once the situation stabilizes in the country.

THE AFGHAN NATIONAL ARMY—A BRIEF

In rebuilding Afghanistan's institutions the United States is the lead agency for reorganizing the Afghan army, Germany is to rebuild the police, Japan is heading the disarming task force along with demobilizing and reintegrating of combatants, Italy is heading judicial reforms while UK is in the forefront of counter narcotics operations. Increase in poppy cultivation in the country is a sad reflection on the effectiveness and efficiency of the British forces in Afghanistan though this is in many ways the most challenging task involving both civil and military effort in the face of stiff resistance as poppy cultivation has been the backbone of income for the Taliban.

The Afghan National Army is rapidly growing into a symbol of nation rebuilding with the strength reaching 30,000 against its goal of 70,000 by 2009. Every month 1000 soldiers are being added. The ethnic composition of the Army however needs to be based on a mix representing overall tribal balance for it to be regarded as a primary national instrument of power. The US which is the nodal agency for building the Afghan Army is committed to provide equipment worth $ 2 billion over the next one to one and half year including a large supply of body armor, protective helmets, M 16 rifles and heavy armored vehicles. A new National Military Command Center has been established and Roshan Safi has been selected as the first sergeant major of the Army recently. At present it is stated that the problem of desertions has been largely overcome, though there continue to be minor infringements till the troops are fully disciplined.

The basic unit of the Afghan National Army is the Battalion or the Kandak, most of which are infantry battalions though one mechanized and one tank battalion has also been formed. A total of 28 battalions of the proposed 31 have already been raised with nine brigades planned, each comprising of 6 battalions. The location of the Corps are stated to be 201 Corps at Kabul, 203 at Gardez, 205 Corps at Kandahar,

207 Corps at Herat and 209 Corps at Mazar-e-Sharif.[24] One brigade each has been allotted to each Corps with a large number of troops deployed in Kabul.

The quality of Afghan troops needs to be improved by effective training and administrative back-up. It is likely to take another three to five years for the Afghan Army to be rebuilt into a national force. Its survival at the end of the day is however still doubtful as divergent forces will continue to pull apart feudal loyalties of the men that has divided Afghan society over the years. The total strength is envisaged to grow to 70,000. The actual requirement may be almost twice the number as reported by the Afghan Defence Minister. The addition of 1000 troops every month is considered as the maximum possible in the time and type of deployment that is required to be undertaken. 3500 troops of the overall American force have been dedicated to train the Afghan Army and the police.

In addition, police forces are also being reorganized to include a Regional command in the south at Kandahar on 31st May and Regional Command East in Gardez on 2nd July. The police are being given training in establishing rule of the law and anti-corruption. The strength of the police is to be raised to 70,000 which at present has already reached 58,000 though all personnel are not adequately equipped. The police have received 45,000 new uniforms, 8000 new vehicles, thousands of weapons and millions of rounds of ammunition.[25] The key problem with the police is pay which is $ 100 per month as against which the Taliban pays $ 250. A shortage of police equipment is said to beset the Afghan police force as only 37,000 are properly equipped. Of the requirement of 85,000 vehicles there are only 2000 which are available to the force.[26]

OPIUM PRODUCTION IN AFGHANISTAN

The UN Office on Drugs and Crime (UNDOC) has indicated that production of opium in Afghanistan was likely to reach a new high of 6,100 tons in 2006, which will be 92 per cent of the world's supply, representing an increase of nearly 50 per cent year on year from 41 per cent in 2005. There is a rise of over

59 per cent in the area under opium cultivation to 165,000 hectares this year from 104,000 hectares in 2005. An issue of concern is the increase of over 162 per cent in Helmand which is being dominated by the Taliban with an increase to 69,324 hectares in 2006 or 42 per cent of the total area. In terms of production in the same ratio this would account for 2,562 tons, which will earn it an income of $ 3 billion. Drugs have a powerful influence in the economy of rural Afghanistan, as Taliban recycles drug money by intimidating rural population and also in many cases buying their loyalty. The war against drugs would thus have to be increased in intensity. The increase in drug production enables the Taliban to pay the fighters $ 8 a day, compared to about $ 4 a day for Afghan Army soldiers and $ 2 a day for the national police.[27]

The inability to control the proliferation of drugs is attributable to international drug smuggling syndicates, corruption and lack of sufficient incentives to farmers for cultivating other crops. Antonio Maria Costa, Executive Director of the UN Office on Drugs and Crime (UNODC), proposed a system of punishment and rewards to solve the problem, thereby 6 provinces out of the total 34 which were drug free being rewarded with greater aid *vis-à-vis* those which had not undertaken measures to reduce cultivation of poppy. As per some reports, this is inducing people to turn to poppy cultivation merely to claim relief, thereby once again playing into the hands of the Taliban.

The opium production was 180 tons before US ousted the Taliban in 2002, while it was 4,100 tons in 2005 and 6,100 tons in 2006 valued at $ 3 billion. The availability of drug money appears to be the key factor in the spring battles, as 6,100 tons of poppy is a lot of money and will fund the Taliban as well as be an useful source of income for the Afghan farmer. Helmand, Kandahar, Balkh, Farah and Badakshan have seen increase in poppy cultivation even though the total area under cultivation has declined from 131,000 hectares in 2004 to 104,000 hectares in 2005. While Nangarhar, Uruzgan and other provinces in central and west Afghanistan showed some decline in production, the total reached 4,100 tons, in 2005 based on an average of 39 kg per hectare yield in the country. At US $ 100 per kg, the total yield works out to $ 410 million, enough to keep any insurgency going for a long while.

ECONOMY, AID DEVELOPMENT AND NATION-BUILDING

The Afghanistan Compact signed at London at a conference of the international community on Afghanistan from 31 January-1 February 2006 enumerated the principles of security, aid and development in the country. This has been the reference point for all agencies in pursuit of peace in the country. Benchmarks and time lines of wide ranging issues have been adopted in the Compact including governance, economic revival and development in all spheres. The unique Afghan culture has been accepted and development is seen to foster the same. The implementation of the Compact however has not made a recognizable difference in the situation in the country. Sufficient period perhaps needs to elapse before tangible benefits are seen on the ground.

The Second Regional Economic Cooperation Conference on Afghanistan was held in Delhi from 18 and 19 November 2006. The aim of the conference was to focus on energy, transport, business and agriculture needs of the country and reassure support to the Afghan government from the international community particularly regional states. The Conference discussed a range of issues concerning Afghanistan and included Iranian Foreign Minister Manuchehr Mottaki, French Foreign Minister Philippe Douste Blazy and Russian Foreign Minister Sergey Lavrov along with key officials of the US and Pakistan foreign services. A parallel meeting of the business and industry federations in India and Afghanistan was also held to focus on private sector investment. A number of countries including China and aid agencies such as Aga Khan Development Network were invited for the Conference and provided much needed boost to assistance in Afghanistan. That the conference was held in India was of significance as this implied a reduction in resistance to a role by New Delhi in Kabul from Pakistan which has considered Afghanistan as its own turf. A realization is perhaps slowly dawning on Islamabad that a stable government in Kabul would be better than instability which has wracked the area for over two to three decades now.

The Indian Prime Minister in his speech assured New Delhi's support to the Afghan Government. The admission of Afghanistan to SAARC has been an important development during the year and underlines its strategic significance as a buffer state between Central and West Asia, China and the Indian subcontinent. Indian's extended vision of prosperity was also highlighted by the Prime Minister which includes the littoral states who should benefit from the 8 to 10 per cent growth envisaged in the country. Indian efforts to promote trade with Afghanistan by establishing the Zaranj–Delaram Highway linking the Garland Highway, the Mazar-e-Sharief Kabul-Kandahar-Herat axis with ports in Iran however has been delayed. The project is now likely to be completed by December 2008.

The impetus that the US army engineers are planning to provide to reconstruction and development projects during the coming year, 2007 (US Fiscal Year Oct. 1, 2006, to Sept. 30, 2007) should be a welcome step in contributing to peace in the region. There are reported to be 600 projects in the pipe line worth $ 1 billion. NATO commanders have been harping on the issue of taking up projects which demonstrate commitment of Western governments to the people of Afghanistan.[28] Some key issues however need to be considered as follows:

Firstly, use of Afghan labor on the projects will reduce unemployment. By providing alternate means of livelihood, this will assist the civil government in meeting the grievances of the people. On the other hand, by providing electricity there will be a visible change to their lives. Roads will encourage trade and development, thereby providing impetus to local economy and also facilitate the fruits of development reaching remote areas. The agencies should consider labor intensive projects and to that extent the use of automated and powered equipment may have to be restricted in the country despite likely delay in completion. Since most projects are due for completion in 2008, creating a security atmosphere to facilitate the same would be important.

Education is a burning issue in Afghanistan. The low level of education at present in the country has denoted the need for emphasis on this aspect. Civil affairs staff and even volunteers on the lines of the Peace Corps could be employed for this purpose. The general educational system will have to be supplemented by a vocational one, thereby weaning away youth of the country from militancy.

One of the long-term tasks of nation-building in Afghanistan is transforming the nation from tribalism. The Taliban is taking advantage of tribalism, by networking loyalties of various tribes and sub-tribes, thereby creating a large support base particularly in southern Afghanistan. The Western approach to this problem has been to buy out tribal leaders, which may only work in the short term. The Afghan tribal is known to switch his loyalties very quickly. However, he will sustain his filial affiliations with people with whom he is sure of building a long term relationship. This is where Pakistan has an advantage despite allegations of its indulging in duplicity. India too has considerable long term goodwill in Afghanistan, however the buffer of Pakistan created after 1947 and zealous blocking of Indian interest in the country by Islamabad has prevented it from taking advantage of this sentiment. Over the past few years considerable efforts have been undertaken by the Indian government to reassert its traditional friendly relationship with Kabul and these seem to be paying some dividends.

India has considerable interests in stability in Afghanistan, not the least of which has been to undermine Pakistani influence which has been predominant for over two to two and a half decades now. India has been supporting liberal forces and has generously endowed the government with aid and development support. The Afghan support groups meet in Delhi needs to be seen in this light.

INDO-AFGHAN RELATIONS

Indo-Afghan relations remained on a high during the year. The visit of President Hamid Karzai from 9 to 12 April 2006 to New Delhi was overtaken by the militants killing Indian engineer, Surya. Despite this a number of issues were discussed including terrorism. India pledged additional assistance of $ 50 million to Afghanistan taking the total aid to $ 650 million. $ 50 million was also given as line of credit. The Afghan President also had meetings with the FICCI and the CII representatives and also visited Hyderabad. This was followed up by the Regional Economic Meet in November 2006. The main problem of developing Indo Afghan relations remains transit facilities through Pakistan which will considerably boost Indo-Afghan interests. Pakistan has been accused of denying road access to Indian goods thereby preventing development of an Indo-Afghan axis which is seen as against Pakistan's interest.

The perils of working in Afghanistan were evident when in April 2006 Kasula Suryanarayana, an Indian communication engineer was abducted and killed by the Taliban. This greatly raised concerns of security of the Indian community. K. Suryanarayana was working for Al Moayed Telecom Company which was executing a project for Afghan telecom services company Roshan Telecom. Roshan is the largest GSM service provider in Afghanistan with a network in 30 cities. The company had apparently not catered for such an eventuality. There was general concern of lack of government support to workers in the telecom, road construction, hospitals and other allied services. Private companies have neglected provision of security and insurance cover. The announcement by the Bahrain based company of Rs. 20 lakh compensation for the slain engineer was an afterthought.

Kidnapping K. Suryanarayana is the third such incident involving Indians working in Afghanistan. The first one occurred in December 2003 when two Indians captured were released by the Taliban while M. Kutty, a border roads worker, was unfortunately killed. Another telecom engineer, Sanjeev was shot dead on 8 November 2003, while Bharat Kumar was killed in a blast in February 2006. There were confusing signals from Taliban which regretted the killing, perhaps a first for the terrorist outfit. This is probably to cover up the operation which could have been conducted by a local group lacking sanction from the hierarchy. The absence of harm to the Indian community after this incident indicates the probability of such a surmise. On the other hand, timing of the killing coincided with the visit of President Hamid Karzai to India which also led to speculation of likelihood of the incident being timed to block increased Indian commitment to the Afghan government.

The Indian road construction team operating on the 217 km Delaram-Zaranj Highway in southern Afghanistan demanded additional security and revised the project cost to Rs. 500 crore. Fifty km of the road has been completed so far. 291 Border Roads Organization workers are protected by 75 commandos of the Indo-Tibetan Border Police. The road is reportedly being constructed in a belt which has heavy drug cultivation thereby leading to resistance from locals, who probably see accessibility as an impediment with the anti poppy cultivation campaign gathering momentum in the country.[29]

A new resurgent India, seeking pastures beyond the emerging shores is defying terror and other hazards to set the countries flag flying high in the neighborhood. These are soldiers of the new great game who are extending the reach of the Indian nation beyond the subcontinent. There are more civilians than soldiers in Afghanistan defining the advent of the Indian business and entrepreneurial leadership in various fields. Many of these personnel are not restricted to Kabul but are spread all over the country, some even daring to go to the Taliban controlled south. This led the Indian External Affairs Minister, Pranab Mukherjee to remark, "I appreciate you have volunteered to come here despite very difficult working conditions and to help establish India's presence in Afghanistan".[30]

There are approximately 2000 to 3000 Indians working in Afghanistan and Indo-Tibetan Border Police personnel deployed for security mainly of the Border Roads personnel constructing the Zaranj-Delaram highway, the Indian embassy in Kabul and the consulates in Kandahar and Jalalabad. Eight hundred Indians in Afghanistan are from Andhra Pradesh.

Indian personnel working in the hinterland should act in the shadow of the PRTs or Provincial Reconstruction Teams in the southern provinces which are garrisoned for providing security to reconstruction projects in Afghanistan. The Indian government should negotiate such an arrangement with NATO or the American forces. Private companies employing Indian personnel should provide insurance cover as insurance companies will ensure that adequate security measures are taken by the enterprises employing the people.

INFORMATION WARFARE AND MEDIA

The Al Qaeda took up cudgels on behalf of the Taliban during the year. It issued threats to nations as Canada to withdraw forces or face attacks at home on similar lines as Madrid or London train bombings. This is not likely to be mere coercion and needs to be taken seriously as the Al Qaeda is generally known to follow up its threats. Canadians who are playing a major role in Afghanistan with their deployment in the most critical area of Kandahar have suffered the ire of the Al Qaeda as well as the Taliban which has also issued a general threat against all European countries who are part of the NATO offensive in Afghanistan.

Al Qaeda's information campaign was timed with increased pressure on the Conservative government in Canada to withdraw troops from a conflict which is not seen of core vital interest to the country. The likelihood of increase in the level of commitment with Leopard tanks and F 18 fighter aircraft being inducted in the theatre also increased the level of resentment. Given the assurances made during the NATO Summit in Riga, Latvia any withdrawal by Canadian or other NATO contingents from Afghanistan is not foreseen in the future.

Mullah Omar, the Taliban leader who had shunned media while in control of Kabul before 2001, is now increasingly using it with greater sophistication. Thus his pronouncements in October of striking against targets in Europe and continued suicide attacks on Kabul in winter did not come as a surprise. While the Taliban reach in Europe is limited, "lone wolf" attacks cannot be ruled out. On the other hand, the targets in Afghanistan are within easy reach and it is likely to continue with its strategy of suicide attacks and vehicle borne IEDs during the winter.

PROGNOSTICATIONS FOR THE YEAR AHEAD—2007

The United Nations Security Council has extended the authorization of the International Security Assistance Force (ISAF) for a 12-month period beyond 13 October 2006 to October 2007. This considerably strengthens the resolve of the global community to bring peace to Afghanistan, through measures which include aid, development and governance in the shadow of security cover. Resolution 1707 (2006), was adopted unanimously by the Security Council indicating widespread support. Chapter VII of the United Nations Charter, also authorizes the participants to use force to fulfil the mandate.[31]

On the other hand, Taliban commanders have been issuing threats of an increase in intensity of operations in the spring of 2007. A Stratfor.com report indicates an interview by Mullah Dadullah, one of Taliban's top commanders stating that it has 500 suicide bombers who can be deployed any time with 12,000 Taliban fighters in readiness for launch. Much of this could be empty boast but cannot be ruled out entirely. Even if the strength envisaged is one-third of what the Taliban commander claims, it would necessitate deployment of at least 80,000 troops by NATO and the Afghan Army combined in southern and western Afghanistan. At present this is restricted to just about 40,000 to 50,000 leaving a clear gap of 50 per cent. Unlike in conventional warfare, in counter-insurgency operations, fire power cannot make up for manpower, hence the deficiency will be more than glaring. Taliban has also published the Layeha or Book of Rules recently which includes 29 simple operational rules for the fighters thus indicating the determination to institutionalize resistance.[32]

The level of violence in 2006 has been estimated to be twice as that in 2005 and is likely to continue in 2007 as per estimates of the Director of the US Defence Intelligence Agency. General Michael Maples has indicated that the insurgents have enhanced their capabilities while at the same time sustaining their support base amongst the Pashtun community, portending heavy fighting in the year ahead. The intelligence chief also underlined the need for support to the Afghan President who is lacking capacity to engage the Taliban rather than political will.[33] The entire struggle is estimated to take a decade rather than a couple of years. It would thus be a hard grind for NATO forces who need to demonstrate a will to stay. Visions of a Soviet like withdrawal in the years to come are highly exaggerated, the key difference being the commitment of the international community to the Afghan cause. This support is not likely to go away easily and as far as NATO governments retain balance, there is less likelihood of any break up in the will to resist. The goals laid down in the various benchmarks as the London Compact and the Millennium Development Goals need to be carried forward diligently by the involved nations.

The summer of 2007 is expected to be a bloody one, with better organized, well-equipped and a "modern" Taliban likely to supplement guerrilla tactics with a mix of conventional attacks, lightning raids and suicide attacks on NATO forces. Reports accepted by the Pakistan Interior Minister Aftab Khan Sherpao indicate that there are over 500 to 600 rebels who were being trained in suicide bombing. Musharraf was reportedly embarrassed by Karzai during their joint meeting with President George Bush when the Afghanistan President attempted to nail him with this evidence.

The key problem in Afghanistan is limited understanding of the complex socio-political relationship between different tribes, communities and clans juxtaposed on a pan Afghan nationality. Nations which have had a limited pan national identity as Afghanistan are difficult to govern or coagulate as modern state entities within a short period. There would always be people, who do not see themselves as part of the overall Afghan Diaspora within the state. To manage differences with a community which considers itself as exclusivist rather than inclusivist is a challenge. Outside forces and particularly the military cannot appreciate the problems and undertake nation-building tasks through force of arms. On the other hand, even the political leadership has limited understanding of the dynamics of other states. Thus imposing solutions from without is always difficult and frequently leads to a failure. Conflict resolution has to come from within and the aim is to create an environment for the same through employment of a subtle mix of arms, development and polity.

The solution in Afghanistan is a long haul wherein the guerrillas need to be fought in their own hit and run style with support of local troops. Softening up the key leaders while sustaining the battle against the Taliban with limited collateral damage till the Afghan Army and the police forces are upgraded to the desired level of modern professional rather than tribal mode of military management remains the way ahead. Tribal leaders should be won over through sops, development, ministerial posts and cash incentives. NATO needs to be committed for a period of a decade or so if they want Afghanistan to emerge as a modern nation state, the alternative is return to Taliban ways with a haven for terrorists.

REFERENCES

1. Detailed coverage of Federally Administered Tribal Areas in Pakistan is carried out in chapter on Pakistan.
2. Jenkins, Simon. UK the Fall Guy.... *The Hindu,* 8 June 2006, New Delhi, p. 11.
3. South Asia Security Trends November 2006. Published online by Security-risks.com.
4. South Asia Security Trends May 2006. Published online by Security-risks.com.
5. South Asia Security Trends July 2006. Published online by Security-risks.com.
6. www.defencetalk.com and South Asia Security Trends February 2007. Published online by Security-risks.com.
7. Based on reports in www.defencetalk.com.
8. Salik Siddiq. *Witness to Surrender*. Oxford University Press. New Delhi, 1979.
9. South Asia Security Trends November 2006. Published online by Security-risks.com.
10. South Asia Security Trends November 2006. Published online by Security-risks.com.
11. http://www.timesonline.co.uk/article/0, 2087-2383232,00.html.
12. South Asia Security Trends January 2007. Published online by Security-risks.com.

13. South Asia Security Trends October 2006. Published online by Security-risks.com.

14. South Asia Security Trends October 2006. Published online by Security-risks.com.

15. Times of India Report. *The Times of India*, 1 May 2006, New Delhi.

16. Based on report in http://www.defencetalk.com/news/publish/article_006809.php.

17. Based on report in http://www.defencetalk.com.

18. Sahni, Ajai. The Stupidity in Afghanistan. *Weekly Assessments & Briefings,* Volume 5, No. 15, October 23, 2006. www.satp.org.

19. South Asia Security Trends September 2006. Published online by Security-risks.com.

20. The Economist Report. *The Economist*, 23 November 2006, London.

21. Based on Report in *The Economist*, London, 23 November 2006 and www.defencetalk.com.

22. Prochazka, Jan. *We Won all the Battle. Czech Armed Forces Today.* 4/2006. p. 17.

23. Based on report at http://www.defencetalk.com/news/publish/article_007063.php.

24. South Asia Security Trends September 2006. Published online by Security-risks.com.

25. Based on inputs from website http://usinfo.state.gov.

26. Based on reports in http://www.defencetalk.com/news/publish/article_006872.php.

27. South Asia Security Trends September 2006. Published online by Security-risks.com.

28. Based on reports in http://www.defencetalk.com.

29. The Indian Express Report. *The Indian Express*, 28 December 2006, New Delhi.

30. South Asia Security Trends February 2007. Published online by Security-risks.com.

31. Based on press release at http://www.un.org/News/Press/docs/2006/sc8826.doc.htm.

32. Taliban Layeha can be downloaded from http://www.signandsight.com/features/1071.html.

33. Based on reports in http://www.defencetalk.com/news/publish/wars/Violence_in_Afghanistan_doubled_in_2006_US_military13008975.php.

Bangladesh: Political Chaos or Prosperity?

2

"The armed forces have been called in to maintain law and order in the country and help in the process of setting up a government desired by the people. I hope they (the army) would do their duty efficiently and live up to their earlier reputation."

Bangladesh President Iajuddin Ahmed on 11 January 2007

"Bangladesh is a terrorism free nation."

Former Prime Minister Begum Khaleda Zia, March 2006

KEY TRENDS—2006

Political

- Instability due to mutual animosities, suspicions and recriminations between two principal political groupings—the Bangladesh National Party and Awami League.
- Interim Administration constituted is seen to be a prop imposed by the Army and Western governments. Stability achieved may thus denote temporary reprieve.
- Holding free and fair elections will be the key to stability in future.
- The Bangladesh Army is seen to be playing an important but behind the scenes role in maintaining stability.

Militancy and Counter-Militancy

- A number of measures undertaken during the year resulted in apprehending principals of major terrorist organizations.
- Success by Rapid Action Battalion has had a salutary impact on militancy.

- Piracy, crime and law and order continue to be major issues providing basic conditions for militancy.

Indo-Bangla Relations

- Indo-Bangla relations, a major factor for peace and stability in India's North East, continue to be a key concern due to perennial issues of infiltration, support to terrorism and demographic invasion.
- Indo-Bangla border fencing will regulate the movement and is seen to resolve a number of these problems.

INTRODUCTION

A healthy growth rate and joint Nobel Peace Prize shared by Mohammad Yunus and the Grameen Bank were perhaps the international high points for Bangladesh in 2006. Regarded some years ago as a basket case, Bangladesh is slowly making its mark on history with its unique model of grass-roots growth denoted by micro credit and bottom up development. However, much more needs to be done for Dacca to be considered as a model developing country. The immense potential of the state has to be harnessed by systemic political and economic governance which can come about if a stable, liberal and democratic government comes to power. The elections will thus decide the future of this nation of teeming millions.

The run up to the elections is likely to be an extremely turbulent period with increase in political activities, law and order and security in the fragile democracy which has been marred by a history of violence over the past three and a half decades. Analysts fear violence and bloodshed. On the other hand, increased role of the army is seen in ensuring stable governance in the country which however will have long-term consequences for stability in the country. While Bangladesh has many achievements to its credit such as alleviation of poverty, self-sufficiency in food and overcoming natural devastations with more than a hundred killed in cyclonic storms in 2006, lack of orderly polity is perhaps the biggest bane accompanied by poor law and order and growth of fundamentalism. Urban land in Bangladesh is a major issue for social conflict as it is a key possession and disputes over plots are resolved only through force and intimidation rather than rule of law just as in other areas of South Asia. The feudal socio-criminal system has pervaded even the business sector and the, 'Mastans' or organized crime warlords are said to be the key to conduct of business through protection rackets which pervades all areas including ironically begging.

Regionally there was much to cheer with Bangladesh admitted to the ASEAN Regional Forum or ARF as its 26th Member. The ARF is a group which is primarily dealing with security issues such as confidence building, peacekeeping, disaster relief, counterterrorism, transnational crime, maritime security and preventive diplomacy. The presence of large-scale piracy in the Chittagong area of Bangladesh makes its membership of the ARF particularly significant and this should facilitate greater contribution of the nation to control of maritime crime.

POLITICAL TRENDS—THE TRAGEDY OF DELAYED ELECTIONS?

The tempo of political activity in Bangladesh were at a peak throughout 2006. The 14-party alliance of opposition parties led by the Awami League demanded resignation of then Prime Minister, Begum Khaleda Zia on grounds of corruption. A nation-wide strike was organized at Mahakali way back in April 2006. Three hundred protestors tried to overrun barbed wire barricades. Dacca also saw a series of clashes between police and opposition activists which left a few hundred injured. Police swung into action when protestors moved toward the Prime Ministers office on 20 April.[1] This pace of protests continued as the year went on with a huge protest rally of opposition activists held in Dhaka on 18 September which demanded electoral reforms before holding elections in the year 2007.[2] This was a part of the 15 months of intense agitation over a sustained period including strikes and protests to ensure free and fair elections in the country. It was continuously alleged by the opposition that the ruling Bangladesh Nationalist Party (BNP) appointed key people to posts in the Election Commission, judiciary and bureaucracy to manipulate public opinion one more time in its favor. Return of the BNP was seen by many as another reign for the Islamic fundamentalists and greater space for jihad elements.

As Begum Kaleda Zia, the BNP Prime Minister demitted office as per norms of the Constitution which decrees that fresh elections will be held under an interim government, the atmosphere was surcharged with political tension. The Elections became increasingly contentious due to intense polarization between the ruling, BNP and the Awami League (AL). The key problem remained that of voters list which is a contentious issue as in all emerging democracies with large-scale allegations of tampering, additions, deletions and other problems. The control of the election machinery thus assumes an important factor in such elections which explains the efforts by BNP to place bureaucrats close to it in power before it gave up office.

The impasse over appointment of retired Chief Justice K.M. Hasan who had been a member of the BNP as the head of the interim government to oversee the elections was broken and a constitutional crisis averted when the President Iajuddin Ahmed assumed the reins of the caretaker government. The initial directions of the caretaker administration appeased the principal opposition party, the Awami League. The President transferred 27 senior bureaucrats and terminated services of Mr. Kamal Uddin Siddiqui, principal secretary, a staunch BNP supporter who had been given extension a number of times by the previous government. The services of a number of key functionaries who had been on contract were also terminated. The Chief Election Commissioner M.A. Aziz and his three deputies were reported to have links with the BNP by the opposition. Some sources even link these functionaries with Islamist parties and the ubiquitous Inter Services Intelligence (ISI) of Pakistan.

Politically the BNP suffered setbacks as a number of leaders broke away from the Party accusing it of corruption and links with Islamic organizations including militants. The formation of the Liberal Democratic Party under Dr. Badrudzoha and joined by Col Oli Ahmad, a key personality from Chittagong, was a major blow to the BNP.[3] The 14-party opposition alliance led by Awami League took to the streets many a times after November over corruption and fundamentalism and there were reports of large-scale political violence in the state.

The ruling BNP coalition comprising of four parties also agitated to put pressure on the interim government. The trend is to project demands, hold negotiations, give an ultimatum for action and take to the streets in case these demands are not met. Street politics and violence was dominating Bangla polity until a clamp down came into effect in January 2007 in the form of proclamation of Emergency and establishment of a caretaker Administration (CA). Some intelligence reports indicated that the BNP had even requested the Army at one stage to take over reins of the country, which reportedly refused the offer.

The Awami League led alliance received a considerable boost with the defection of prominent members of the Bangladesh Nationalist Party as reported in the November issue of Security Trends.[4] The BNP partially made it up with an attempted coalition with the Jatiya Party led by former president H.M. Ershad with a possible deal of awarding the Presidentship to Ershad. This reportedly led to a conflict with the Jamaat which has a stronghold in the northern parts of the country as per a report by Bibhu Prasad Routray in sair.org. There are also reports of clashes between the BNP and the Jamaat activists in various parts of the country during the period. Jatiya Party finally joined the Awami League led 14-party coalition. The other constituent of the ruling combine, Islami Oikya Jote (IOJ), has already broken off from the BNP. The poor economic performance of the BNP has also contributed to its loss of popularity which is likely to suffer from the incumbency factor.

The main townships of concern for law and order were assessed as capital Dhaka, Kushtia, Meherpur, Magura, Kurigram, Narsingdi, Narayanganj and Bagerhat. Clashes were also reported from Rajshahi, Tangail, Sirajganj, Satkhira, Bogra, Netrakona, Dinajpur, Patuakhali, Khagrachhari, Noakhali, Faridpur, Mymensingh, Jhenidah, Kishoreganj, Pabna, Gaibandha, Barisal, Gazipur, Sylhet and Rangpur.[5]

The Bangladesh Nationalist Party (BNP) had survived its term with a coalition with the Islamic parties so far and appears to have been considerably weakened with a split of a section of the liberal bloc. Sheikh Hasina who leads the 14-party alliance of which her own party the Awami League is the principal constituent is likely to reap the harvest of success due to the anti-incumbency factor by successfully undermining many of the ills of the election machinery in the country which was in the grips of BNP loyalists. Allegations of bogus voters list are rampant and vary from 12.2 million as projected by National Democratic Institute Washington to 14 million indicated by the Awami League.

The deployment of the Army seems to have had some impact, which was done by the caretaker President Mr. Iajuddin Ahmed despite protests by his advisors since 10 December 2006. The Army had indicated that it would be controlling the capital Dhaka, all the district headquarters with the Navy controlling a large number of coastal districts in the country and the Air Force controlling the airports of Dhaka, Chittagong and Jessore. The agitation over the issue had seen over 35 people killed in the violence and the Army deployed more than once in December 2006.

The final rounds of protests commenced with withdrawal of 2,370 of the 4,146 nominations filed for elections, indicating clear grass-roots support to the move by Awami League leadership. The series of bandhs and blockades undertaken by the Awami League alliance brought life to a virtual standstill after nationwide protests from 5 January which were to be followed up on subsequent days till the elections. The Interim government had no option but to deploy the Army after police failed to check the protestors which swamped the capital Dacca as well as other major cities.

Repeated rounds of protests and civic unrest however finally led to proclamation of Emergency by President Iajuddin on 11 January. Other key officials including the Chief Election Commissioner M.A. Aziz resigned or were replaced by a new Caretaker Administration under Fakhruddin Ahmed. All five poll officials of the Bangladesh Election Commission resigned on 31 January setting the stage for review of the electoral process. The new administration planned to revamp the poll process including drawing up a new voters list and using transparent ballot boxes. Primarily composed of apolitical persons including the interim chief, a former governor of

Central Bank of Bangladesh, leading businessmen, a newspaper owner and chairman of Security Exchange Commission, the government began firmly by arresting a number of corrupt officials with alleged links with the underground and political activists including supporters of both the groupings. The Interim administration is reported to have the tacit support of the Bangladesh Army as well as Western governments primarily the United States and Britain.

Militancy, Counter-Militancy and Terrorism

Bangladesh much as other countries in South Asia is affected by many waves of insurrection over the years. A large number of madrasas were reported to foster fundamentalist teachings deviating from scriptures of Islam which speaks of enlightenment through brotherhood and sacrifice. Of equally great concern is the harsh treatment meted out to intellectuals in the country some of whom are reported to have been ill-treated giving people an impression that Bangladesh is likely to be a second Taliban controlled Afghanistan. There are also a number of leads after train blasts in Mumbai, India in July 2006, which denoted that the perpetrators of violence had links with Bangladesh. All this portends a troubled period on India's eastern borders, what with allegations of a large number of terrorist camps based in the country and continuous cross-border firing.

However, some of the militant organizations as Jama'atul Mujahideen Bangladesh (JMB) and Harkat-ul-Jihad Islami Bangladesh (HuJI-B) have been marginalized during the BNP rule. Despite this Bangladesh continues to be a hot spot as a base for terrorism in the country over the years and is said to be influenced by the ISI. There were also reports that the banned JMB had regrouped and was planning to strike during the elections just as it had done in August 2005. These attacks are likely to be deadlier than the ones in 2005 as the organization is reported to have considerably refined its techniques.

The law and order structure is so corrupt that a para military organization, the Rapid Action Battalion, is credited as the only successful enforcement agency but alleged to have resorted to extra judicial killings to enforce rule of the state. This has led to a large number of accusations of human rights violations. But many see this as the only hope for people against the Godfather, "mastan" system of business. Mastans are said to be main conduits of the criminal–politician–police nexus representing growing challenges for the government. The Rapid Action Battalion has been credited with bringing even terrorists of various Bangla factions to book and hence has earned some respect of the people. This, however, is suitable for targeted operations against known and identified terrorists and criminals, the general law and order situation continues to remain at the mercy of the political-police and criminal coteries at all levels.

The most encouraging news from within Bangladesh during the year indicated that JMB supreme commander, Abdur Rehman, surrendered on 2 March and on 6 March the Jagrata Muslim Janta Bangladesh (JMJB) commander Siddiquil Islam alias Bangla Bhai also surrendered during an encounter with the Rapid Action Battalion. This was a significant boost to anti-terrorist operations in Bangladesh, leading the Prime Minister to announce that, "Bangladesh is a terrorism free nation".[6] No doubt this was a hyperbole, but it proved that the state if determined could act against terrorist organizations as over the years doubts were being expressed due to its alliance with Muslim fundamentalist organizations and a corresponding soft approach towards their strong arms.

The apprehension of the terrorist leaders was also supplemented by judicial action which resulted in sentencing seven terrorists by a Bangladesh court on 30 May. Judge Reza Tarik Ahmed proclaimed death sentence on perpetrators of murder of two judges in the bomb attack on Jhalakati in southern Bangladesh on 14 November 2005. The chief of the outlawed Shayek Abdur Rahman of Jamaat-ul Mujaheedin and Siddikul Islam Bangla Bhai of JMJB were amongst the seven punished. The bomb attacks had been a part of the series that rocked the country in the latter part of 2005. The strident signal send out by the judiciary is laudatory as frequently judges have been lenient against terrorists. Perhaps bombing of the judicial complex was too close physically as well as emotionally for the judiciary in Bangladesh to remain silent.

The fanaticism of the terrorists in Bangladesh can be assessed by the statement by the military commander of the JMB, Ataur Rahman 'Sunny' in the Sessions Court on 20 April 2006. Sunny pleaded guilty on charges of possession of firearms and ammunition and said that he possessed these to pursue his goal of an Islamic Bangladesh. This trend is likely to create a hierarchy of 'virtuous' terror which will be very harmful in the long run as terrorists will claim martyrdom.

Bangladesh Special Task Force along with the Army also raided the Rangamati Hills and killed 10 insurgents of the National Liberation Front of Tripura. While this was a positive action, it is well known that the Bangladesh forces have not been very active against some of the other North Eastern groups as ULFA and NSCN (IM).

Another danger in Bangladesh is that of piracy. Nine incidents of piracy in and around Chittagong port were reported in the first quarter of 2006 and Chittagong remained the hot spot for maritime crime with over 40 incidents reported during the year.[7] Vigilant maritime surveillance and patrolling is thus called for with assistance of the Indian coastguard and the Navy if need be.

Bangladesh as a Hub of Terror. Western sources as Selig S. Harrison have been quoted by www.crossfirewar.com to have indicated in a *Washington Post* article that Pakistan's ISI has established an effective network in Bangladesh. The issue of Bangladesh emerging as a hub of terrorism in South Asia directed against India also gained ground during the Year. The Indian Minister of State for Commerce, Jairam Ramesh categorically referred to fears of forces in Bangladesh aligning against Indian interests. The serial blasts in Varanasi, India on 7 March were said to have been masterminded at the behest of Asadullah, a HUJI leader, who was also alleged to have been behind the blasts in Delhi in October 2005.

Islamic fundamentalist groups as the Jamaat-e-Islami are the link used by the ISI in Bangladesh to support armed groups in India's North East. The Jamaat is reported to be gaining in influence in the government with two officers allegedly sympathetic to the Jamaat, Major General Mohammad Aminal Karim and Brigadier General A.T.M. Amin appointed as the Military Secretary to the President and Director of the Armed Forces Intelligence Anti-Terrorism Bureau respectively.[8] The two appointments are particularly significant as the President plays a significant role in elections scheduled in the country in 2008. The anti-terrorist operations being primarily undertaken by the Special Task Force of the Army are also said to be over seen by the Anti-Terrorism Bureau. A network of madrasas and Islamic charities funded by Saudi Arabia and other Gulf states are also reportedly proliferating in Bangladesh.

The existence of such camps not only in Bangladesh but also in Pakistan was also confirmed in a report to the Indian Parliament by Union Minister of State for External Affairs, E. Ahmed, which indicated that there were 52 terrorist training camps in Pakistan and POK. In Bangladesh there were reportedly 172 camps cum sanctuaries and a list of 307 criminals and insurgents was provided to the Bangladesh Rifles by the Border Security Forces authorities in 2005. Bangladesh has been consistently denying their existence over the past many years.

The persistent pursuance of terrorist cases by the Bangla judiciary needs to be commended. While generally the judiciary is reasonably favorable towards deviants in society seeking a path of reform and in many cases it has shown unusual clemency, in Bangladesh the resoluteness of the judiciary towards terrorists who had launched bomb attacks in 2005 needs commendation. The operations by the Rapid Action Battalion have also borne fruit, thereby providing a high level of deterrence which needs to be sustained.

INDO-BANGLA RELATIONS

General Trends

The key issues affecting Indo-Bangla relations are as follows:

- Infiltration and illegal migration into Assam and other areas in the North East.

- Support to terrorism. A large number of apprehended terrorists in India seem to suggest that they had some connection with Bangladesh.
- Balancing relationship with China and Pakistan *vis-à-vis* India.
- Support to Indian terrorist outfits such as the ULFA. Reports indicate that ULFA leaders have even bought property in Bangladesh and operate with impunity.

The high point in Indo-Bangla relations during the year was the visit of the Bangladesh Prime Minister to India. Indo-Bangla relations long under a quandary of mutual suspicion were placed on an even keel with the first visit by Begum Khaleda Zia, the Prime Minister, to New Delhi from 20 to 23 March 2006. The agenda for Bangladesh was very clear, as observed from the speech of Khaleda Zia at the official banquet hosted by Manmohan Singh. It was trade and more trade. She wanted duty free access to exports from Bangladesh to narrow the trade gap.[9] These requests provide India with a strategic leverage to correct the skewed trade deficit with Bangladesh of $ 1.5 to 2 billion, thereby contributing to improvement of relations and forcing Dacca to view Indian apprehensions of fostering terror from its territory more seriously. India handed over a list of 170 terrorist camps in Bangladesh.

INDO-BANGLA BORDER STABILITY

Stability of the Indo-Bangla border is a key to many issues governing Indo-Bangla relations. One key indicator of instability is border firing. The spate of firing on the Indo-Bangla border continued during the year. Two incidents, Chopra in North Dinajpur District on 22 March, and in Kuchlibari area of Cooch Behar District on 28 March, were reported. In June 2006 the area of Hakimpur and Ichhamati River were the hot spots. The Churtia sector in West Bengal also saw exchange of fire between the Border Security Force of India and the Bangladesh Rifles. The provocation apparently has been an attempt by a number of youth to cross over into India. Reports of firing in the West Bengal sector of the border in Nadia district were also received thus denoting proliferation of this trend.

The Bangladesh Rifles (BDR) on the other hand accused the Indian Border Security Force of pushing in 15 Indian Muslims from the Baikari border on 11 November with 19 Indian Muslims reportedly pushed in the previous week.[10] The Bangladesh human rights group Odhikar has also alleged that over 413 Bangladeshis have been killed by the Indian Border Security Force (BSF) in the past five years, a report which remains largely unsubstantiated. The total kills were reported to be 479 of which the BSF is alleged to have killed 413, 381 Bangladeshis were reportedly injured, 449 arrested, 531 abducted and seven women raped by BSF men. While 83 people including 8 children were said to be missing and 40 fell victim to looting by the BSF and criminal gangs from India.

The prominent trend indicated in infiltration was that militants operating in the North East generally favored north Bengal for infiltration, while those operating in other parts of the country particularly in Jammu and Kashmir favored the south Bengal border. This indicates a clear division of area between groups based on an informal understanding between the organizations as well as support networks which are assisting them.

The stand off between the Border Security Force and the Bangladesh Rifles does not seem to end. Perhaps the stakes in the people and goods running racket across the border is so well entrenched that it is creating local insecurities resulting in firing. A similar clash used to occur regularly on the Indo-Pakistan border in the 1980's which tapered off with construction of the fence. There is thus a need to fence the Indo-Bangla border on a war footing. There was some cheer however in the form of a visit by the Indian Home Minister, Shivraj Patil to Panbari, a post of Bangladesh Rifles in the Tin Bigha corridor. This should be considered a landmark event after the clashes in 2005 which saw killing of a Border Security Force Officer, allegedly by the Bangladesh Rifles in this area.

There are also reports of encroachments by Bangladesh on Indian territory. A report by the Assam Revenue Minister Bhumidhar Barman that Bangladesh has encroached upon 499.83 acres of Indian territory also caused great consternation.

299.04 acres of Pallatal tea estate, 11.73 acres of Pramodnagar tea estate in Karimganj district and 189.06 acres in Dhubri district, under Mancachar revenue circle was reported to have been encroached by Bangladesh. Coming from revenue officials, the authenticity of the report cannot be doubted and denoted the lebensraum approach of the Bangladesh Rifles. On the other hand, the situation in the Katogorah sector of the Cachar district was tense with troop build up and digging of trenches by the Bangladesh Rifles and evacuation of 250 families.[11] Bangladesh Rifles was also reported to be arming civilians in the area of Harinagar in Cachar district after it claimed 216 acres near the Surma river. India has claimed that the land is falling in its own area. Bangladesh Rifles is continually reported to be plodding its farmers to till Indian land to establish their claims in the area.[12]

INDO-BANGLA BORDER FENCING

The Indo-Bangla fence is a vexatious issue, but it should resolve the long-standing requirement of a physical barrier which would not just dissuade but prevent move of Bangla migrants to Assam. The situation in other parts of the Border is also uncertain as there are no definite indications of the likely time of completion of the fence. The entire stretch of Indo-Bangla border fencing is said to be slated for completion by 2007. However, there are major delays in construction especially due to resistance from Bangladesh Rifles. Over the year, there were reports from some areas of Bangladesh Rifles disrupting the fencing work. There are constant efforts by the Bangladesh Rifles to interfere with the public works as per Engineer-in-Chief, B.N. Majumdar.[13]

The border situation may show some signs of improvement in case the ongoing fencing work is completed by the end of the year as indicated during a recent tripartite meeting between the Centre, the All Assam Students Union and the State Government. The fencing of the Indo-Bangla border will be constructed on the lines of the fencing in Jammu and Kashmir with a grid of electronic surveillance. This was indicated by officials of the Border Security Force which is in the process of upgrading the fencing along the 4,096 km Indo-Bangla border. The procurement plan includes 900 hand held thermal imagers costing Rs. 28 lakhs each, 27 LORROS (long reconnaissance and observation system) costing Rs. 2 crore each which is essentially used by the Army for observation and direction of artillery fire and 5000 light weight night vision devices which are costing Rs. 1.5 lakhs each. The requirement of surveillance devices for Army and the BSF on the Jammu and Kashmir frontier keeping in view the high level of infiltration is no doubt justified. However, the level of targeted infiltration on the Bangladesh border is limited. Thus, spending a budget of over Rs. 38,100 lakhs or Rs. 381 crore needs reconsideration.

The local resistance to construction of fence in West Bengal is also contributing to this problem in a major way. District officials are unable to get approval of locals for parting with their land for construction of fence and there is also heavy resistance from people who have to cultivate land which is 150 meters ahead of the boundary fence towards the international border. Small land holdings and politicization of the issue further complicates the problem which was not evident when the fence in Punjab was constructed in the late 1980's. This had resulted in considerable reduction in the inflow of terrorists into Punjab and consequent decrease in the level of terrorism in the state which was brought under control in early 1990's. Impact of elections in Bangladesh in 2007 is likely to be considerable and the BSF is expecting some inflow and disruptive activities by the groups.

Other Issues

The Indian establishment continued to stress the support received by terrorists in Bangladesh as M.K. Narayanan highlighted this at a special interaction with the police officers of southern states in Bangeluru (Bangalore) during the year.[14] The significance of this statement in the south is relevant as a number of Bangladesh laborers have migrated to the economic growth spots in this area.

A.K. Mitra, Director General of the Border Security Force (BSF), in a press conference in Delhi during the year also claimed that in the past five years 1.5 lakh (150,000) people entered India from Bangladesh through the legitimate route of integrated check posts on the Indo-Bangla border but had not returned to their native country. The number of personnel who had entered illegitimately could be anybody's guess. The estimates vary and run into millions. The trend of concern is however said to be migration of a large number of terrorist groups to Bangladesh which is forming the hub for training and consolidation.

Indo-Bangla border security was the focus of attention in two exchanges between representatives of both the countries, Home Secretary level talks from 24 to 26 August 2006 and talks between Inspector Generals of India's Border Security Force and Bangladesh Rifles. The key issue discussed during the Home secretary level talks was cooperation of Bangladesh to combat terror, which assumed importance after allegations that there was involvement of a Bangla hand or support in the train blasts in Mumbai on 7 July 2006. Extradition of militants such as Anup Chetia, Paresh Barua and Arabinda Rajkhowa of the ULFA, fencing and a ceremonial guard of honor during retreat were some of the other items on the agenda.[15] Allegations of Bangladesh being a preferred base for Islamic terrorists fleeing from India led to the need for stressing upon Bangla authorities the importance of exercising control thereby preventing use of territory by elements which were inimical to both states.

Final Review

Bangladesh is likely to see political uncertainty over a period in 2007 till an acceptable government comes to power and starts functioning smoothly. This period of flux could be exploited by inimical forces linked with militants to cause disruption during the election process. The Army had geared itself for such an eventuality earlier and has demonstrated resoluteness as well as restraint to achieve order. The success in apprehension and successful charge sheeting of militants including Bangla Bhai and other influential terrorists involved in the blasts in 2005 needs to be followed up to ensure that spread of terrorism is nipped in the bud. In case reports of Army's refusal of assumption of power as offered by the BNP are true, it is likely to remain neutral.

Indo-Bangla Relations. Illegal migration and infiltration is a major issue in Indo-Bangla relations. There is a need to evolve a permanent solution to the problem. The boundary fence is taking too long and would certainly be a good measure but since a large tract continues to be unfenced, particularly the enclaves and adverse possessions by both sides, provocations will continue. Mechanisms which are evolved at the higher level will also not be effective as implementation on the ground is frequently marred by local issues such as cattle running, people smuggling and so on. Local politicians and criminal elements invariably attempt to rope in weaker elements amongst the border guards to create opportunities for nefarious activities. A holistic solution will be needed in long-term interests of Indo-Bangla security as well as relations. This will also provide much needed relief to the explosion of illegal migration to India, particularly in the North East and the metropolitan cities.

Conclusion—Key Issues before Interim Government

The key issues before the Interim government would be as follows:

- *Resurgence of the economy*. While the focus so far has been at the micro level, Bangladesh is languishing as it does not invoke confidence in foreign investors so far in the macro fundamentals of its economy. Major investments from India such as the Tata group are awaiting political stability.
- Control over extremist forces which had been gaining ground of late particularly with allegations of a soft approach by the BNP over the past five years of its rule.
- Macro level law and order is a major problem with Chittagong port being the hub of piracy and criminal networks.
- Reports also indicate a large base of Al Qaeda and the ISI which has been operating in Bangladesh with some agencies also reportedly implying that it has become a hub for terrorism. While these reports appear to be

exaggerated, there is a need for the government to dispel this notion.

REFERENCES

1. South Asia Security Trends May 2006. Published online by Security-risks.com.
2. South Asia Security Trends October 2006. Published online by Security-risks.com.
3. The Indian Express Report. *The Indian Express*, 28 October 2006, New Delhi.
4. South Asia Security Trends November 2006. Published online by Security-risks.com.
5. Based on inputs from sair.org, weekly reports.
6. Based on reports in www.satp.org/satporgtp/countries/bangladesh/index.htm.
7. With inputs from ICC International Maritime Bureau Report available at www.icc-ccs.org.
8. Bhatti, Khalid. A new haven for reactionary Islam. Accessed at http://www.socialistworld.net/eng/2006/11/20bangla.html.
9. Excerpts of Speech of Bangladesh Prime Minister. *The Hindu*, Marketing Supplement, 31 March 2006, New Delhi, p. 2.
10. Based on reports in http://www.bangladesh-web.com.
11. The Hindu Report. *The Hindu*, 30 July 2006, New Delhi Edition.
12. The Hindustan Times Report. *Hindustan Times*, 28 July 2006, New Delhi, p. 9.
13. Based on inputs from sair.org.
14. Report *in The Hindu* accessed at http://www.hindu.com/2006/10/20/stories/2006102010550100.htm
15. The Economic Times Report. *The Economic Times*, 24 August 2006, New Delhi.

Nepal: Restructuring Revolution to Peace

"We want India to help institutionalize the people's demand for a democratic republic in Nepal. The question is not whether India has a role in establishing peace in Nepal. It must have such a role."

Nepal Communist Party Chairman Prachanda

"I being the Prime Minister with the consent of the seven parties want to assure all that I will never deviate from the democratic principles for which I have been fighting for the past 60 years."

Nepal's Prime Minister, Girija Prasad Koirala.

KEY TRENDS—2006

Politics and Governance

- Review of Constitution and parliamentary processes need to be fully established.
- Political controls at the grass-roots also need consideration.
- Governance needs to reach down to the village level to revive economic activity.
- Pacification of the Madhesi uprising led by the Madhesi Janadhikar Forum would be key to peace and stability in the year ahead.

Militancy and Counter-Militancy

- Process of disarming of Maoists successfully completed.
- Effective measures to control Maoists cadres in the hinterland necessitated.
- Effectiveness of Army and police has to be honed.

Indo-Nepal Relations

- A role for India in bringing peace and prosperity in Nepal is being increasingly accepted.
- Indo-Nepal Treaty due for review will be the acid test.
- India's continued economic commitment to Nepal will attain positive leverages.

INTRODUCTION

Nepal's historic return to parliamentary democracy was heralded on 28 June 2006 raising hopes of rapid normalcy in South Asia's second mountain kingdom after strife for over a decade. Street side protests in Kathmandu acted as the tipping point for an obdurate King Gyanendra who had refused to see the writing on the wall to abdicate power to people's representatives. Though analysts have raised fears ranging from continued rounds of fractious negotiations to reopening of a new phase of civil activism on the streets in Terai, there is enough evidence indicating a permanent return to peace which will unlock the riches in what is one of the poorest states in South Asia. Some cynics have even predicted a return to militancy in case the demands of the Madhesi are not met in full, though at present this appears to be a gross over reaction.

Politically the agreement between the Seven Party Alliance (SPA) and the Maoists is based on strong foundations of the 15-Point Agreement which was followed by the 8-Point Agreement and then the Comprehensive Peace Agreement (CPA) which have provided the framework within which various contentious issues can well be resolved to establish, a "multi-party governing system, civil liberties, fundamental rights, human rights, press freedom and democratic norms and values including the concept of rule of law". Present indications reveal that differences are narrowing down and there is much optimism of longevity of the political process. However, a number of serrated interregnums are expected and only a strong commitment by the SPA and the Maoists will see stable polity emerging at the national level with balanced power sharing arrangements in 2007. The problem is likely to arise from growing influence of the Royalists, parties loyal to the monarchical form if not directly to the King who are showing greater organizational coherence. These forces are likely to come into direct confrontation with the Maoists, for whom any reference to the monarch is anathema. The signs of dissonance in Nepal today are ominous. These relate to polity, law and order, disarming and reemployment of Maoist cadres and emergence of factionalism with break away groups as the Janatantrik Terai Mukti Morcha (JTMM) and the Madhesi Janadhikar Forum mobilized over perceived discrimination between the Terai and Hill communities which are increasingly threatening to play spoiler.

The likely dates for Constituent Assembly polls were some time in June 2007 but postponed to November. However the first step appears to be initiation of the Maoists in the Government, which will come about only after the Maoists give up their arms. This will be a major exercise needing extreme patience, rectitude and persistence by all sides. India will also have to play a role in exercising subtle pressure on Kathmandu, so that the SPA is adequately bolstered to insist on the same. There is also a need to restore economic activity and administration in the state at the earliest. This continues to be in disarray, though tourism has considerably picked up. An economic package by India will be an essential requirement and a generous endowment on the lines of the Marshall Plan will do Nepal a world of good.

STRATEGIC SEQUENCING OF PEACE IN NEPAL

From Confrontation to Solutions

Nepal was in turmoil in the beginning of the year, however the situation gradually improved to indicate peace and even normalcy by December 2006. On 2 January 2006, the Maoists terminated the ceasefire and carried out a series of attacks on government posts in the country especially around Katmandu, the capital. The Nepali government reacted violently to crack down on political leaders as mass agitations gripped the nation on 20 and 21 January. The Maoists continued their attacks on government forces camps in Hatuwgadhi in Eastern Nepal on 27 January and in Palpa in western Nepal on 31 January 2006.[1]

The local body elections in Nepal in February 2006 proved to be a farce. The royalist-loyalist axis prevailed as expected in what was purely an administrative exercise in portraying pseudo democracy. King Gyanendra had wanted to prove to the world that there was democracy in Nepal. The results on the other hand gave a different message, that Nepal will not accept an engineered democracy.[2]

Violence continued in March as a report in *The Times of India* gave graphic details of a pitched battle between Government forces and the Maoists on 27 March. The report was by Bhojraj Bhat, who was on the scene of a Maoist rally in Thokarpa village, 80 kms from Kathmandu. The meeting was attended by about 2000 rebels including allegedly members of the elite strike force. The Nepal army struck with a swoop of four armed helicopters for an hour and half at noon and followed it up at 3 p.m. A paratroop landing also took place at around 5 p.m. as per Bhat. The rebels are reported to have managed to melt in the jungles.[3] Though the timings stated do not appear credible as flying post noon is difficult in mountainous areas of Nepal. Some of the other key incidents were killing of 13 Nepali soldiers in a clash with Maoist guerrillas in Bhakumdebeshi on 20 March. Ten police officers and 23 Maoists were reported dead at Birtamod, 600 kms from Kathmandu.

Political activity denoted coagulation between the SPA and the Maoists and a mass agitation was scheduled on 6 April but was postponed. By now the political battle lines in Nepal were clearly drawn up. It was the SPA and Maoists versus the monarchy. By turning the three-pointed confrontation into a two-pronged one, there was greater hope for a political solution.

The tipping point of militancy in Nepal was reached with the people taking to the streets to win freedom from monarchy in the last week of April. This forced King Gyanendra to announce reactivation of the Parliament which partially assuaged the SPA as well as the Maoists who were quick to announce a three-month long ceasefire on 26 April 2006. This was followed by reassembly of Parliament and swearing in of Girija Prasad Koirala, the grand old man of Nepali politics on 30 April 2006.

Nepal's full parliament had a historic swearing in ceremony on 28 June 2006, wherein the Monarch's throne was replaced by the national flag.[4] This saw restoration of democracy in Nepal after 4 October 2002, when King Gyanendra had adjourned the Parliament, followed by assumption of absolute powers on 1 February 2005.

Elections to the Constituent Assembly were also announced along with measures to bring the Maoists into the mainstream. While announcing the truce, Chairman Prachanda is reported to have said, "Our party once again, through this statement, announces a unilateral ceasefire for three months with immediate effect." This was being done to facilitate the "people's struggle" for a constituent assembly and a democratic republic "so as to lead the struggle to a historic conclusion" and for encouraging the parliamentary political parties to announce unconditional constituent assembly. During the ceasefire, the People's Liberation Army assured the masses that it would not launch any offensive action.[5]

Political Restructuring Paradigm

Looking at Nepal a year ago, not many were hopeful that the revolution which had subsumed over 13,000 lives would result in peace and order in the near term. Yet the pace of normalcy over the past one year has been truly gratifying. The process of disarming Maoists is well under way and a new dawn awaits Kathmandu today. The deliberate course of political restructuring in Nepal ensured that normalization was as smooth as it can come about under extraordinary circumstances. There are many lessons from Nepal which can be applied to the myriad revolutions across the globe.

Essentially the approach was top down. The first step was to have a comprehensive peace agreement. This was to ensure adherence to common agreements made earlier between the Seven Party Political Alliance (SPA) and the Maoists such as the 12-point, 8-point and 25-point codes. The overall aim was to transform the ceasefire between the Nepal government and the Maoists into a permanent truce. A Five-Point Agreement was reached on 9 August 2006 seeking assistance of the United

Nations for management of arms and armed personnel, ceasefire and elections to the Constituent Assembly. The Interim Constitution Drafting Committee (ICDC) submitted a draft constitution to the peace negotiating teams of the Government and the Maoists on 25 August. Consisting of 26 parts and 172 articles, the 76 page report was considered highly contentious as the King was granted ceremonial powers and the fate of the monarchy was to be decided by a referendum. This was on expected lines as it was anticipated that once the euphoria over uprising in Nepal subsides, the Royalist would be able to gain some ground and ensure that monarchy was retained at least in a ceremonial form.

The commitments outlined in the various common agreements were reaffirmed and restoration of multi-party democratic system was also assured through the Comprehensive Peace Agreement (CPA) signed between the Prime Minister Girija Prasad Koirala and Maoist Chairman Prachanda on 21 November 2006. This outlined the framework for restoration of democracy, peace and progress. The principal decisions related to formation of the interim legislative parliament as per the provisional Constitution, with the King absolved f all rights of administration. The Maoists as well as the Nepal army were to return to barracks. Seven main camps at Kailali, Surkhet, Rolpa, Nawalparasi, Chitwan, Sindhuli and Ilam along with three smaller camps were nominated. The arms and ammunition of the Maoists were to be stored in these camps to be monitored by the United Nations.[6] This process is nearing completion. The Peace Committee of Nepal prepared a draft of the Agreement on Ceasefire and Human Rights and Abidance to Humanitarian laws which was signed between the Nepal government and the Maoists. The terms of ceasefire included end of armed rebellion and demobilization of the armed forces with prohibition of the following activities:

- Acts of attacking or using arms directly or indirectly against each other.
- Seizing or raiding places where the arms of other side have been stored as per mutual understanding, with or without arms.

- Acts that would cause mental pressure or loss to any individual person.
- Acts to place ambushes targeting each other.
- Actions involving killing or violence.
- Acts of abduction, arrest, imprisonment, disappearance.
- Destruction of public, private, governmental or military properties.
- Aerial attacks or bombarding.
- Mining or sabotaging.
- Acts of spying each other's military activities.

In addition human rights were also guaranteed and a National Peace and Rehabilitation Commission was set up for dispute resolution. There were some hiccups in the process with the Maoists opposing unilateral nomination of ambassadors to various countries. The UN increasingly assumed a significant role in restoration of governance in Nepal with a three-member UN team having extensive discussions with the Nepal government as well as the CPI (Maoists). Thus the initial resistance by the Maoists for UN supervision of the polls in the country was overcome.

The expectations of stability continue to be belied by recent political and militant happenings in the state over the past few months particularly an increasing Terai and Hill divide. But these appear to be temporary impediments to return to stability and smooth governance. The maturity and statesmanship demonstrated so far in resolution of a fractious dispute which has engaged the attention of the world for many years is admirable and could be replicated elsewhere albeit with local modifications.

Role of Nepal Army

The acceptance of Maoist political writ in the country by the Army appears to have hastened King Gyanendra's decision to make peace with the agitators. A report by Siddharth Varadarajan in *The Hindu* on 27 April 2006, indicated that the King was persuaded towards peace by the Chief of the Royal Nepal Army, Pyar Jung Thapa, who with an ear to the ground correctly assessed that the mass agitation was clearly going out of hand. The, 'Nepali street' phenomenon finally broke the wily King's back.

Nepal's Army adjusted to its return to the barracks, as the new Chief of the Army Rukmangad Katuwal indicated that it will cooperate with the Government in the peace process. A change of attitude in the role for restoring peace and stability in the country is noticeable. The Army stands a lot to gain from a rapprochement with the Maoists as it will retain its present high status in Nepali society. The lure of deployment with UN contingents has also been providing monetary incentives to the forces.

The Army is also being brought effectively under Cabinet control, with the Army Chief to be appointed at the pleasure of the Cabinet under the new Military Bill which was presented to the House of Representatives on 18 August. Any mobilization of the Army will also require approval of the Security Special Committee of the House within 30 days.[7] Simultaneously a battalion sized contingent of the Army was dispatched for duties in Lebanon. UN commitment has been a favorite ploy used by the King to keep the Army happy with the greater pay packet on offer.

The problem may not be that of controlling the Army which maintains strict discipline, despite some provocation by its antagonists, the Maoist cadres. Controlling splinter Maoist groups which do not seem to be amenable for greater checks will need considerable efforts. The Royal Nepal Army has offered to absorb armed Maoist cadres. This may not solve the problem as militias are not amenable to military discipline. It may be more appropriate to create para military forces or development task forces after disarming the Maoists. This will provide an acceptable intermediary between an armed force and a police force.

Some rancor between the Nepal Army and the Maoists can be well understood. However, it cannot be allowed to persist as the resultant power struggle will go against stability in Nepal in the days and months ahead. The Maoists have to accept the role of the Army in a democratic set-up and the Army too will have to trim its sails to stay afloat in the turbulent days ahead without being undermined into oblivion. On the other hand, both sides need to be cautious as the Royalists who are presently in retreat may find this as a golden opportunity to stir the pot. A collision between the Army and the Maoists would set a disastrous course.

THE WAGES OF REVOLUTION

Fatalities in Nepal, 2001-2006

The total casualty figures in Nepal as indicated by South Asia Terrorism Portal are 12,826, killed as per Table below.[8] These figures are generally matching with those provided by various other agencies at approximately 13,000.

Summary of Casualties in Nepal

Year	Civilians	Security Forces	Maoists	Total
2001	50	198	803	1051
2002	238	666	3992	4896
2003	214	307	1584	2105
2004	380	481	1590	2451
2005	232	310	1301	1843
2006*	61	181	238	480

* Data till December 15.

The number of casualties during the ceasefire period starting 26 April as per report published by the National Human Rights Commission of Nepal are said to be 43. This included 11 persons killed by the Security Forces and 15 by the Maoists. The balance were killed either by unidentified personnel or by splinter groups within the country. The NHRC also alleged that incidents of torture and harassment continued and the Maoists had not completely dismantled their ruthless politico legal mechanisms such as People's Courts and continued extortion and abductions. "Tax" collection, an euphemism for extortion by the Maoists, was also said to be rampant and the key districts affected were said to be Kailali, Nepalgunj, Bhaktapur, Dolakha, Rupendehi and Kaski.

THE YEAR AHEAD

Nepal is having a number of problems at the grass-roots. There were reports of clashes breaking out between various Maoists groups in many areas. The hold of the central Maoist leadership on the periphery is likely to be limited and it is possible that there would be a number of autonomous groups who would not like to lose unbridled power that they have wielded over the years. The situation is likely to be extremely volatile once Maoists hand over arms which will not only make them defenseless but also raise fears of revenge killings by the Royal Nepal Army and other groups who are not likely to surrender their weapons. There is a need to ensure that local pressures are not allowed to lose gains made in bringing the overall struggle to a political solution.

A report in the sair.org has stated that there are a number of incidents of extortion, pressure on contractors and resistance of return to law and order in districts.[9] The districts where such incidents have been noticed include Siraha, Magdi, Sankhuwasabha, Sarlahi, Bardiya, and Dhangadhi. In addition, splinter groups are also raising their heads. Of particular concern is the Janatantrik Terai Mukti Morcha and Madhesi Janadhikar Forum which is fighting for greater autonomy for the Terai region. These groups will not lay down arms placing the Maoist cadres at their mercy. Thus the complexity of the situation in Nepal needs greater energies of those involved in policy and decision-making in the country as well as its neighbor India and the United Nations. There is a need for effective engagement by the international community through the UNO before internal differences blow out of proportion. A joint Royal Nepal Army and Maoist force could prove ideal to control the hinterland, but will not be acceptable politically, culturally and militarily. However, in a revolutionary struggle this can be managed and it is more appropriate to take a conciliatory stand rather than aggravating differences based on a history of hostility even when the antagonism is merely few months old.

The Maoists are also facing two problems, a cadre which is increasingly alienated from the central leadership, thus recently it had to apologize to the widow of the French mountaineer, Jean Christopher Lafaille for extortion by its rank and file, and the growth of organizations in Terai which are not likely to surrender their arms on its bidding unless another phase of bloody conflict is undertaken. The fragility of the situation in Nepal was evident particularly in the Terai where Nepalgunj witnessed clashes between the residents and rural migrants. The continued nexus of Maoists with contractors and other commercial interest groups also remained a matter of concern. Reports of Maoists insisting on district authorities awarding contracts to their favored contractors continue unabated. Attacks on members of political parties are also continuing.

Reports indicated free toll collection by Maoists even in Kathmandu as also double "taxation" on Nepal's transit points with India as well as Tibet. The pseudo state authority established by the Maoists as per influential Nepali editor Yubaraj Ghimire is undermining influence of the state in Nepal. The large number of spoilers in the Nepali political scene is highlighted by the statement by a previously unknown group, the Nepal Janatantrik Party (NJP) in Dhangadhi, Kailali district adjacent to the sugar belt in Uttar Pradesh which supports the King. The pro-monarchy Rashtriya Prajatantra Party has remained neutral so far. In an apparent bid to improve their sullied image, the Maoists in Nepal took to patrolling crime pockets and also undertook a cleaning campaign in the capital. How effectively this campaign will affect the districts will determine the fate of the polity in Nepal. Thus the situation continues to be anomalous.

Indo-Nepal Relations

India had played an influential role to bring Maoists towards resolution of the impasse in talks with the SPA. Sitaram Yechury, Politburo Member of CPI (M), in India, is said to have played a significant role. A four-point formula popularly known as the "Yechury Formula" had highlighted the way ahead with recall of Parliament, implementing various agreements reached, talks with Maoists and legislative measures to provide greater autonomy to Parliament.[10] This was after an abortive attempt to broker peace through the Prime Minister's envoy, Karan Singh. At the crucial stage Indian envoy, Shiv Shankar Mukherjee had a one on one meeting with the Maoist leader Prachanda. The agenda was reportedly to emphasize the need for security to Indian businesses in Nepal. The need to push the process of participation in parliamentary democracy was also highlighted by Shankar Mukherjee. A subtle message also appears to have been conveyed to Prachanda that surrender of arms was the only way out for participation in the election process.[11]

India underlined its commitment to Nepal during the visit of the Nepalese Prime Minister, the ageing G.P. Koirala in June 2006 soon after taking over.[12] The emphasis during the visit was on an economic package for recovery to include grants, credit, soft loans and new projects including rescheduling loans. Military aid did not appear on the overt agenda. Works on 137 small and big projects in Nepal with Indian assistance is to be speeded up. India has reportedly recommended disarming Maoists as a precursor to holding elections.

A package of Rs. 8.5 billion has also been offered to Nepal for infrastructure development in the Terai region. This will supplement the Rs. (Nepal) 1,500 crores aid announced during the visit of the Nepali Prime Minister to India. India's total aid to Nepal was Rs. (Nepal) 1,800 crores in 139 projects at various stages of implementation in the fields of health, education and infrastructure.

Indo-Nepal relations received a major fillip with the Maoist leader, Prachanda denoting a change in stance from the earlier antipathy of the Party towards New Delhi. Prachanda, Chairman of the Communist Party of Nepal (Maoist), stated, "The Indian government stood by Nepal earlier and played a positive role in helping us forge a common understanding with the political parties. The people of Nepal know that without the direct or indirect help of India, the 12-point understanding which became the basis of joint action with the political parties would not have been possible. India must not give up that role."[13] Two key Maoist leaders were also released from West Bengal after cases against them were dropped. This should augur well for the future of Indo-Nepal relationship with the Indo-Nepal Treaty also due for review in 2007. Thus there is all possibility that there may be an extension of the present Indo-Nepal Treaty till the new government in Kathmandu is able to take a decision on the same. The Joint Technical Level India-Nepal Boundary Committee is reported to have met in Kathmandu to finalize the border demarcation by June 2007. An interim meeting is to be held in March 2007 so that the final task is completed in due time.

India has been attempting to obtain hydro power from Nepal over the years, however the militancy in the state and lack of interest in the administration has prevented progress in this sphere. The restoration of order should provide some hope of reconsideration of India's proposals by Nepal. A Xinhua report indicated that in Power Summit 2006 in Kathmandu, India's Ambassador to Nepal had indicated the country's willingness to sponsor power projects up to a capacity of 250 MW for Nepal's use. These are likely to be the 240 W Naumure project and the 60 MW Kankai project. The electricity generated will be used exclusively by Nepal. Seeing the reluctance of the Maoists towards cooperation with India, it would be prudent to tread cautiously and adopt a cooperative approach which is of critical significance both for India as a measure of energy security and Nepal providing it much needed revenue for development.

The Indian Lok Sabha was informed by the Home Minister, Shivraj Patil, that there was a major effort to increase security on the Indo-Nepal border in all the bordering districts of Bihar, Uttar Pradesh, Uttaranchal, West Bengal as well as Sikkim. The number of Shashtra Seema Bal (SSB) battalions was being doubled to 38 and road and border construction work was to be concluded at a rapid pace. Six hundred and fifty-seven kms of roads in the border districts of Bihar had been identified as of operational significance which would be upgraded. However, despite this emphatic assertion, the situation on the ground continues to be pathetic. Free cross-border movement of personnel as permitted in the Indo-Nepal Treaty of 1950 takes place without any restrictions. The SSB is facing considerable difficulty in establishing its posts in the area as it is unable to acquire land and also lacks operational focus. There is a need for joint posts integrating the SSB, customs and police which is lacking. An attempt was made in Uttar Pradesh which has been reasonably successful at Rupaidiah border post which could be further explored in other points on the Indo-Nepal border.

India's policy of continuous engagement during the past decade despite much provocation from the Monarchy as well as the Maoists has paid rich dividends. It has facilitated peace in the state as well as improved Indo Nepal relations. The intimate links between political parties in India and Nepal has also facilitated renewal of warmth. India needs to explore how this model can be applied to other neighbors such as Sri Lanka which is passing through a much longer and more intense phase of insurgency.

REVIEW AND PROGNOSTICATIONS

Restoration of peace and normalcy in Nepal will be a long drawn out process as law and order and administration in the districts has completely collapsed. There are many complicated issues such as disarming Maoists, restoration of the government, administrative infrastructure in Kathmandu and then the provinces followed by the districts and finally economic rejuvenation and spread of benefits of peace to Nepal's countryside. The primarily agrarian economy seems to be in dire straits over the years though tourism will provide some immediate hope as the summer season is approaching. The priority should thus be to ensure that the key constituents including the Maoists and the Army confirm their allegiance to the Koirala government and power of command flows from the hands of the prime minister. The priority should be economic rejuvenation and rebuilding institutions. An election under indigenous cadres under international observation and not supervision is the way ahead. With political activity in Nepal having resumed, the key issues would be as follows:[14]

Immediate Time Frame—Internal

- Strengthen the political process by greater interaction between the Maoists and the SPA.
- Employ Maoists in restoration of civil administration in the country rather than merging with the Royal Nepal Army.

- Commence revival of administration in the country including the districts to restore governance.
- Commence economic activity including tourism.
- Improve law and order, safety and security of common citizens.

Medium-Term—Internal and External

- Aid and assistance from international community for revival of the country.
- India should play a key role in the same albeit from the sidelines.
- Attempt to bring Royalists on board.
- Evolve framework for holding elections.

Continued extortion, labor and union problems generally attributed to lack of control in the hinterland had led the Nepalese business community with FNCCI (Federation of Nepalese Chambers of Commerce and Industries) in the lead, threatening a five-day strike in September 2006 protesting mayhem by Maoist elements and the criminal fringe which always thrives during periods of uncertainty.[15] The crisis was averted with deft political maneuvering by the Prime Minister. These problems are recurring with regularity. The ability of the central Maoist leadership to control its cadres at the district level will finally determine prevalence of order, for the police which had been overshadowed by the Army during the period of struggle has not regained control of the countryside. Reestablishment of rule of law thus is a primary necessity which needs consideration at the highest level, for the number of reports of extortion and crime are increasing each day.

Providing gainful employment to the disarmed cadres will remain another vexatious issue. Unless the cadres are provided with alternate sources of legitimate income and institutional measures to assimilate them in a law abiding society are undertaken, mere disarming would not lead to peace and stability. The first requirement thus appears to be to provide them some authentic source of income to stop extortions. Past experience suggests that it is difficult to wean away youth who have been accustomed to toting guns with impunity to adjust to the normal routine of earning bread through the grind of hard labor. Reskilling the force with vocational training could be one way, more creative integrationist measures would have to be evolved rather than mere absorption in the armed forces. The insistence by the SPA to start the process with disarmament is indeed the right path. Disarming will however prove difficult as present indications suggest that mass laying down of arms by the cadres on instructions from the leadership in Kathmandu may not come about smoothly.

Arresting activities of break away factions as the JTMM which are seen to raise the ante over the past few months with calls for secession of the Terai region is another area of confrontation. The danger in Terai looms from varied ethnic communities as the Madhesi and Tharu tribal. Controlling these and similar movements, more of which will come about in the fractious geography of Nepal with limited communications between various parts of the country will be the final challenge which the Maoist and SPA combine would have to address with firmness.

The other issues in Nepal are functioning of the Government in the provinces and districts which needs to be revived at the earliest. Development works also need to commence so that the economic stress in the country is reduced. There are continued reports of the Maoists holding people's courts in the outlying areas and also seeking funds for maintenance an euphemism for extortion. This is creating stress in the ruling coalition. The ability of the Central Committee of CPM to control its cadres in outlying districts has not yet been tested. This will come as a true test of the leadership of Prachanda, with the CPI (M) attempting to transfer itself from a rebel outfit to an elected government in due course.

Confidence building between the SPA and the Maoists will be severely tested in the coming months with the Madhesi agitation gaining prominence. The Royalists are also gaining ground and there would be a number of spoilers coming into play. There are increased accusations of the Madhesi Janadhikar Forum acting at the behest of the Royalists and Hindu fundamentalists in the Terai.[16] The Nepal Army is also not likely to give up its primacy in state polity so easily, having tasted power over the past so many years. Thus, the complexities in Nepal indicate a turbulent period ahead. The challenge is to ensure that these remain in the political rather than the military field. International mediation is essential if peace is to be retained. Security is the essence of administration and the people need to feel safe to carry out their normal functions economic and political.

The impression gaining ground is that Maoists will continue with their agitation mode of politics to gain concessions from the government on various aspects. So far Prime Minister Koirala due to his stature has been able to pacify the Maoists as well as various political parties in the government. What happens after Koirala remains a question as the leader is suffering from poor health.

Conclusion

While internecine conflict is not new to South Asian states, Nepal today is the exception as this is impeding growth and development. Others as Sri Lanka and Bangladesh have shown reasonable progress despite being embroiled in varying shades of terrorism. The Nepali political combine must bury the differences and take the benefits of peace to the hinterland, before the potential of a hundred mutinies erupts once again.

REFERENCES

1. South Asia Security Trends February 2006. Published online by Security-risks.com.
2. South Asia Security Trends March 2006. Published online by Security-risks.com.
3. The Times of India Report. "Copters were...". *The Times of India*, 1 April 2006, New Delhi, p. 24.
4. South Asia Security Trends July 2006. Published online by Security-risks.com.
5. South Asia Security Trends May 2006. Published online by Security-risks.com.
6. South Asia Security Trends December 2006. Published online by Security-risks.com.

7. With inputs based on a PTI report.
8. Adapted from date provided by South Asia Terrorism Portal.
9. *Weekly Assessments & Briefings,* Vol. 5, No. 6, 21 August, 2006. sair.org.
10. Cherian, John. Indian Flip flop. Accessed at http://www.hinduonnet.com/fline/fl2309/stories/20060519004801000.htm.
11. The Indian Express Report. *The Indian Express*, 1 November 2006, New Delhi.
12. South Asia Security Trends July 2006. Published online by Security-risks.com.
13. Interview of Prachanda accessed at http://www.tibet.ca/en/wtnarchive/2006/9/15_7.html.
14. South Asia Security Trends May 2006. Published online by Security-risks.com.
15. South Asia Security Trends October 2006. Published online by Security-risks.com.
16. Poudel, Keshab. Silent Moderation and Violent Extremism. Accessed at http://peacejournalism.com/ReadArticle.asp?ArticleID=15422.

Pakistan: To Be or Not To Be

"Don't push us.... It is not the '70s. We will not climb mountains behind them (militants), they will not even know what and from where something has come and hit them."

Pakistan's President Pervez Musharraf,
On Countering Baloch Militancy.

"Places of worship of all religions including Hinduism were an integral part of the culture of Pakistan and its geographical history. Maintaining such properties in good condition is a government priority in order to turn them into sites for bonding between religions."

Pakistan President Pervez Musharraf

KEY TRENDS

Political Trends

- Political flux in the country with elections scheduled in 2007 for the parliament as well as the post of President.
- Softening of policy of the leadership on Kashmir is evident.
- Greater accommodation for assimilation of perceived alienation amongst communities as Hindus evident.

Militancy Trends

- Two track terrorism policy is continuing though focus of security is shifting from the Eastern border with India to Western border with Afghanistan.
- Balochistan, North West Frontier Province and Waziristan continue to pose challenges of militancy, separatism, tribalism and fundamentalism in varying degrees.

- Internal sectarian violence and terrorism is another dimension.

Military Build Up

- Two tracks of military build up are evident—induction of American equipment through liberal arms aid. Upgraded F 16 fighters are being inducted through this stream.
- Development of indigenous capability through Chinese assistance is the second track—JF 17 is the key joint project in progress.

Internal Polity

Coagulation of political forces in Pakistan grew apace with a 36-Point Charter of Democracy proclaimed by old rivals Benazir Bhutto and Nawaz Sharif from London. Their voices from abroad pepped up their supporters at home and are expected to provide some melodrama in the forthcoming elections in Pakistan in 2007, both for the assembly as well as the post of the President. These leaders seem to be playing upon a rift in the Pakistani military hierarchy with a proposal to establish a commission to investigate the Kargil intrusion by Nawaz Sharif and claim that he was kept in the dark by the military and became aware of it through former Indian Prime Minster, Atal Behari Vajpayee.[1] However, the situation continued to be in a flux throughout the year with conflicting reports indicating a compromise between Benazir Bhutto and President Musharraf. 2007 will certainly be a tumultuous year for Pakistani politics. Pakistan government demonstrated better acceptance and need for assimilation of the Hindu community in society and positive measures were being undertaken for greater inclusiveness.

Pakistan Occupied Kashmir had its eighth assembly elections in which 369 candidates are reported to have participated on 11 July 2006. The candidates had to owe allegiance to the Constitution due to which JKLF candidates were banned from participation. While the POK people came to grips with lack of development and economic penury as news from across the border of lower prices of goods and better access led to a feeling of frustration. This however could not be mobilized during the elections. There were rumblings in the northern areas which were also controlled. The hold of the Army over Pakistan polity is thus seen to be absolute during the year.

The key issue is the hold of the Punjab-Sind lobby on Pakistani polity over the years. An inclusive polity including representation from Balochistan, Gilgit and other areas will meet the genuine aspirations of the people. The elections in 2007 provide a golden opportunity for the same. Unless legitimate efforts towards this end are undertaken, the militancy in the politically fringe but otherwise important provinces will grow over the years. Army's Corps commander caucus is the key decision-making body in Pakistani polity. Thus an alliance which is favorable to the Army is once again likely to be the winner. Pakistani's have evolved a unique model of democracy with political success determined by affiliation with the Army generals rather than a ground swell of support from the masses. Alleged corruption by political leaders in the past can also be one of the key reasons for continued army domination of society.

Terrorism and Counter Terrorism

President Musharraf, acknowledged the growing threat of what he called, "extremism" in an interview on Khyber TV as early as in May 2006.[2] The chickens thus finally come home to roost. This will be a cold reality for states adopting terror as a policy, whosoever breeds terror will have to finally exterminate it in his own brood some day. Pakistan's internal situation thus remained in a state of flux. The intensity of clashes between government forces and tribal in Pakistan's Balochistan and North West Frontier Province grew over the period with total casualties in the first couple of months of the year reported to be 529 till 19 March 2006. These included 251 civilians and 225 terrorists as against 648 persons killed including 430 civilians and 137 terrorists in 2005.[3] This is an alarming, four-fold rise in the level of violence, denoting a new phase in the conflict on Pakistan's Western Frontier.

Pakistani authorities conducted an air raid in the province of Bajaur, north of Waziristan, adjacent to the Afghan province of Kunar. There were allegations that a large number of students who were of the age from 15 to 16 years had been killed in the strike. Eighty-six people were present in the madrasa of which only 3 survived. There were number of protests in Khar, the principal township of Bajaur and effigies of the US President were burned. The local Taliban leaders also proclaimed that suicide squads will strike Pakistani security forces just as the militants are attacking Americans in Afghanistan. Apparently the raid was based on inputs provided by American intelligence. Pakistan, Afghanistan and the United States have an intelligence sharing arrangement.

The equity of Jihadi organizations as the Jamaat ud Dawa considerably increased due to extensive relief work undertaken in earthquake hit areas during the initial months of the year as per a report by the International Crisis Group quoted in *The Hindu*.[4] There were also fears that this would cement the military-terrorist network. With substantial relief aid flowing into Earthquake Reconstruction and Rehabilitation Authority, utilization of these funds had to be carefully scrutinized. Some reports also indicated that the Jamaat was placed in the relief loop by the Army as a convenient tool of propaganda for the organization. The sympathy generated for the Jamaat was expected to raise its stock amongst the local populace. With continuing poverty, recruits for terror were expected to be easier to come by. However events moved faster than anticipated and thus the Jamaat could not effectively cash on whatever goodwill it earned in relief work.

The antipathy between Western governments and the Jamaat also played into fears of resurgence of a group allied to the Lashkar thereby checking its growth. Jammat ud Dawa is also said to have been involved in the plot to target aircraft using chemical explosives. The JuD, a front for the banned LeT or Lashkar-e-Taiyyaba, is not free from controversy. It has been felicitated for its role in providing relief to the earthquake victims in Pakistan Occupied Kashmir, while at the same time funding terror on the other side of the Line of Control in Indian Kashmir.

This finally led to ban on Jamaat ud Dawa (JuD), and its so-called welfare arm, the Idara Khidmat e Khalq or IKK vide the United States Department order No. 13224. This invited strong reactions from the Jamaat leadership in Pakistan which fumed against Mushraff and Bush.[5] The Lashkar-e-Taiyyaba which draws support from the JuD has already been banned under the United Nations Committee Order 1267. India may seek a similar ban on the JuD in coordination with the United States in the United Nations, which will force Pakistan too to proscribe its activities. As the JuD is the matrix of suicide and jehadi terrorism in Pakistan it marginalization should be essential component of India's foreign policy objectives which have to consider state as well as non-state threats.

The arrest of eight terrorists reportedly belonging to Al Qaeda in Pakistan who had planted rockets at Rawalpindi and Islamabad during October indicated the spread of Al Qaeda in the country. These rockets were to be armed through mobile phones. Four rockets were recovered from Ayub Park in Rawalpindi, two from National Arts Council and another two from Shakarparian hill. Decoding of mobile phones had led the intelligence agencies to the culprits.[6] This was indicated by the Interior Minister of Pakistan, Aftab Ahmad Khan Sherpao. All individuals were reported to be Pakistanis and had aimed to create panic in the city.

There were a number of suicide bombers being trained for targeting government and military forces in Pakistan. Reports indicated that military installations and units in areas as Peshawar, Nowshera, Risalpur, Dir, Dera Ismail Khan, Abbottabad, Rawalpindi, Islamabad, Jhelum, Kharian, Lahore, Multan, Hyderabad and Karachi were under threat.[7] Reports also indicated that the Taliban is training 12 muslims from Western countries in Afghanistan for conducting suicide attacks. They were nine British, two Norwegians and one Australian and were to organise cells in their countries, assisting the Taliban in extending their activities in the region. These reports need to be read against the backdrop of a statement made by Taliban chief Mullah Omar that the organisation will soon launch attacks in Europe. The increased presence of NATO forces has upset the designs of Taliban for reestablishing themselves in Kabul and these reports are also designed to undermine resistance back home in Europe.[8]

There was also some focus on maritime threats. Pakistan Navy conducted a joint naval exercise with the US Navy for two weeks essentially coordinating measures on counter-terrorism, human and drug smuggling on the sea routes. This was carried out in three phases to include harbor, sea and analytical skills. Two ships and one submarine each was used by both sides, the sea phase of which was conducted in Pakistan's territorial waters.[9]

Pakistan's Two Track Terrorism Policy. Pakistan is following a two track policy on insurgency and terrorism. It is ensuring that the needs and aspirations of the Western forces particularly Americans are met so that they continue to turn a blind eye towards nuclear proliferation and terrorism in Kashmir. Islamabad has also cooperated with the British in investigating London chemical air strikes plot exposed on 10 August. The Pakistan Army has also assisted Americans in exterminating a large number of Al Qaeda operatives in its own area and overtly denied a base to them. At the same time, it is ensuring that militancy by Kashmiri separatists, Islamic fundamentalists and the Taliban prospers so that its stakes in Afghanistan as well as in India continue unabated. This policy of neighborly antagonism as the key to survival does not bode well for instability in South Asia as well as within Pakistan. Common wisdom states that the wages of breeding terror elsewhere are invariably paid at home.

Balochistan

Balochistan the mineral rich province in the West with the strategic Gwadar port, gas and projected Iran-India pipeline saw constant strife between the tribals and Pakistan Army during the year. There is a three-pronged struggle which has pitched government forces against the tribal Bugtis who's Nawab Akbar Khan owns 40 per cent of the land in Sui gas fields and the Balochistan Liberation Army. Four hundred Pakistani soldiers are reported to have died in the battles in

Balochistan in the past few years as per an Economist report. Nawab Akbar Khan took to the hills in protest and waged a guerrilla war from the mountain lairs while the Baloch National Army demanded autonomy.[10] Sharing revenue from oil and natural gas in the region and greater sovereignty for the Baloch are the key issues. The tribal are concerned over loss of control over oil and gas most of which is falling in the Bugti belt. Government operations in the region have reportedly neutralized 40 Farari or absconder camps and obtained surrender of over 500 armed tribesmen.[11]

In April Balochistan Liberation Army (BLA) was banned in Pakistan after it was declared a terrorist organization, under Section 11 (b) of the Anti-Terrorism Act 1997.[12] The BLA has been accused of sabotage and rocket attacks on government, civil and security forces. Ironically, Pakistani government which has been sponsoring the cause of Kashmiri separatists as freedom fighters and pronouncing killed terrorists as martyrs is faced with the dilemma of, "one man's terrorist being another man's freedom fighter" in Balochistan.

Killing of the tribal head of the Bugtis, Nawab Akbar Khan Bugti in August 2006 appeared to be a gross miscalculation by the military-bureaucratic elite as there were widespread protests over gunning down of the septuagenarian in the remote mountain areas of the province. This gave a temporary fillip to the political agitation in Balochistan but did not have a sizable impact on the ongoing insurgency in the area. The Pakistan Army having declared the killing as a grand success hastily withdrew the statement after seeing the violent reaction in Quetta and other parts of Balochistan. This also led to coagulation of all anti-government forces in the troubled province which the Bugti-Mengal-Marri (BMM) tribal triumvirate attempted to capitalize. In the larger Pakistani polity, despite elections scheduled in 2007 this is unlikely to have a major impact.

After the initial outrage over killing of Nawab Akbar Bugti, Balochistan appeared overtly peaceful as the tribal leaders seem to have been assuaged by the conciliatory approach taken by the Pakistani government after its initial *faux pas* of declaring it as a great victory. No overt linkages between the BLA and the Taliban have been noticed so far. The Taliban are primarily Pushtun Muslim groups who are mainly Sunni while the BLA comprises of the Baloch tribes, Marri and Mengal. Their source of funds is indigenous as well as foreign from the Baloch diaspora. There are no indications of the Al Qaeda having links with the BLA either. Al Qaeda being a Sunni organization, there is likely to be limited interaction with the Balochi liberation organizations. Some reports also indicate that the British are funding the BLA primarily to assist them in the insurgency in southern Afghanistan, as Balochistan and Quetta is considered as the base for Taliban Southern Command fighting in Kandahar. Reports also indicate that the Pakistani intelligence agency ISI has established safe houses for the Taliban in Quetta. This has created resentment in the Baloch population as there is limited affinity towards the Pushtuns.

The lie in the Pakistani governments proclamation that a jirga held during August has declared allegiance of the Baloch community to the ruling junta in Islamabad was exposed with another grand Jirga on 21 September 2006, which proposed to move the International Court of Justice over violation of the original agreement of accession of the Kalat state with Pakistan in 1947.[13] Such reopening of old and disputed legacies always represent hardening of stand of a party to any dispute. The situation ahead thus appears to be highly volatile and the alienation feared after the killing of Akbar Bugti appears to have taken firm roots in Balochistan.

Comments—Baloch Situation

BLA and Baloch struggle is primarily led by the three Baloch tribes, Bugti, Mengal and Marri against Pakistan government authorities for equity in national power sharing. The Baloch struggle draws its strength from the initial resistance offered to amalgamation with Pakistan in 1947 followed by intermittent rebellion against the Pakistani state and the latest uprising based on economic exploitation of the area. Balochi polity is extremely fractured with a large number of tribal and sub-tribal interests continually at conflict with the government.

Thus there is adequate scope for the Pakistani government to divide the Balochi resistance by playing one tribe and sub-tribe against another.

However, this cannot be a long-term strategy and Pakistan will have to consider the overall status of Balochistan in its national scheme. What the Balochi rebellion is seeking is not independence, the call for which is only a bargaining chip but greater influence in national economy, polity and policy making mechanisms including the Army. Thus a policy which could meet these aspirations would see peace returning to the troubled province provided Islamabad has the sagacity to follow the right course.

Sources say that Iran may also be interested in this region as it has a large Baloch population in its eastern provinces. Pakistan has been accusing India of sponsoring the insurgency in Balochistan by supplying arms and resources. Pakistan has also been saying that India has established widespread presence in Afghanistan through a number of consulates with the aim of creating problems in neighboring Pakistan.[14] Reports also indicate that there is British interest in Balochistan as it is seen to be directly affecting British operations in southern Afghanistan.

Pakistan is following the American model of counter-insurgency operations in Balochistan using strike aircraft and attack helicopters to drive the insurgents deep into the hills. The military precision with which the Pakistani government is tackling the militancy is seen by the killing of Akbar Khan Bugti whose death was surrounded by mystery but which can be reasonably believed to have been carried out by Pakistani Special Forces assisted by air and attack helicopter support. Pakistan's use of excessive military force is based on its previous experience in the 1970's when the insurgency in Balochistan was effectively quelled by the Pakistan Army. This time around it is hopeful that use of air power will produce equally decisive results.

The lessons of history, however, seem to have been lost on the military junta. Air power has to be in support of ground and naval operations unless it has a strategic purpose. An exclusive air campaign is unlikely to gain substantial results as despite intelligence, it is very difficult to engage a large number of targets accurately particularly in urban and underdeveloped terrain as Israel realized recently in Lebanon. On the other hand even when used to assist forces on the ground in insurgency situations, it only antagonizes the local population and creates an occupation mindset thereby increasing the intensity of resistance.

Two scenarios can be envisaged in Balochistan in the future which are as follows:

(a) *Scenario* 1. Successful politicization of the Baloch militancy by Pakistani administration by a process of political and economic sops taking on board all the tribal groups including the BMM (Bugti, Mengal, Marri) combination, accompanied by firm action to quell terrorist activities in the area. This is the ideal scenario which may not produce immediate results but is in Pakistan's national interest. Delicate balancing of inter-tribal equations will be essential.

(b) *Scenario* 2. Politicization by promoting inter-tribal rivalry combined with military force to quell the BMM and the BLA. Playing a grouping of minor tribes against the BMM to drive a wedge between the two would give a semblance of crisis resolution but will not be in long-term interest. This will strengthen the Baloch resistance and increase militancy. This is perhaps the strategy which the Pakistani military has been following so far and is likely to result in a long drawn out battle.

Waziristan and NWFP

The situation in Pakistan's tribal areas adjoining Afghanistan continued to be serious with over 300 terrorists killed since March in Army operations. Approximately 5000 fighters are known to have united to fight the Pakistan Army which has for the first time ventured in this area traditionally dominated by the tribal. Reports indicate that there are 80,000 troops deployed most of whom are likely to be from the Para military Frontier Corps.[15] The United States is reported to have provided Pakistan considerable equipment including 10 Huey Cobra helicopters and 3 Cessna Caravan planes. Use of armed helicopters has been proliferating. It is being justified by the presence of Al Qaeda fighters in the area. A CIA controlled Predator Unarmed Armed Vehicle struck on Damadola village on 13 January 2006 killing 18 people. The mission was launched to target Ayman Al Zawahiri, the second in command of the Al Qaeda but Zawahiri is said to have escaped. This resulted in massive anti-US protests in Pakistan.

The growth of jehadi culture in Pakistan and its continued employment of technology was more than evident with the raid on 156 FM stations in the Pashtun tribal area. The Pakistan Electronic Media Regulating Authority (PEMRA) has in coordination with the local authorities seized 94 stations which were operating illegally in the tribal areas transmitting religious and political views, fanning sectarian hatred and anti-national sentiments.

The terrorists in North Waziristan, announced a ceasefire for a period of one month ostensibly to allow the tribal jirga to reach a peaceful settlement in the extremely volatile area in the strategic Pushtun lands astride the Durand Line in June 2006.[16] Taliban spokesman, Abdullah Farhad said that the security forces should return to bases, check posts should be abolished, all personnel arrested should be released and incentives for tribal leaders should be restored. The terrorists however will retain the right to attack in self-defense. Ceasefire is a, "time out" tactics employed by terrorist groups, either when they are under pressure or want to shift their strategy. The aim of the Taliban is clearly to bide for time, seek free movement in the area and keep the tribal happy by getting them additional resources.

The jirga held consultations with the Taliban commanders at an unknown location east of Miranshah and both parties are said to have agreed to an extension of the ceasefire in July 2006. The situation in South Waziristan, however, remained contentious with the Taliban commanders having issued a warning to government tax collectors to stop collection of taxes on goods moving in and out of Waziristan.[17]

In August, Pakistani forces mustered services of the former leader of the opposition in the Pakistani National Assembly, Maulana Fazlur Rehman to work out an agreement with the Taliban now firmly entrenched and virtually running an Islamic Republic in North Waziristan. The ceasefire initially announced on 25 July 2006 was extended till 10 September 2006. An Agreement was signed on 5 September, the main points of which were as follows:

- Cessation of all land and air operations against the Taliban.
- All Taliban prisoners arrested during operations to be freed and a clemency granted for all terrorists irrespective of crimes.
- The Taliban were to turn in heavy weaponry but are allowed to carry small arms.
- Pakistan to pay reparations to the Taliban and tribes for losses during the operation.
- The Army to withdraw from all check posts and a paramilitary force to assume control.
- Tribal leaders and Ulema to assume responsibility to ensure that there will be no more attacks on security forces and government property.
- Disputes to be settled through the Frontier Crimes Regulations (FCR) instituted during colonial times and the Taliban would dismantle other kangaroo courts.
- Pakistan to restore all privileges and rights of tribal.
- All foreigners will either leave North Waziristan or respect local laws.
- All movement through the mountains into Afghanistan will be stopped.
- The Taliban and Ulema will return stolen government property such as vehicles, wireless sets, and arms.
- A 10-member committee will monitor adherence to the agreement and will include political administrators and tribal elders.[18]

Pakistan planned to mine the border with Afghanistan to prevent militants from crossing into Afghanistan. However, there were widespread protests by Kabul as well as the United Nations. The problem is the legitimacy of the Durand Line. A fence will also divide the Pushtoons living on both sides of the border. Pakistan claims that it has deployed 80,000 troops and established 800 check posts to prevent trans border infiltration. However, all these efforts have apparently not given results.

Afghanistan constantly complained Pakistani involvement in the upsurge of Taliban in the country over the past one year. In the latest round of mutual suspicion, Afghanistan President Karzai is reported to have accused Pakistan of providing a safe house to Mullah Omar, the Taliban chief in Quetta and sanctuaries in Karachi as well as the North Waziristan town of Miranshah.

The Taliban had organized in three distinct groups by the end of the year as under:

(a) *Taliban—Pakistan.* Primarily comprising of Pakistanis, this is the group which is dominant in Waziristan and has successfully negotiated with the Pakistani government in September, thereby gaining virtual control of northern Waziristan. This apparently has the support of the tribal in the area, acquired through coercion, willing acquiescence and bribes.

(b) *Taliban Afghanistan—Eastern Command and Southern Command.* The Taliban in Afghanistan appears to be divided into two groups, one operating with its support base in Quetta and the second group with its base in Miranshah, north Waziristan. The northern group is predominant in the eastern provinces in Afghanistan along with other splinter Afghan groups as the Wana Shura and Hekmatyar's Hezb I Islami, while the southern group in Kandahar and Helmand.

Comments on Waziristan

This policy of making peace with the tribal leaders and/or Taliban in northern Waziristan came under intense debate during the year. The controversial deal on 5 September with the

Pro-Taliban militants, which Pakistani authorities claim is with the tribal leaders resulted in the Army withdrawing from the region. Reports indicate that Taliban are assuming slow and gradual control in the area. The Taliban is now known as the Pakistani Taliban as opposed to those who operate in Afghanistan who come under the name of Afghan Taliban.

The first resistance came from Afghan leaders who complained that after the deal, there has been increase in Taliban activities particularly in the areas adjacent to northern Waziristan. Perceptive observers such as Ahmed Rashid have indicated that a coalition of extremist groups, the Pakistani and Afghani Taliban, Central Asian and Chechen rebels along with the Al Qaeda will be calling the shots in this area. The Taliban is attempting to establish its own administrative infrastructure in much the same way as it had done in southern Waziristan after April 2004.

The agreement between the Pakistan government and the Taliban in north Waziristan was regarded as a watershed in the border areas. The Pakistan Army spearheaded the same, though observers see it as a surrender in the face of stiff resistance, it has been facing in the area over the past couple of years in which it has lost over 700 soldiers. It was also said that this was to force the Al Qaeda to leave Waziristan or live peacefully in the area. One hundred thirty detained tribals were to be released by the government in return for local assistance in reining in the foreign elements.

The Agreement also had a clause that there will be no trans border movement of the people to Afghanistan, for which no specific mechanism has however been devised. This is not likely to bring much relief to neighboring Afghanistan, a fact which has increased the tension in relations between Pakistan President Musharraf and Afghan President Karzai who has been categorically insisting that the Pakistani Agreement is detrimental to Afghan security. This was apparent when on 20 September, US helicopter gun ships chased 10 suspected Taliban terrorists to Lawara Mandi in Waziristan where they were arrested. This was an intrusion by US helicopters of Pakistani air space. It was also reported that five bodies of prominent locals were brought to Miranshah from the Paktika province of Afghanistan. One of these is said to be that of the militant commander, Maulana Abdul Kalam of north Waziristan. The tribesmen are reported to have been killed in a fire fight with the Allied forces in Afghanistan. That the Agreement may have tacit US support was underlined by the statement by the US Assistant Secretary of State Richard Boucher that the deal had a potential to work.

Reports in December indicated that the Taliban were routinely crossing the Pakistan-Afghan border to launch strikes and returning to the base across the Durand Line in Pakistan. Thus, Waziristan is said to be providing safe sanctuaries to the Taliban. At the same time there is increased Talibinisation of the area with reports of over 100 tribal killed on allegations of being spies and government agents.

The Agreement in north Waziristan was a defensive measure by Pakistan to seek a reprieve for its forces deployed in the tribal areas, which were making hardly any headway in the counter-insurgency battle in one of the most rugged terrains of the World with an enemy who is a master of deceit, cunning, tactical acumen and fanaticism. The Taliban had effectively exploited intervention by the Pakistan Army in a frontier agency, where local tribal have been fiercely independent to instigate the tribal leaders to fight the Army. The options before the Pakistan Army were thus to engage the Taliban-tribal combine for a long war to bring it to heel or win a peace apparently with a lot of monetary persuasion and deflect the Taliban towards Afghanistan. This is what has been achieved in the bargain and just as the Agreement, Pakistan Army made with the Taliban in south Waziristan; it will only heighten the state of the resistance to NATO forces in southern Afghanistan in the future.

The Pakistan Army will also be able to move its troops to Balochistan leading to a possible suppression of the rebellion. The release of large number of army troops is also significant prior to the elections scheduled in 2007. This will enable the army to continue its hold on the Pakistani power structure in the future.

Pakistan's short-term strategy will only lead to extending its status as a failed and ungovernable state over the next one to two decades. By bringing order to the Western border it could have built a symbiotic relationship of trust and confidence with the regime in Afghanistan contributing to long-term security. Now that it has chosen to hunt with the hares, the situation is highly vitiated. There is no hope ahead for the people of Balochistan and Waziristan which will continue to be at a level of development comparable with any poor African state.

PAKISTAN ARMED FORCES BUILD UP

Missile Superiority

Pakistan's Strategic Planning Division (SPD) asserted to its parliamentarians that it was ahead of India in the nuclear and missile programmes. It also indicated that Pakistan was solely controlling these strategic assets and had adequate number of missiles and nuclear weapons to meet its needs. Details of the Command, Control and Communication system and expenditure incurred on such systems were also given. The minimum deterrence policy of Pakistan was said to be the key factor for promoting national security and preserving peace and stability in the region.[19] This presentation by the SPD to the political hierarchy in the country is probably the first of its kind in Pakistan. The aim is obviously targeted at raising awareness of the high level of deterrence of Pakistan's nuclear capability both within and outside the country. The concerns of the parliamentarians were also addressed by assuring good health and welfare of the renegade nuclear scientist A.Q. Khan, who was reported to be under reasonable health and safe custody.

Pakistan's quest for military parity with India continued with reports of successful test of the Hatf VI or Shaheen II which is reported to have a range of 2,000 kms.[20] This is said to be a nuclear capable surface to surface ballistic missile and most likely to have been built with Chinese assistance. The successful testing of Babur, the Pakistani version of a cruise missile signifies Pakistani efforts to gain parity with India in the missile capability dimension of conventional and nuclear capabilities. This will enhance deterrence and until the Indian forces are able to create a missile shield, Pakistan with first strike intent will hold the edge against India in an accidentally triggered nuclear or conventional exchange.

The Hatf II or Ghaznavi, a short range ballistic missile with a range of 290 kms was tested by the Strategic Missile Group. The Ghauri and Shaheen I had also been tested during the same period as the operational readiness of the Strategic Missile Group was being assessed. The presence of the Chief of the Air Staff, Air Chief Marshal Tanvir Mahmood Ahmed indicated that the missile forces are likely to be managed by the Strategic Missile Group under the Pakistan Air Force. This is perhaps the first time that the Pakistan Army is set to lose its preeminence in decisions relating to a strategic system.

In November, Pakistan Army Strategic Force Command (ASFC) conducted military exercises which culminated into firing of the Hatf IV or Shaheen I by the Strategic Missile Group on 29 November. This has been a follow up of the successful firing of Hatf V or Ghauri which is said to have a range of 1300 kms.[21]

Pakistan Arms Aid by the USA

Pakistan is reported to have received $ 3.6 billion in military aid for operations from January 2002 till August 2005 which is 25 per cent of Pakistan's Defence budget. $ 900 million are likely to be used from Pentagons' massive $ 439 billion FY 2007 budget for reimbursements to coalition supporting nations of which Pakistan will be a major recipient.[22]

Pakistan signed a deal for supply of F 16 aircraft with the USA. However, it has been reported that it would be required to provide unprecedented guarantees to ensure that technology of the advanced F 16 C/D models was not shared with China and the F 16 would not be armed with nuclear weapons. Any overseas mission for the aircraft will also require approval of the US government. There were a number of issues which were discussed by the US government with Congressional representatives which have not been made public. Most of these are likely to be related to transfer of technology to Pakistan and use of F 16 as nuclear weapon carriers against other states.

Pakistan has been seeking more offensive aircraft and helicopter capability from the USA for launching counter Al Qaeda operations in its border areas. The use of air power by Pakistan was more than evident with the killing of Akbar Khan Bugti in the air raids in Balochistan. Whatever the guarantees, the US plea of equity and a new relationship in south Asia between India, Pakistan and Afghanistan indicated that the deal was eventually cleared by the Congress.

This F 16 deal includes 16 new aircraft and refurbishing the current fleet of 34 aircraft. An option for an additional 18 aircraft has also been indicated. The total deal is worth $ 5 billion. Thus Pakistan is slated to have around 34 new F 16 aircraft in its inventory which would imply an accretion of two more squadrons, in addition to the existing two F 16 squadrons which may well turn the balance in air parity in south Asia in its favor.[23]

The early warning, avionics and armament package on the refurbished F 16 aircraft is also impressive. This will include the AMRAAM air to air missile and 54 APG-68(V)9 Radar for Block 50/52 F 16 manufactured by Northrop Grumman. The $ 99.5 million firm fixed contract for 54 *AN/APG-68 (V)9 Radar Systems* was granted to Northrop Grumman Electronic Systems in Linthicum Heights, MD. The breakdown of 54 radar units will be 36 for the newly sanctioned F 16s, plus 7 spare for the new aircraft, 10 spare for retrofits of older F 16s and 1 additional radar. Defenseindustrydaily has also indicated that Pakistan will order 60 more units under the F-16A/B Mid-Life Update (MLU) modification and Falcon Star Structural Service Life Enhancement kit programme which will be the APG-66(V)2 radar.

The APG 68 radar offers better detection range and resolution. The faster processors provide high degree of inputs at five times more processing speed and ten times advanced memory capacity over the present version of the radar. There is resistance to electromagnetic interference and counter-measures which have been built in the system. This gives it enhanced capability for air to air or air to ground operations particularly useful in a target rich and beyond visual range environment.

The increase in range offered is said to be to the order of 30 per cent, tracking four *vis-à-vis* two targets and larger search volume with better track while scan capability. The single track capability is also said to be much improved.

In the ground attack mode the new radar is said to act as a sensor utilizing its high resolution synthetic aperture radar to locate and recognize ground targets beyond visual range and even further upstream. The resolution will be two feet. This has an all weather capability and will provide real time source for targeting of long range, precision guided weapons. The detection range in sea surveillance mode has also been increased and with increased ground moving target identifying and mapping capability will provide a powerful tool to the pilot to home on to and strike at the targets. The accuracy is greatly enhanced due to auto bore sight capability and dynamic tracking is also improved due to an inertial measurement unit.[24]

The Bush Administration defended its decision to sell F-16 aircraft to Pakistan as a key element of the Government's strategy to broaden the strategic relationship in south Asia with India, Afghanistan and Pakistan, as per hearings by the House Foreign Relations Committee on the subject held on 20 July 2006. The aim of the decision is to strengthen the hands of President Musharraf America's key ally who is seen to be under increasing pressure in Pakistan internally what with the campaign against the Baluchis and the tribal in Waziristan in full swing. Many people in Pakistan believe that the Islamic upsurge of violence in the country is a result of partnership with the USA. The elections in Pakistan in 2007 are also said to be a cause of concern for Musharraf. Accretion in F-16 inventory will enable him to keep the Armed Forces, the key policy makers in Pakistan in good humor. This acquisition will upset the balance of air forces in the region, with the Indian Air Force superiority greatly whittled down after the MIG 21 aircraft being dated.

Naval Accretions

Pakistan is building up its armory in a very systematic manner with a view to project itself as an alternative power centre in south and central Asia. The key is naval and air capability in tune with the upcoming hubs of Gwadar-Pasni ports on the southern coast of the country. The Chinese interest in this area is well-known and infrastructure development is taking place with Chinese engineering assistance. Simultaneously the southern areas will also see a network of oil and gas pipelines crisscrossing from Iran to Pakistan and hopefully to India. The naval procurements to operate from these bases include the following:

(a) *Submarines.* Marlin SSK from Armaris of France is the preferred option likely to be exercised to induct three submarines. These are diesel-electric versions, single hulled, with air independent propulsion and are likely to cost between $ 1 billion to $ 1.2 billion. Class 214 submarine has also been offered by Germany firm Howaldtswerke-Deutsche Werft (HDW). Chinese, Italian and Russian firms are also actively seeking this high value order. The submarines will be equipped with Harpoon anti-ship missiles from Boeing, 300 of which are being cleared by the US Congress for sale at $ 370 million to Pakistan. Fifty of these missiles will be submarine launched. Pakistan is already operating the French Agosta 90 B class submarine since 1994, thus the induction of another French type of submarine will be favored.[25]

(b) *Harpoon Anti-Ship Missiles.* The Defense Security Cooperation Agency notified the US Congress of a possible Foreign Military Sale to Pakistan of Harpoon Block II Anti-ship Missiles along with associated equipment and services for a total value of $ 370 million. These include 50 UGM-84L (submarine-launched), 50 RGM-84L (surface-launched), and 30 AGM-84L (air-launched) Block II Harpoon missiles; 5 Encapsulated Harpoon Command Launch Systems; 115 containers and assorted equipment. The press release indicated that the proposed sale will contribute to US foreign policy and national security by assisting Pakistan improve its security.[26]

(c) *S 100B—Argus AEW & C.* Pakistan is to get 14, S 100B Argus AEW & C airborne early warning aircraft from Sweden after protracted negotiations. Seven aircraft will be with the Pakistan Air Force for AEW & C role. SAAB aircraft had competed against the Bombardier Dash-8/Q 200. A key capability of the aircraft in AEW role is the ability to scan ground as well as air activity simultaneously. Pakistan Air Force surveillance capability will be considerably enhanced with the induction of the AEW & C providing it valuable early warning.[27]

Other Military Equipment and Systems

Pakistan's acquisition of the Swedish Erieye, Saab 2000 AWACS in June 2006, despite widespread opposition at home over the cost of the project, against the backdrop of diversion of funds from earthquake relief is likely to be supplemented by a deal with China for its indigenously built AWACS jet, Y-8. Chinese prototype was reportedly demonstrated to the Pakistanis at the Air Force Base in Chaklala. A successful demonstration of this aircraft could possibly lead to Pakistani acquisition on very favorable terms from China, given the strategic nature of Sino-Pakistan defense relationship. While this may enable Pakistan to increase the density of airborne surveillance platforms, the quality of coverage will be dependent on the ability to integrate two possibly divergent systems, the Erieye and the Y-8 as well as the capability of the electronic surveillance and command and control systems likely to be deployed on these platforms.

Pakistan is planning to modify P 3 maritime patrol aircraft into Airborne Early Warning platforms using the Northrop Grumman Airborne Early Warning Suite designed for E2C Hawkeye. A notification to the effect was given by the Pentagon to the US Congress. Pakistan had been supplied eight P3C Orion maritime surveillance aircraft from the US Navy surplus which increased its overall strength in this class to 10 aircraft. Three are to be modified into AEW platforms which will be used to support aircraft and surface ships. The Pentagon notification however indicated that these were only for maritime purposes. Pakistan has also been considering buying a Chinese AEW platform and the Swedish Saab 340 with the Ericsson Erieye AEW system.

Pakistan's anti-tank capability is set to enhance considerably with induction of 2769 Radio Frequency (RF) TOW 2A missiles and 415 RF Bunker Busters. 121 TOW launchers will be modified to fire the RF guidance system. These are reportedly being inducted for employment against terrorists on the AH-1S Huey Cobra attack helicopter system. Pakistan Army is following the American concept of air and helicopter strikes on indigenous guerrillas, a measure which has been assiduously avoided by the Indian armed forces due to its negative fall out.

Pakistan is slated to buy an unspecified number of J-10 fighters from China which are known as F-10s in Pakistan. This will also supplement the F 16 that Pakistan is planning to buy but the same was postponed in the wake of the October 2005, Earthquake.

Pakistan's interior minister, Aftab Sherpao demanded additional armed helicopters during his recent visit to the United States on 24 July 2006. This was essential to boost joint anti-terror and anti-narcotics operations being undertaken by both the countries on the Pakistan Afghanistan border, he claimed. The drug dealers in the area are said to be well armed and hence it was essential that more armaments were allotted to defeat the network.[28]

PAKISTAN STRATEGIC INFRASTRUCTURE

Khushab Nuclear Reactor

Pakistan is said to be building a new reactor which is capable of producing large quantity of plutonium at Khushab. A satellite imagery of Pakistan's nuclear facility at Khushab in central Pakistan denoted a partially completed heavy water reactor. This has been a cause of concern for India as well as the nuclear non-proliferation lobby in the United States. A report in the UNI however, stated that the US government had downplayed the significance of the information by a Washington based think tank, Institute for Science and International Security.

This is likely to enable production of 40 to 50 nuclear weapons a year. This is said to be a twenty-fold increase in capability to produce nuclear weapons from the present two to three per year.

The Khushab facility is said to have a capacity for 1000 megawatts or more and will provide Pakistan the ability to make plutonium warheads. Pakistan is said to be having 30 to 50 uranium warheads which are difficult to mount on missiles. The advantage of plutonium bombs over uranium bombs is clear. As against 15 to 20 kilograms of material required for making a uranium bomb, plutonium weapons can be built with as little as 5 kilograms, which also makes it easy to fit warheads on missiles. These can also act as triggers for the larger hydrogen or fusion bombs which are many times more powerful than a fission weapon. This will place Pakistan in the super league of the atomic club in years to come. Many Congressmen in the United States including Gary Ackerman have expressed great concern over this development, particularly with Pakistan also being supplied with F 16 aircraft which are nuclear capable. The construction of the reactor has led to fears of a nuclear arms race in the South Asian region, with India and Pakistan engaged in numerical parity, simultaneously India attempting to equate its capability with that of China.[29]

SINO-PAKISTAN RELATIONS

A Free Trade Agreement was one of the key achievements in cementing the long-standing political relationship between China and Pakistan during the visit of President Hu Jin Tao to Islamabad in November.[30] The manufacturing sector was specifically selected for mutual cooperation with household appliances, automobile and textile being the key areas. In the energy segment exploration of fossil fuels, coal, hydro power, nuclear and renewable energy sectors were also identified for cooperation. Establishment of a Pakistan Consulate in Chengdu is also planned to improve access for Pakistani citizens to China's Western region.

China-Pakistan Free Trade Agreement (CPFTA) is seen as a possible measure by Beijing to enter the lucrative South Asian market particularly through the Special Export Zone (SEZ) in Lahore, which could be targeted at South Asian and Indian markets. The SEZ in Lahore could meet the 35 percent value addition required by Pakistan as per a report in the website www.whatisindia.com. The report also stated that it would be essential for India to monitor future exports from Pakistan and develop economic intelligence specifically targeted at the Lahore SEZ.[31] India is mainly exporting raw materials such as minerals and iron ore to China which constitutes 60 per cent of the total trade of over $ 17 billion. While this trade may not be affected, it is feared that China could use the cheaper Pakistan route to flood Indian markets, bringing back fears of a charge of the Dragon which had led to many small scale entrepreneurs in India in 2000 to close their shops when cheap Chinese goods first entered Indian markets.

A key agreement was signed between China and Pakistan in the field of defense production to include development of an airborne early warning surveillance system. Pakistan has already sought a Saab turbo prop aircraft with Ericsson airborne radar which is expected to be delivered in 2009. Pakistan has an agreement with Chinese aviation firm CATIC for development and production of JF 17 Thunder fighter aircraft. Eight of these are expected to be delivered by 2007 and the production has already started in Pakistan in January 2006 with serial production slated to begin by January 2008.

Signing of a bilateral agreement for construction of an additional 200 km of the Karakoram Highway from Rai Kot to Sazeen was also a major landmark. This would entail investment of $ 325 million. The 335 kms stretch from Khunjerab to Rai Kot is already under renovation. Visitors who had been on this route recently complained of severe damage to the road which has become virtually impassable. The Gilgit and Skardu road is also being passed on for renovation to China by Pakistan which will considerably improve communication links in the northern areas. The overall plan is to connect Gwadar through Kashghar (2,600 kms) to Beijing 8,500 kms away. A quadrilateral agreement with Tajikistan and Kyrgyzstan for movement of goods is also under process.

A military exercise, code-named "Friendship-2006" was held from 11 to 18 December 2006 in Abottabad, north of Islamabad. The aim of the exercise was to coordinate the concept and training for counter-terrorism, strengthen cooperation between China and Pakistan in the field of non-traditional security and safeguard peace and stability of the region. Chinese People's Liberation Army troops have been part of an exercise in Pakistan for the first time. The exercise is said to have enhanced counter-terrorism skills. These exercises are based on a memorandum of understanding between the Chinese and Pakistani leadership for joint training. China and Pakistan already have a long-standing agreement on defence including defence production. Many analysts believe that Pakistan's current missile prowess is wholly based on Chinese support. On the other hand even Pakistani tanks as Al Khalid are said to be designed in China and manufactured from knocked down kits.

The JF 17 Project a joint project between Chengdu Aircraft Industry Corporation and Pakistan Aeronautical Complex is set to commence production in March 2007. The engines for this joint venture are reportedly being provided by Russia which has already signed an agreement with China, despite protests by the Indian side.

China is also likely to extend assistance to Pakistan in the field of peaceful nuclear development, provide four F22P frigates to the Pakistan Navy, upgrade the Karachi Dockyard and transfer technology for indigenous production of naval craft. The deal is said to be worth $ 600 million.[32] When seen along with Chinese assistance in development of Gwadar port, the presence of China on the northern shores of the Arabian Sea demonstrates significance placed by China on the flow of oil through the area, which China would like to have some control through Pakistani proxy. This will be a powerful leverage for the Chinese and in turn provide a boost for Pakistan's naval facilities both commercial and military.

Pakistan is reported to have acquired the capability to build French Agosta class submarines including the technology rights for transfer and marketing at a later stage. Pakistan has two Agosta class submarines with the third being built in the

Karachi docks. A total of four submarines are to be inducted in the Pakistan Navy.[33] Pakistan is also slated to purchase six new frigates from China and Greece. The modernization of the Pakistan Navy has been undertaken keeping in view its overall plan of upgradation of its armed forces and the strategic role that Pakistan has slotted itself in as the frontline state for Islamic as well as Western powers in the region. This requires a delicate balancing act, which President Musharraf has been performing successfully so far.

Signing of the Sino-Pakistan Defense Pact by Chairman of Pakistan's Joint Chiefs of Staff Committee, General Ehsanul Haq and Lt Gen Zhang Qin Sheng, Assistant to the Chief of the General Staff of the People's Republic Army, denotes strengthening Sino-Pakistani defense links. The Pact between China and Pakistan includes strategic defense cooperation and military assistance agreement. This was the culmination of the fourth round of defense and security talks which included cooperation in the field of defense and military assistance.[34]

China-Pakistan Nuclear Cooperation

China is reported to be providing Pakistan with a nuclear largesse of six nuclear plants. A declaration to the effect was reported during the visit of the Chinese President Hu Jin Tao in November 2006. This will provide a total of 6300 megawatt (MW) of nuclear energy in the sites selected by Islamabad. These plants will be under scrutiny of the IAEA. Pakistan Atomic Energy Commission is targeting 8800 MW of nuclear energy by 2030. The likely locations are Qadirabad-Bulloki link canal near the Qadirabad headworks, the Dera Ghazi Khan canal near the Taunsa Barrage, the Taunsa-Punjnad canal near Multan, the Nara canal near Sukkur, and the Pat Feeder canal near Guddu and the Kabul river near Nowshera.[35] The proposed size of the nuclear plants is quite large, each generating over 1000 MW of energy. This indicates Chinese expertise in developing large sized nuclear plants. Apart from increasing the nuclear energy capacity bank in Pakistan, it will also enhance strategic Sino-Pak cooperation.

Gwadar Pasni Area

Development of the Gwadar Pasni area in Pakistan has led to considerable consternation in American and Iranian circles as the intent of China of increasing its presence in the region through a, "string of pearls" strategy gets well established. A railway line is also proposed to be constructed to link Gwadar Pasni area with rest of the country.[36] The United States is wary of China's ability to monitor shipping traffic in the area as also have a better control of the strategic outposts in the region. Gwadar is also worrying Iran which sees a competition to its own port Chahbahar being developed with Indian assistance. Thus, there will be two sea outlets for oil and gas of central Asian states, one through Iran and the other through Pakistan. There is also intense resistance to development of Gwadar by the local Baloch tribal who deprived of the fruits of riches in minerals and oil on their land earlier are now resisting outside presence.

Improvement of Karakoram Highway

The Karakoram Highway was built in 1978 and the 809 kms long road is said to be largely in a state of disrepair. It is also said to have suffered heavy damage during the earthquake in 2005. A memorandum of understanding was signed between China and Pakistan for upgradation of the Karakoram highway. The first stage will see the 335 kms road between the Raikot Bridge and the Khunjerab pass rebuilt and upgraded. The width is slated to be expanded to 30 metres and the transportation capability will be increased three times.[37]

Energy Developments

Pakistan's ambitious Energy Security Plan which envisages an increase in nuclear power generation from 425 Megawatts at present to 8,800 megawatts by 2030 received a fillip with the approval for Chashma Nuclear Power Plant Unit 2 by the International Atomic Energy Agency (IAEA). This is being built with Chinese assistance and succeeds the Chashma 1 which has similar safeguards. Pakistan already has two research and two nuclear power plants under safeguards of the IAEA. There is intense scrutiny of Pakistan's nuclear programme after its nuclear scientist Abdul Qadeer Khan was found guilty of collaborating with North Korea and Libya. The Pakistan government however, succeeded in staving off any allegations of its involvement by shifting the entire blame on A.Q. Khan. (www.defencetalk.com)

The Iran-Pakistan-India (IPI) suffered a set-back with both India and Pakistan refusing to accept the proposal by the consultant appointed by Iran, Gaffney Cline and Associates for a price formula for the gas which Iran proposes to sell to India and Pakistan. Pricing and open ended contracts were the major issues on which there were disagreements. Iran had proposed a price equal to 10 per cent of Brent Crude oil price and in addition a fixed cost of US $ 1.2 million British Thermal Unit (BTU).

REFERENCE

1. South Asia Security Trends June 2006. Published online by Security-risks.com.
2. South Asia Security Trends June 2006. Published online by Security-risks.com.
3. South Asia Intelligence Review. Weekly Assessments & Briefings Volume 4, No. 36, March 20, 2006.
4. Reddy, B. Murlidhar. "concern __"*The Hindu*. 20 March 2006. New Delhi. p. 11.
5. South Asia Security Trends May 2006. Published online by Security-risks.com.
6. South Asia Security Trends December 2006. Published online by Security-risks.com.
7. South Asia Security Trends January 2007. Published online by Security-risks.com.
8. South Asia Security Trends May 2006. Published online by Security-risks.com.
9. Based on report in www.defencetalk.com.
10. The Economist Report. *The Economist*. 1 July 2006.
11. Report in www.satp.org.
12. South Asia Security Trends May 2006. Published online by Security-risks.com.
13. South Asia Security Trends October 2006. Published online by Security-risks.com.
14. Reported in www.crossfirewar.com.

15. South Asia Security Trends May 2006. Published online by Security-risks.com.
16. South Asia Security Trends July 2006. Published online by Security-risks.com.
17. Based on reports in sair.org.
18. Based on reports in www.whatisindia.com.
19. South Asia Security Trends August 2006. Published online by Security-risks.com.
20. South Asia Security Trends May 2006. Published online by Security-risks.com.
21. South Asia Security Trends December 2006. Published online by Security-risks.com.
22. Indian Express Report. *Indian Express*. 30 October 2006.
23. Based on a report in http://www.defencetalk.com/news/publish/article_006676.php.
24. With inputs from www.defenseindustrydaily.com and defense-update.com).
25. Based on France OKs Sub Talks With Pakistan Islamabad Wants U.S. Harpoon Missiles To Arm Subs. PIERRE TRAN, http://www.defensenews.com/story.php?F=1840676&C=thisweek.
26. Based on press release http://www.dsca.mil.
27. With inputs from defenseindustrydaily.com.
28. South Asia Security Trends August 2006. Published online by Security-risks.com.
29. Based on report at http://www.defencetalk.com/news/publish/article_007061.php.
30. South Asia Security Trends December 2006. Published online by Security-risks.com.
31. Based on reports in www.whatisindia.com.
32. Times of India Report. *The Times of India*. 24 May.
33. South Asia Security Trends August 2006. Published online by Security-risks.com.
34. Indian Express Report. *Indian Express*. 25 August 2006.
35. South Asia Security Trends November 2006. Published online by Security-risks.com.
36. South Asia Security Trends August 2006. Published online by Security-risks.com.
37. South Asia Security Trends August 2006. Published online by Security-risks.com.

Sri Lanka: Back to the Wars of Ealam

5

KEY TRENDS—2006

"(The President) remains unshaken in his resolve to achieve peace in Sri Lanka and is undeterred in his efforts to combat all forms of terrorism and violence."

Statement of Presidential Secretariat after attack on Gotabaya Rajpaksa, President's Brother and Defence Secretary

"(Marginalization of the Ceasefire Agreement)...has also compelled the Tamil people to resume their freedom struggle to realize their right to self-determination and to achieve statehood"[1]

LTTE statement on 22nd February 2007

Political

- Sri Lanka politics is in a flux with floundering of the Memorandum of Understanding between the ruling Sri Lanka Freedom Party (SLFP) and the opposition United National Party (UNP) due to large number of alleged engineered defections from the opposition to the ruling party.
- This will create problems of political consensus in the south effectively negating progress of negotiations with LTTE.
- LTTE considerably weakened in eastern Sri Lanka and influence restricted to the north. Karuna remained one of the principal points of political contention for the LTTE.
- Ban of LTTE by the European Union and death of principal ideologue Anton Balasingham also indicates political loss abroad.

Militancy

- LTTE continues to follow a joint strategy of suicide attacks and conventional strikes using artillery.
- Strikes from the sea on Sri Lankan Navy have also been effective.
- Northern LTTE held area will be the main battlefront in 2007.
- Air strikes could be anticipated.

Counter-Militancy

- Sri Lanka Armed Forces are gaining ground through effective use of air and fire power along with resoluteness of battle hardened troops in conventional operations.
- Deep penetration strikes or raids are also used to effect.
- Karuna faction guerrillas are providing the Sri Lankan Army considerable advantage in eastern Sri Lanka.

Economy and Development

- Economy has suffered due to loss of tourism. However, other macro indicators do not indicate a slowdown.

GENERAL

Introduction

Sri Lanka returned to civil war after four years of fractious peace. Employment of air against the Liberation Tigers of Tamil Ealam (LTTE) marked a new stage in conflict in the troubled Island. Sri Lankan Armed Forces (SLAF) and political hardliners wanted a hard-hitting response to repeated acts of violence by the LTTE. The bloodshed was initially seen as brinkmanship by the LTTE to gain maximum concessions from the Sri Lankan government particularly to rein in breakaway Karuna faction in the South. The LTTE always works on an either/or plan. In case things do not go in favor, it continues with lethal strikes and then follows up with a terror offensive and a ground war. In 2006, however this strategy did not bear fruit. The government forces were spoiling for war, which sane political voices on both sides of the fence had been avoiding. The Sri Lankan Armed forces were reasonably prepared for this eventuality and the war was bloodier than the previous ones.

The conflict was expected to intensify after Heroes Day Speech in November 2005 by LTTE supreme leader Prabhakaran in which he outlined a strategy of confrontation. During the initial stages it was marked by a series of deep penetration raids on isolated small posts and IED attacks. This conflagrated into full blown battles in the east in Muttur and Sampur area and gradually spread to the north. By the end of the year, the LTTE had lost many of its strongholds in eastern Sri Lanka as well as control of the A15 Highway. Northern parts of the Island except for Jaffna however, continued to be in its firm grips.

The government strategy was twofold. Accretion in fire power was used to penetrate LTTE strongholds in the north and the east. At the same time the A9 Highway was closed which placed LTTE at a twofold disadvantage: Denying revenue levied from vehicles plying on it and also suffering the ire of the people of Jaffna who are supplied entirely by air and sea.

On the political front also there was limited hope. Sri Lankan politics appeared in a flux with a large number of defections, allegations and counter-allegations against the ruling Sri Lanka Freedom Party? While Mahendra Rajpaksa consolidated power after winning the elections with a reasonable majority and attempted to create a consensus by evolving a Memorandum of Understanding (MOU) with the opposition parties, this advantage was whittled away through political short-sightedness. LTTE on the other hand was considerably undermined politically after it was banned by the European Union and the Supreme Court in Sri Lanka negating co-joining of the North and East provinces.

Breaking the cycle of violence in the foreseeable future appears extremely difficult. The LTTE despite having suffered some recent military setbacks is capable of waging a guerrilla campaign supplemented by suicide attacks. While the SLAF after having tasted victory in eastern Sri Lanka is yearning to strike the LTTE in the north. There is not much hope at present that an understanding will be reached.

POLITICAL TRENDS

The political activities in the Island during the year began with United Peoples Freedom Alliance led by the Sri Lankan Freedom Party (SLFP) under Mahendra (Mahinda) Rajpaksa winning 145 of the 165 council seats in election results declared on 31 March 2006. This provided the President necessary political strength to pursue a peace agenda.

Mahendra Rajpaksa also consolidated his hold on Sri Lankan polity after being nominated as the undisputed leader holding both the posts of President and head of the party. This provided him considerable flexibility in negotiations. The offer of a 14-day truce and direct negotiations with the LTTE made by the President on taking over appeared to be a positive outcome of removal of insecurities. However, the year saw a reversal of this trend.

The Sri Lankan government appointed a multi-ethnic panel to advise the government on evolving a power sharing formula for Tamil dominated north and east. This was apparently due to pressure from the Indian side to undertake some tangible measures to restore peace in the troubled Island, which saw death toll rising over 60,000. India's Foreign Secretary Shyam Saran is said to have visited Colombo on 3 July to evolve a political consensus.[2] The iridescence of both sides however did not produce any immediate results.

A significant political achievement was national consensus arrived at between Sri Lankan President Mahendra Rajapaksa's Sri Lankan Freedom Party (SLFP) and former Prime Minister Ranil Wickremesinghe's United National Party (UNP) which was to facilitate a common national agenda with a 6-point Memorandum of Understanding for a federal solution to resolve the vexatious ethnic issue on the island.[3] This was largely seen to overcome the absence of consensus amongst Sri Lanka's political parties which was claimed by the LTTE as being one of the key factors for lack of progress in peaceful resolution of the crisis. However, the positive atmosphere did not last long as by the beginning of 2007 an altered political equation was emerging in Colombo with large-scale defection in opposition ranks and abandonment of the Memorandum of Understanding.

LTTE Politics

The ban by European Union (EU) considerably undermined LTTE's political position internationally. The LTTE had considerable financial and political support in EU based on the large Tamil diaspora. European Union countries have always been permissive allowing militants to operate within sovereign states under the freedom fighter paradigm even when they used extreme violence as the LTTE has been doing over the years. The ban is thus a significant blow to self-determination movements around the world which are propagating political freedom through barrel of the gun.

At home there are increasing signs of unrest against the Tigers due to their repressive approach. It is unlikely that there would be an open revolt in the immediate future. An increase in internal displacement has also placed the Tigers at a disadvantage. Politically too the LTTE suffered a major setback with the decision of the Sri Lankan Supreme Court on 16 October 2006 that the merger of the northern and eastern provinces effected in 1987 was not legally valid.[4] This considerably weakened its legal case for a separate homeland for the Tamils in the north and the east.

The LTTE celebrated "Maveeran Varam" or Great Fighters week coinciding with the birthday of the supreme leader Prabhakaran in November.[5] The feudal character of the organization with its total allegiance to the supreme commander is evident with the tribute to the martyrs coinciding with the birthday of the leader. Nonetheless, this event provides a perspective of thinking of the leadership particularly the Heroes Day speech.

The Heroes Day speech by V. Prabhakaran on 27 November 2006 was as expected a vituperative outburst on inequities of the ethnic relationship. The main theme was abandonment of the path of peace to achieve Ealam as this has not resulted in reduction in Sri Lankan chauvinism as per Prabhakaran.[6]

Prabhakaran acknowledged the extraordinary situation faced by the movement of simultaneously engaging in war as well as peace, though in modern times, this is not an unusual scenario. The closure of supply routes received due mention as also splitting of Tamil homeland. The economic embargo and the war of arrests and disappearances alleged to be unleashed by the Sri Lankan government was also highlighted. Lack of determination of the government in the south for peace is a major consideration despite three changes in the regime, the manner in which these have been marginalizing the Tamil movement was very lucidly portrayed by Prabhakaran. The other key facets being exclusion of LTTE from donors meets, international isolation, para military (Read Karuna) operations and the ultimate aim of Sinhalese government for a military solution thereby making the Ceasefire Agreement defunct. The ban by Canada and EU received prominent mention and appears to have hurt the leader the most. The rejection of the call to rein in the para military forces and open the A9 Highway comes up for serious criticism by the leader. These will continue to be the bargaining chips in any future negotiations.

The recent All Party Conference created by the Sri Lankan government to arrive at a consensus along with the Memorandum of Understanding signed by the principal parties in the country was also critically castigated. The Heroes Day speech portends resumption of open hostilities in the days ahead. The most clear indication of the same is not a declaration of war but abandonment of the policy of peace and castigation of two timing policy of simultaneous war and peace. So far indications are that Prabhakaran has not given up negotiations with the Sri Lankan Monitoring Mission.

Economic Trends Affecting Polity

The economy in Sri Lanka which was expanding rapidly but had a temporary setback with outbreak of conflict. The inflow of tourists came down and there was large scale inflation reported. The LTTE came under a funds squeeze after ban by the European Union. Closure of the A9 Highway further denuded its coffers. The Sri Lankan government's unwillingness to open A9 was an effort to prevent the LTTE from running its extortion and tax collection racket as well as deny free movement to rebels. The A9 Highway which runs from Colombo to Jaffna through a large swathe of LTTE territory north of Vavuniya thus remained the key area of contention between the Sri Lankan government and the LTTE. The talks in Geneva have broken off primarily because the government was not willing to give in to this principal demand by the LTTE. The significance of the A9 is evident with it forming the key line of supply to the beleaguered Jaffna peninsula where the Sri Lankan government is holding out despite heavy pressure from the LTTE over the years. Jaffna is symbolic in that it is considered the most significant Tamil township in Sri Lanka.

President Mahendra Rajpaksa used the economic card deftly by announcing a Rs. 100 million package on 27 April 2006 for a task force to restore essential services in the Eastern Province. This differential in the east was designed to soften the population which was being successfully weaned away from the hold of the LTTE with the break away Karuna faction gaining ground over the years.

India's greater involvement in development in Sri Lanka was evident with a contract signed between the National Thermal Power Corporation (NTPC) and the Ceylon Electricity Board (CEB) for a joint venture power project in Trincomalee. The NTPC is due to invest $ 500 million in Trincomalee, a name derived from Tamil for Holy Triangle Hill. The location proposed by Sri Lanka, Sampur is controversial, as till recently it was under the control of the LTTE. However, the Indian side preferred China Bay which already had Indian Oil presence and is well connected by rail, road and port.[7] India's economic involvement in Sri Lanka in the power sector can be a good vehicle for greater say in the area.

Sri Lanka continued to enlarge economic cooperation with other regional states with an agreement with Myanmar amongst other states. Direct trade with Myanmar, scheduled as the intermediary route via Singapore, is no longer considered necessary. Myanmar and Sri Lanka are members of BIMST–EC, a sub-regional grouping comprising of Bangladesh, India,

Myanmar, Sri Lanka, Thailand, Nepal and Bhutan. However, trade between the two has been at a low key mainly due to logistical problems of transit and smooth trade regulations.

REVIEW OF POLITICAL TRENDS

Building a southern consensus is perhaps the first step towards evolving a lasting political solution. The problem is not just selling the southern consensus to the LTTE but also to Sri Lankan chauvinists, the right wing Jathika Hela Urumaya (JHU) and the left wing Janatha Vimukthi Peramuna (JVP). The draft proposal for devolution of powers which was drawn up by the All Party Conference was discussed in January 2006 and through this process a common Sri Lankan view should have emerged thereby providing concrete proposals to be put across to the LTTE. However, Sri Lankan fundamentalists particularly the Buddhist clergy, the JHU and the JVP, the main leftist group remain increasingly belligerent. The LTTE also dismissed the proposals of the All Party Conference. This could have formed the backdrop for further negotiations which may eventually reduce the resistance of the LTTE as well as the Sri Lankan opposition. However, trends indicate that a political consensus is no longer possible with the ruling party accused of triggering defections by the opposition. The death of Anton Balasingham, LTTE ideologue who is said to have been Prabhakaran's alter ego is considered to be a setback for the moderate voices in the organization. The statement by Prabhakaran in his memory indicated intensification of the struggle in the future as he grieved his loss, "(at a time he was) needed-most, as our freedom struggle intensifies". Many analysts thus see the death of Balasingham as probably a blow to chances of peaceful resolution of the conflict in the Island. A political solution to the Sri Lankan impasse thus appears to be remote in the near future.

Peace Efforts

Efforts to conclude peace between the LTTE and the Sri Lankan government continued apace during the year. These even included Sri Sri Ravi Shankar, the Indian spiritual leader and master of the Art of Living movement, who was flown in by a Sri Lankan helicopter to meet the LTTE chief Prabhakaran in his jungle hideout.

Two rounds of peace talks were also held during the year 2006 on 22 and 23 February and 28 and 29 October. These appeared to be an effort by both sides to appease the Sri Lankan Aid group and avert international pressure thus ending without any substantial gains. A review would reveal that there was lack of seriousness on the part of the LTTE as well as the Sri Lanka government to engage in a dialogue. Thus in February, the LTTE proposed that the Karuna faction should be disarmed before proceeding with negotiations well knowing that the Sri Lankan government could not possibly agree to such a proposal as this would have meant that the rebels were under its control. In October the LTTE insisted that the A9 Highway be reopened. Sri Lankan government sought broadening of talks to include a general devolution of powers including human rights violations while LTTE focused on opening A9 Highway.[8] The latter could have been considered favorably, but the hard-line stance adopted by the Sri Lankan government which considered the humanitarian crisis in Jaffna as a creation of the LTTE prevented a breakthrough. Sri Lankan government has been insisting that truce will have to include iron clad guarantees personally from the LTTE supremo Prabhakaran, a stand which has probably been taken keeping in view the need to establish credibility in negotiations.

Talks were also scheduled on 24 and 25 April in Geneva but LTTE backed off claiming that it had not been able to carry out effective pre-parley meetings with its leaders in the east as they were not provided safe transportation to attend confabulations in the north. This was also seen by observers as an attempt to rein in the Karuna faction which was inflicting heavy damage on LTTE cadres in the east.[9]

The SLMM (Sri Lanka Monitoring Mission) led by Norway was considerably weakened after withdrawal of monitors from members of the EU which had banned LTTE. Finland, Sweden and Denmark pulled out representatives after the LTTE indicated its inability to permit representatives from European states to continue in the mission. This was a big setback to the peace process as 35 of the 55 members are said to be from EU countries. With a depletion of strength the SLMM had further problems in monitoring the ceasefire, which appears to be floundering. The SLMM was attempting to bring a semblance of peace and nudge both parties towards a political solution by ensuring that there was physical distance between the warring groups. Despite repeated breakdown in the ceasefire agreement, the main mediator, Erik Solheim of Norway expressed confidence in April that the renewed wave of violence did not imply an end to ceasefire and underlined that both sides had assured that peace talks would continue.[10] However, this did not have the desired impact.

International pressure on LTTE mounted with the International Donor Group on Sri Lanka backing the peace process. However, this had limited impact as both sides continued to exercise the option of breaking the deadlock through fighting. A Norwegian peace envoy even attempted to broker a deal with the LTTE, visiting the Tigers stronghold in Killinochchi, as open fighting broke out with shelling of the area held by the LTTE by Sri Lankan government forces during height of fighting in August 2006. The government did not want to create another pressure point in terms of control of water by the LTTE by acceding to the ceasefire. Thus the truce was not followed up and the LTTE which was said to be in the process of opening the waters was prevented from doing so by artillery shelling.

Till reasonable alternatives to LTTE's role as the principal arbitrator of the future of Sri Lanka's Tamils emerge, it is unlikely that peace talks would lead to substantial success. International pressure on the LTTE should continue and the next step of its ban by the European Union after the ban by Canada needs to be followed up with greater urgency. The situation however needs to be watched from day-to-day rather than creating high level of expectations either way.

STATE OF MILITANCY AND WAR

General Trend

The militant activity during the year shifted from IED and deep penetration attacks to artillery duels, sneak raids and conventional attacks using artillery and air strikes. Both sides were increasingly using heavy guns, tanks and even multi-barrel rockets to pound each other's positions. The Sri Lankan Air Force is also employing newly acquired Kfir fighter aircraft to strike at LTTE positions, most of which are camouflaged in school buildings and other public areas or deep in the jungles. Renewed escalation of conflict which started with attacks by each side on water works at Muttur near Trincomalee and then escalated to Jaffna also led to blockade of A9 Highway by the Sri Lankan forces thereby denying the beleaguered population in Jaffna crucial supplies. The government aim was to put pressure on the Tigers who had been depending on this lifeline for supplies as well as for extorting large sums in the form of toll taxes.

Pounding LTTE positions causing heavy destruction to troops and equipment followed by blocking of supplies as well as funds to the Tigers appears to be the Sri Lankan government's strategy. The LTTE aim during the year was to consolidate control of the air and sea space astride the areas held by it. Thus it launched a number of sea borne strikes on the Sri Lanka Navy. Senior military and political leaders were prime targets of suicide attacks by the LTTE. The government backed Karuna group and the Sri Lankan Army is also apparently following a strategy of targeting the leadership, as a number of LTTE leaders particularly in the east have been eliminated. The LTTE will carry out suicide attacks, IED and mine attacks on Sri Lankan targets. The so-called deep penetration strikes by the Sri Lankan forces/backed groups are also likely to continue.

The Sri Lankan Armed Forces focused on weakening the hold of the LTTE in the Eastern provinces and securing the sea space. Towards this aim, breakaway Karuna faction was employed to advantage to conduct intelligence operations and penetrate the LTTE network in the east. Another key objective was opening the A15 Highway between Batticaloa and Trincomalee which was under LTTE control for long. By the end of the year the Sri Lankan Armed Forces had succeeded in attaining a major part of their objective by use of force.

Military Capability Enhancement

The Sri Lankan government considerably enhanced military capability by building up the air force. The most recent acquisition was four MiG 27 from Ukraine at a cost of $ 6.8 million which will boost its present inventory of 13 aircraft to include Kfir Israeli jets and F 7 Chinese ground attack aircraft.[11] The Sri Lankan Air Force has experience of flying MiG 27 aircraft and thus would be able to easily adapt to the same. India on its part has shored up the air defenses of the Sri Lankan forces by providing Indra low level air defence radars. An increase in the LTTE armory was indicated with 100 pieces of artillery, 20 122mm guns and 80 heavy mortars as per assessment by the Sri Lankan Army Chief Sarath Fonseka.[12] However, despite this, the general consensus is that the Sri Lankan Armed Forces have attained considerable edge over the LTTE, especially as the terrorist organization has lately lost support in the East.

Control of the Sea

One of the key militancy trends during the year was attempts by the LTTE to control the sea. The attack by Sea Tigers on a convoy of Sri Lankan naval ships which destroyed one Fast Attack craft of the Navy and killed 17 sailors on 11 May was the second during the month by the Sea Tigers after a suicide assault destroyed a naval ship on 5 May.[13] The MV Pearl Cruiser which was carrying 690 troops to Jaffna was the main target. However, the fast attack craft surrounding the ship evaded the Sea Tigers averting a major tragedy. In retaliation, the Sri Lankan Air Force bombed the Tiger's clandestine air strip at Ernamadu near its political headquarters at Kilinochchi. The tactics of launching suicide strikes by fast attack craft could have been effective, but the intervening patrol craft avoided a major disaster which would have certainly brought civil war to the country. These clashes at sea continued during the month of June with a fierce battle waged in the Kalpitiya lagoon off the north western coast on 28 June 2006 which saw 17 people killed. The LTTE is reported to have attacked a Sri Lankan navy patrol craft in the area.[14] These attacks also have a political significance with the LTTE claiming control and sovereignty over sea and air space. It also proclaimed that it was a state and not a non-state actor as proclaimed by the Sri Lanka Monitoring Mission from time to time.

The Sri Lankan Navy has been ferrying troops to Jaffna after the intervening land route has been under the control of the LTTE. The LTTE being landlocked is also dependent on the sea for supplies. The LTTE has a sea wing which is said to have a fleet of shallow seacraft which control the waters opposite its areas. Twelve hundred Sea Tigers are reported to have lost their lives in the battle off the sea coast. Twenty-two deep sea vessels registered under front companies are said to bring in supplies which are ferried by local fishing vessels to off load cargo in mid sea from ships and then transport to the bases to keep the insurgency going in north and north central parts of the country. The north-eastern seas are thus critical to both sides.[15]

Use of Air Power by Sri Lanka Armed Forces

The Sri Lankan Air Force employed strike aircraft as Kfir to advantage in attacking LTTE targets with considerable precision. This proved to be a major factor in blunting the edge of the guerrillas. The tactics of aerial bombardment was commenced by the Sri Lankan Air Force after 25 April 2006, when a suicide bomber targeted Army Chief Sarath Fonseca. The Sri Lankan Air Force carried out a number of air attacks on LTTE held areas thereafter. One such strike on 27 July 2006 in the Verugal river region in Trincomalee and Keppapulavu in Mullaitivu district in retaliation of the LTTE closing sluice gates of Mavil Aaru dam which supplies water to land held by Sri Lankan farmers was particularly effective during the crucial phase of the battle for control of the waters. India did attempt to pressurize the Sri Lankan government to avoid aerial bombardment but with limited effect.

The Flash Points

The first flash point was in the east, where LTTE had blocked the waters of the Maavilaru canal to the town of Muttur since 20 July 2006. However, the main operations were launched by the Liberation Tigers of Tamil Ealam (LTTE) on 11 August in the north to seek an entry into Jaffna, the heart of

Tamil homeland, with limited success. The combination of land and sea attacks which lasted for a period of over two weeks failed to achieve any territorial adjustments despite heavy casualties on both sides. The airbase at Jaffna, Pallaly and the naval base at Killaly were the key objectives for the Tigers. This could have been a diversionary operation to wean away attention of the government forces from Muttur or an attempt by the LTTE to take advantage of a weakened government force to gain control of Jaffna. However, this was not to be and Sri Lankan forces averted a major disaster.

The LTTE then attempted to disrupt activities in the Trincomalee port under government control by heavy artillery shelling to counter which Sri Lankan forces launched operations for capture of LTTE's gun positions to include the areas of Pacchanoor, Thoppur and Mahindapura on 28 August.[16] The aim of the three-pronged offensive was said to be to capture positions of the LTTE in the areas of Muttur east and Sampur accompanied by air bombardment.

Capture of Sampur

The capture of Sampur by the Sri Lankan Armed Forces was the first regular operation launched after the ceasefire of 2002 with coordinated employment of all the three services. This is a major transformation in conduct of operations by the Sri Lankan Armed Forces. Army and air operations were very effectively synchronized and artillery fire played a major role in causing heavy casualties to the LTTE. On the other hand, the Sri Lankan Navy has been deterring attacks from the sea by the Tigers. This new found confidence of the Sri Lankan Armed Forces seems to have come from improved planning, training and coordination of operations at all levels. Induction of Kfir fighter aircraft from Israel and multiple rocket launchers has considerably enhanced the fire power. LTTE devoid of anti-aircraft missiles or weapon systems has been severely affected by the air strikes in particular. Sampur is the key to the Trincomalee harbor and hence both the LTTE and the Sri Lankan Armed Forces were keen to secure it.

The Muslims in the east fear renewed attacks by the LTTE as they are suspected to be aligned with the government by the outfit and against an Ealam. The Ealam movement has been weakened in the eastern part of the Island after defection of the Karuna faction; hence the LTTE is particularly sensitive to the Muslim issue in the area. The losses in Muttur and Sampur have added to the hostility between the LTTE and the Muslims leading to large-scale migration from the area by the latter.

The SLMM blamed the Sri Lankan Armed Forces for violation of the 2002 ceasefire by opening a new front. The LTTE as well as the SLAF have been violating the ceasefire regularly. The battle was rejoined with the Sri Lankan navy claiming to have sunk 11 Tamil Tiger vessels and killed a large number of rebels in fierce sea battles on 25 September.[17] The A9 Highway connecting Vavuniya and Jaffna via Killinochchi and Muhamalai was one of the key issues as it enables the LTTE to collect toll 'tax' on the extremely busy road.

Beyond Sampur

The wave of fighting in Sri Lanka dubbed as Ealam War IV by many observers started on 11 August and subsumed the peace process as well as a large number of lives on both sides. The Government forces buoyed by success in gaining control of Sampur attempted to remove domination of Trincomalee harbor by the LTTE and engaged it in a series of sharp and intense battles. This has been the most severe fighting in the Island after the 2002 ceasefire. At least 400 combatants are reported to have died between 6 and 11 October in the northern area of Jaffna and Mankerni in eastern Sri Lanka. The LTTE is reported to have beaten back a series of attacks by Government troops apparently to break siege of the Jaffna peninsula. This fighting continued intermittently despite both sides sitting across the table for talks in Geneva on 28 and 29 October.

Fighting in the east in the area of Mankerni is likely to have been initiated by the breakaway Karuna faction going by the long winded name Tamil Makkal Viduthalai Pulikal (TMVP). The attack is claimed to have been carried out without any provocation and could possibly have been planned as a diversion by the TMVP to support Army operations in the north. Both attacks resulted in a stalemate and heavy casualties on both sides.[18] The defection of the Karuna faction led by Vinayagamoorthy Muralitharan, a key aide of Prabhakaran, had a telling impact on the LTTE's influence in the east where it has lost considerable ground during the year.

Exchange of fire between the LTTE and Sri Lankan troops led to abortion of the supply convoy which was dispatched to the beleaguered people in Vakarai on 29 November. The convoy which had been organized by the ICRC and the UNICEF as well as the World Food Programme could not proceed because of cross firing. About 30,000 civilians were in urgent need of food in Vakarai after intermittent clashes in the area after 8 November. A suicide attack was also launched on the brother of the President, Rajpaksa at the end of the month though he escaped unhurt.[19] The LTTE has had a consistent policy of elimination of key personalities including high-level government officials, political leaders and military top brass.

After Sampur, Vaharai in the Trincomalee area which controls the A15 Highway remained the focus of operations, with the LTTE and the Sri Lankan forces engaged in artillery duels and raids which displaced a large number of people. The villages of Somapura, Sirimangalapura, Serupura and Mahindapura had to be evacuated as the spate of attacks continued. Kantalai and Kurunegala received a large number of refugees.

Suicide Attacks

Suicide attacks continued to be one of the main strategies employed by the LTTE. Analysts were looking towards a possible date for ceasefire when the LTTE struck a serious blow to the peace process targeting a high dignitary, this time the Chief of the Sri Lankan Army, Lt General Sarath Fonseka on 25 April.[20] A women suicide bomber jumped at his car as the Chief was to visit the army hospital where a maternity care clinic was in progress. The Sri Lanka government in response to the LTTE suicide attack launched air strikes on targets in LTTE controlled areas in eastern Trincomalee. Twelve people were reportedly killed in these attacks as per Tamilnet.[21]

The LTTE plan for attack on Fonseka was well thought out. It always strikes at what in military terms is known as the, "centre of gravity". Fonseka as head of a belligerent army was having increasing stakes in polity of the country and was thus a prime target. He has been a proactive chief with wide experience of combat in the north and has refurbished the army. He is a strong proponent of the continuance of the High Security Zone. The LTTE struck with due precision, killing five of the escort, the Army Chief escaped with grievous injury. The government was apparently prepared for such an eventuality as indicated by the speed with which air strikes were launched. Another failed attempt targeted the brother of the Sri Lankan President and secretary in the Defence Department of the government in November.

However, the LTTE succeeded in eliminating Sri Lankan Deputy Chief of the Army, Major General Parami Kulatunga in a suicide strike. This led to increased restrictions on movement which replicated measures undertaken prior to the 2002 Accord. The LTTE also attacked a convoy of sailors which saw over 103 people dead and wounding scores of others on 17 October.[22] The attack took place at a transit point in Trincomalee district on sailors returning home from the frontline. This was followed by another attack by a sea borne suicide squad at Galle causing very heavy casualties.

A suicide attack was launched allegedly against the Pakistani High Commissioner in Colombo, Bashir Wali Mohammad, just as the cricket tri-series between Sri Lanka, South Africa and India was set to commence in the capital. This led to withdrawal of South Africa from the tournament and the Indo-Sri Lanka series failed to take off due to heavy rains. The LTTE is said to have been targeting the Pakistani envoy due to alleged assistance by the country to Sri Lankan Armed Forces particularly in terms of artillery, rocket launchers and training in use of air power.

The failure of a number of suicide attacks by the LTTE in Sri Lanka during the year provided an indication of how defence can be organized against such an operation. While intelligence is regarded as the key, shielding the main target is the principal security measure against a targeted attack by a suicide bomber. Thus, in the failed attempt on the brother of the President, it is said that the guards protected him against contact by the suicide bomber, thereby he escaped unhurt with only blood spattering on his shirt.

Impact of Suicide Attacks. The Sri Lankan government's hardening stand on confrontation with the LTTE could be the result of increased suicide attacks on government officials close to the hierarchy. Targeting Fonseca, the Chief of the Army, was intended to drive the army towards a confrontational course during the beginning of the campaigning season in 2006, while in December, the brother of the President Rajpaksa, Gotabaya, Secretary of defence was attacked but fortunately escaped unhurt. The statements from the President and his brother in the wake of this incident indicated the resolve of the government, "to defeat all efforts of the LTTE to achieve its bloodthirsty aims by grossly misleading the international community" and "unshaken in his resolve to achieve peace in Sri Lanka and is undeterred in his efforts to combat all forms of terrorism and violence". The President's commitment was underlined by his son joining the Sri Lankan Navy setting a singular example. The Sri Lankan government also re-imposed Prevention of Terrorism Act (PTA) which had been held in abeyance since the ceasefire in 2002. This is seen by monitors as an act in violation of the truce and the LTTE were quick to point out that this will induce a cycle of violence which may turn the conflict more bloody.

State of Violence—A Review of Casualties

The number of casualties in Sri Lanka during the year has considerably gone up and has been the highest going by data provided by South Asia Terrorism Portal. Thus at 3,920 killed in 2006, the total is higher than 3,791 casualties during 2000. The data is tabulated as given below and is also represented graphically. The figures for 2006 are up to 30 November.

Fatalities between 2000 and 2006[23]

Year	Civilians	Security Forces	Terrorists	Total
2006	949	752	2219	3920
2005	153	90	87	330
2004	33	7	69	109
2003	31	2	26	59
2002	14	1	0	15
2001	89	412	1321	1822
2000	162	784	2845	3791

Graph Showing Fatalities 2000-2006

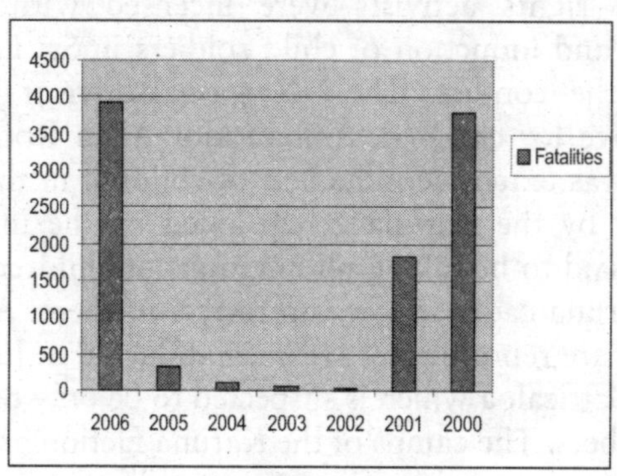

The state of LTTE casualties announced during the Martyrs Week is also revealing. The Tamil Tigers remembered a total of 18,742 comrades killed which also included 299 suicide bombers and 4,065 women combatants known as freedom birds. Although 818 were reported to be killed in 2006, the government has recorded figures of 2,018 dead. The killings during the year 2006 up to November are said to be 3,400 in a total figure of 60,000 casualties overall since 1972.[24]

SUMMARY OF FATALITIES

LTTE has a long history of violence. Statistics provided by the Sri Lanka government and culled from the South Asia Terrorism Portal reveal that LTTE had violated the ceasefire 5,464 times between February 22, 2002 and February 4, 2006. About 562 people were killed in these incidents which included

174 soldiers. The crime graph ascribed to the LTTE also included 117 attempted murders, 620 abductions, 46 attempted abductions, 106 cases of extortion, 2,199 conscriptions, 875 cases of injury, 22 instances of torture and 128 cases of intimidation. The data circulated by the Sri Lanka Monitoring Mission (SLMM) has indicated 3,535 violations during the period February 1, 2002 and February 28, 2006. A disturbing factor is 803 cases of child recruitment and 212 cases of child abduction. The violations attributed to the Sri Lankan Security Forces on the other hand during the same period were 169.

Child Soldiers—A Human Tragedy

Human rights activists were incensed with large-scale abductions and induction of child soldiers in Sri Lanka by all parties to the conflict. The UN special advisor to the UN representative for children, Ambassador Allan Rock indicated that there was extensive induction of children in the war zone particularly by the Karuna group aided by the military. The military is said to be taking photographs of children in villages and the Karuna cadre follows up to recruit them. About 60 to 70 children are reported to have been abducted in June and 135 in May in Batticaloa which is suspected to be only one-third the actual numbers. The camps of the Karuna faction are located in government controlled areas thus providing some credibility to the allegation. There were numerous allegations against the LTTE on similar accounts.

Karuna Factor

Karuna is LTTE's bête noir. His forces have effective influence in the eastern districts of Batticaloa and Amparai districts and are said to control the area on the Batticaloa coast from Chenkalladdy to Valaichennai. The fratricidal conflict between Karuna's followers and the LTTE has already caused some heavy losses in leadership to the LTTE with Senadhi, Kaushalyan and Nedimaran killed in the eastern districts. This apart the veneer of total loyalty to the cause and inviolability of supreme leader is losing sheen as Karuna defected despite being a senior organizer in the LTTE hierarchy. The pressure on its eastern Wing and lack of effective control over these areas has made control over Karuna one of the principal demands in talks by the LTTE. The impact of Karuna's rebellion against cadre unity is a major factor as this militates against the LTTE's philosophy of total control and being the sole representative of the Tamil community in Sri Lanka.

REGIONAL PLAYERS

Role of India

India's policy triad in Sri Lanka rests on commitment to the Island's sovereignty through a federal structure, considerations of sensitivity of the Tamil population in India and preventing major power incursions into Sri Lankan polity and structure. The complex interplay of these factors has been evident in India's Sri Lanka policy over the years. In the interest of human security, India has to subtly get into the act like it did in Nepal recently and attempt to bring the intransigent parties to the peace table, shedding off its inhibitions of a repeat of the failure of Operation Pawan in the 1980s. The key to resolution will not be direct intervention but pressure on the principals. Undoubtedly, the leverages available with India in this case are limited but need to be fully exploited. Political leaders of Tamil Nadu could be roped in to do a "Yechury"[25] in Sri Lanka. There is also greater pressure for Indian participation in the peace process with the Sri Lankan Foreign Minister making two trips to India during the year. The LTTE's political voice, the late A Balasingam raised controversy virtually regretting the assassination of Rajeev Gandhi. However, Indian wariness is understandable given the experience of the past. How long will India avoid getting involved in Sri Lanka is a mute question, there is no way that the solution will see resolution without Indian intervention. The Sri Lankan government on its part offered a two-week truce to the Tigers on 25 June 2006 to which the LTTE responded with characteristic negativity.

The Tamil Factor

The Tamil factor in Indo-Sri Lanka relationship was evident with Tamil Nadu government's pressure on the Central Government to close the Central Reserve Police Force (CRPF) camp which was providing training to the Sri Lankan police.

The outbreak of conflict saw a large number of refugees coming into Tamil Nadu. The total had crossed over 4,000 by the end of June and a steady stream followed thereafter. Maximum refugees approximately 70 per cent came from Trincomalee, while the remainder coming from Mannar and Jaffna.[26] This put pressure on the refugee camps in the areas of Rameswaram some of which were filled to capacity.

Indian Tamil parties are also being increasingly wooed by the LTTE. Some pro LTTE voices have been heard from the traditionally pro Sri Lanka Tamil parties as the Pattali Makkal Katchi (PMK), the Marumalarchi Dravida Munnetra Kazhagam (MDMK) and the Dalit Panther's Party of India (DPI). Overtures to the Tamil Nadu Chief Minister, M. Karunanidhi were also reported. The interview of Anton Balasingham wherein he declared that the assassination of Rajeev Gandhi was a historical tragedy, appears to be a part of the same process. LTTE is aware that to get the Indians on board they would have to make amends for the historical error of targeting Rajeev Gandhi. The LTTE aim appears to be very clear, cement sympathy amongst the likes of Vaiko and other leaders favorable to it in India. The attempts to reach out to central leadership in India however did not bear fruit. Members of Parliament of the Tamil National Alliance in Sri Lanka, a political grouping close to the LTTE, also attempted to meet the Indian Prime Minister a number of times but were forced to return to the island disappointed.

There were also hectic negotiations between the principal Tamil parties and Indian government emissaries including National Security Advisor M.K. Narayanan and Foreign Secretary Mr. Shiv Shankar Menon. This followed an initial discussion which Menon had with Sri Lankan government in Colombo with a view to test waters for a political agreement worked out between New Delhi and Colombo. The sentiment of the Tamils in India also received some consideration with the Tamil Nadu Chief Minister M. Karunanidhi meeting the Congress President and UPA Chairperson Sonia Gandhi on the same day. At best it could result in a tactical arrangement of supplies to Jaffna and opening of A9 Highway in exchange for joint naval surveillance. On the other hand, a comprehensive package could have been worked out with the Sri Lankan government which could be offered to the LTTE. However Prabhakaran's statement on the Heroes Day speech of abandoning the path of peace does not bear confidence of such a move succeeding in the near future.

Indo-Sri Lanka Dialogue

Sri Lanka's main request to India during the year was provision of relief supplies to Jaffna and patrolling of the waters in the Palk Straits as well as off the Islands sea board in the north and east. During his visit to India during the month, Sri Lankan President focused on the need for assistance from the Indian Navy to defeat designs of the Sea Tigers, who he claimed were indulging in gun and drug running which was harmful for Indian Tamils as well. The pro-LTTE Tamil parties as MDMK leader Vaiko strongly represented against such a support to the Sri Lankan Navy and met the External Affairs Minister Pranab Mukherjee on the eve of the visit of the Sri Lankan President. In case India decides to provide such assistance it will be undertaken without much fanfare and covertly. On the other hand, it may undertake to patrol the waters in the outer periphery while the Sri Lankan Navy does so inwards. What would be the reaction in case of a clash or suspected run in is hard to guess. But the move will lead Tigers planning to off load their cargo deeper into the sea in the oceanic areas and hence may prove to be deterrence at best.

The Sri Lankan President's visit to India as the Chief Guest of the Asian Mayors Conference was utilized by the Indian government to express its concerns about the growing humanitarian crisis in the country. India is keen to avert civilian deaths and a supply crisis in the Jaffna peninsula and is preparing a 7000 tons supply convoy to the area. India is following a policy of being an "interested bystander".[27] Though how long it can continue to do so remains to be seen as there is pressure from within Tamil Nadu on the government to play a more proactive role and see that the sufferings of the Tamil people due to the astringent policies of the Sri Lankan government are reduced. The MDMK which is more vocal on the issue held a day long fast protesting the visit of the Sri Lankan President and opposed the likelihood of any joint patrolling of the Palk Straits by the Indian and the Sri Lankan Navy as proposed by the Sri Lankan President before his visit to India. The gratitude expressed by the Chief of the Tamil Tigers in his Heroes Day speech for the support provided by the Tamil people needs to be seen in this light.

The Sri Lankan government is also reported to have made a request to New Delhi to ship relief to the population in Jaffna denied of supplies due to closure of the A9 Highway, their life-line. This package will comprise of rice, dal, sugar and milk powder which will be a great relief to the beleaguered population. The aid was to be delivered through the Indian and the Sri Lankan Red Cross. The LTTE however has threatened to attack ships coming with supplies, placing the entire relief mission in a jeopardy.[28]

India's attempted breakthrough in the Sri Lankan impasse with Prime Minister Manmohan Singh meeting the Sri Lankan President Mahendra Rajpaksa on 30 November 2006 in a closed door meeting which involved only the principal functionaries from both sides, the foreign ministers and the Indian foreign secretary could produce some results by preparing the Sri Lanka leadership for a better compromise. The Sri Lankan President is reported to have indicated the devolution package evolved by the All Party Representatives Committee which is a possible political solution to the crisis. The Indian side reiterated its stand for a negotiated settlement acceptable to all sections of the Sri Lankan society.

Review of India's Role in Sri Lanka

Indian back channels need to start the process of joint negotiations, to overcome LTTE's one point agenda of Ealam and whittle it down to autonomy. India has to ultimately take the plunge in the interest of the hapless people of the island and perhaps recognizing this, negotiations have been reported. India has been reluctant to play a role in the internal polity of Sri Lanka after the experience of the 1980s when it faced resistance from both the parties in Sri Lanka, the government and the LTTE and within India for its Peace Keeping Mission cum Force Projection in the hapless island to the south. India however is well poised at this juncture to act as a catalyst (not mediator) in Sri Lanka. The Indian government is also willing to deal with all Tamil parties in Sri Lanka by adopting a balanced approach. The LTTE is undertaking efforts to come closer to the Tamil political parties in India. There were some positive signals aimed at the ruling Tamil Nadu Chief Minister, M. Karunanidhi who had not been favored by the LTTE earlier. The growing rift between Vaiko's MDMK and the Dravida Munnetra Kazhagam (DMK) is also seen as a part of this new equation. However, given the history of India's engagement of the LTTE, there are considerable apprehensions over the organizations credibility. The possible course which India could take is as denoted below:

- Form a National All Party Committee for evolving a consensus as was organized in the case of Nepal. The Tamil Parties, DMK and AIDMK should be allotted a major role in the discussions, not necessarily in mediation.
- Establish the base level for talks as India's commitment to sovereignty of Sri Lanka; however devolution of powers and federalism can be discussed.
- Violence to be shunned by both sides. This needs to be emphasized.
- The first steps should be renewed commitment to cease-fire, cessation of hostilities of all types by both sides and suicide attacks in particular by the LTTE.
- Step-by-step approach will pay better dividends.

The Indian government has considerable leverages which it needs to exploit and bring the crisis in the island to a quick conclusion before further loss of lives. India's strategy appears to be to avoid further humanitarian tragedy and thus it is expected that despite resistance from the Tamil Nadu government as well as the pro-LTTE Tamil parties, there may be some assistance extended to the Sri Lankan government. The most appropriate would be to provide food aid which is required urgently by the six Lakh population in Jaffna, while naval joint patrolling can follow.

The principal issue will remain that of taking LTTE on board. LTTE leader V. Prabhakaran has already declared in his address on 27 November 2006 that there was no scope for any compromise and hinted that an all out war was the only solution to obtain desired Ealam by Tamils. The Sri Lankan government on the other hand feels that the LTTE does not represent the total spectrum of Tamil opinion. While the Norwegian mission is doing its best to successfully continue with the ceasefire, for a final settlement, India will have to be involved given the peculiar nature of the conflict.

The stages for emergence of solution could be renewed commitment to ceasefire by both sides, gradual de-escalation, opening of Jaffna blockade by allowing traffic on the A9 Highway with joint check posts and patrolling and simultaneous political negotiations towards a common devolution package. The Quebecois type of arrangement of a nation within United Sri Lanka could be one of the formats attempted.

Role of Other Players

Pakistan is reportedly providing extensive assistance to the Sri Lankan Armed Forces for building up military capability. Pakistan's advisors are also reported to be assisting the Sri Lankan armed forces in conduct of operations. President Rajpaksa visited Pakistan commencing 31 March ostensibly to strengthen bonds of friendship. Sri Lanka may also be looking for arms to fight the LTTE as India has been consistently denying offensive arms to Lankan forces given the sensitivity of the 56 million ethnic Tamilians in the country.[29] While the sovereign claims of the government of Sri Lanka to seek arms for national security cannot be questioned, the timing of the visit with talks scheduled in Geneva in April did not bode well for peace. Chinese firm, Huanqiu Contracting and Engineering Corporation has been awarded the contract for construction of Hambantota port reportedly after India had refused the same offer. The funding is to be on government to government basis. This will provide China a foothold in Sri Lanka which will considerably enhance the Chinese interests in the area.

A Final Review

Sri Lanka will see a low burning sim war or a high intensity insurgency, which ever way the same is defined which may even fracture into an open civil war, which will continue in the months ahead. A peace initiative will have to commence with a graduated return to ceasefire which should be designated as avoidance of strikes on civilian targets by both sides, followed by strikes on leaders and so on.

The Sri Lankan government has proposed devolution of powers to the provinces as a possible final solution to the Tamil crisis in the country. Presently it is following a four-pronged approach as follows:

(a) Continued military strikes against the LTTE primarily fire assaults.

(b) Exploit the split in the LTTE in the east to marginalize and isolate it within the Tamil community. The President's allusion that the LTTE is not the sole. representative of the Tamil people needs to be seen in this light.

(c) Simultaneous international and regional marginalization of LTTE.

(d) Seek devolution of powers politically within the island which should lead to a federation minus structure.

The Sri Lankan government's decision to seek a military solution to the problem is based on a number of factors which have recently gone in its favor to include the following:

(a) Ban on the LTTE by the European Union.

(b) Increase in military potential with induction of heavy artillery, multi barrel rocket launchers and Kfir jet fighters.

(c) A perceived weakening of the LTTE military potential as seen in its recent defeats in Muttur and Sampur.

(d) The squeeze felt by the LTTE due to closure of the A9 Highway and blockade of Jaffna.

(e) Split in the LTTE particularly the emergence of the Karuna faction in eastern part of the Island.

LTTE Strategy

Sri Lanka will see intensification of the conflict ahead after the speech by LTTE supremo V. Prabhakaran rejecting truce. In all likelihood, Prabhakaran will ask his forces to go in for an all out offensive in 2007.

LTTE should understand that the path for autonomy is through political negotiations. However, it appears that this recognition is a long way off and any subsiding of violence will be a tactical ploy by this outfit. Sri Lankan political parties showed increased resolve to work out a peace agreement and a number of meetings of the political coordination committee emphasizing the need of a peaceful solution with the LTTE were held. However, this advantage was wasted through the politics of defections in the early part of 2007. International pressure to avert a civil war in Sri Lanka needs to be sustained. The trigger for open conflict will be a major attack by the LTTE. It thus needs to be dissuaded from such an assault and is the key issue in the immediate term. The activity of the Karuna group is the most contentious issue in the LTTE-Sri Lankan government stand off. The LTTE believes that this group is supported and is acting on behalf of the Sri Lankan Army, while the Sri Lankan government says that it is an internal dissident faction of the LTTE. As Karuna represents a direct threat to the LTTE's monolithic ideology, the focus of its resistance will continue to be downsizing of the group in the year ahead.

Conclusion

Many observers believe that only pressure by international players will bear on both sides, the Sri Lanka government and LTTE to negotiate lasting peace. The Norwegian mission is acting as an effective facilitator but lacks the strategic strength to force both sides to give up the path of violence. USA, India and the aid caucus in particular can influence the situation. India obviously prefers to wait and watch for a suitable opportunity for a breakthrough. Till such an opening emerges, it is unlikely that situation in Sri Lanka will show any signs of improvement. The daily cycle of violence amidst apparent normalcy including a surging Colombo stock exchange is likely to continue to denote perhaps that all is normal in the country.

REFERENCES

1. http://www.tamilnet.com/img/publish/2007/02/CFA_LTTE_5_YEARS.PDF.
2. South Asia Security Trends August 2006. Published online by Security-risks.com.
3. With inputs based on reports in http://www.whatisindia.com.
4. South Asia Security Trends November 2006. Published online by Security-risks.com.
5. South Asia Security Trends December 2006. Published online by Security-risks.com.
6. South Asia Security Trends December 2006. Published online by Security-risks.com.
7. Report by M. Rajendran. *Hindustan Times*, 30 December 2006.
8. South Asia Security Trends November 2006. Published online by Security-risks.com.
9. South Asia Security Trends May 2006. Published online by Security-risks.com.
10. South Asia Security Trends May 2006. Published online by Security-risks.com.
11. With inputs from www.defense-update.com.
12. With inputs from sair.org.
13. South Asia Security Trends June 2006. Published online by Security-risks.com.
14. South Asia Security Trends July 2006. Published online by Security-risks.com.
15. Report by Amantha Perera on Sri Lanka in sair.org.
16. South Asia Security Trends September 2006. Published online by Security-risks.com.
17. South Asia Security Trends October 2006. Published online by Security-risks.com.
18. With inputs from *Weekly Assessments & Briefings*, Volume 5, No. 14, October 16, 2006. sair.org. Return to Arms. Guest Writer: Amantha Perera.
19. South Asia Security Trends December 2006. Published online by Security-risks.com.
20. South Asia Security Trends May 2006. Published online by Security-risks.com.
21. Based on reports in Tamilnet.

22. South Asia Security Trends November 2006. Published online by Security-risks.com.
23. Source: Institute for Conflict Management database. Accessed through www.satp.org
24. Hindustan Times Report. *Hindustan Times*, 22 November 2006, New Delhi.
25. Yechury implies the soft negotiating strategy adopted by Sitaram Yechury Indian left wing leader with the patronage of the Government to resolve the crisis in Nepal using the leftist links from October 2005 to April 2006.
26. Based on reports through sair.org. 10 July 2006.
27. Bagchi, Indrani. *The Times of India*, 29 November 2006. New Delhi.
28. With inputs from http://www.whatisindia.com.
29. The Times of India Report. "Rajpaksa...". *The Times of India*, 1 April 2006. New Delhi, p. 24.

India's Regional and Global Trends: Rising Aspirations

6

"I too have a vision regarding India and Pakistan. I earnestly hope that the relations between our two countries become so friendly and that we generate such an atmosphere of trust between each other that the two nations would be able to agree on a Treaty of Peace, Security and Friendship. This will become the instrument for realizing our collective destiny and the basis for enduring peace and prosperity in the region."

Indian Prime Minister Manmohan Singh

KEY TRENDS

- India's global and regional policy identified as greater economic, political and military engagement. The focus shifts towards energy and economy.
- Closer Indo-US, Sino-Indian and Indo-Pakistan relations define the period.
- The Hyde Act has opened greater scope for cooperation between the United States and India in a number of strategic fields including nuclear energy and defence procurements.
- Sino-Indian relations progress apace with focus on economic engagement and trade with opening of the Nathu La border post.
- Indo-Pakistan relations continue to be punctuated by Kashmir and terrorism. The positive aspect is that the process of dialogue continues.
- Indo-Myanmar relations are punctuated by the shadow of China as Myanmar calibrates relationship with New Delhi based on impact of its compact with Beijing.

- Closer integration of Indian relationship with Japan, Australia and IBSA provides more leverage to New Delhi to broad-base foreign policy.
- Energy and nuclear diplomacy have emerged as the key areas of focus of India's foreign policy in the years ahead.
- Military diplomacy as a significant facet of India's foreign policy manifests in agreements with diverse nations as Germany and Japan and large number of military exercises.
- Greater Indo-Singapore cooperation in the field of military training is likely to be seen in the future.

INTRODUCTION

Globalization implies security through greater interaction in the regional as well as global sphere. This exchange so far restricted to politics and economy is now expanding to a number of other fields. Many new issues in foreign relations are thus coming up such as energy, nuclear, military diplomacy and joint training. These are the new contours of foreign policy in the days ahead which provide a country much leverage. India was seen to assimilate these in diplomatic engagement during the year. Thus a survey of India's Global and Regional Policy, Indo-US Relations, Sino-Indian Relations, Indo-Pakistan Relations, India's Dialogue with countries such as Germany, Myanmar, Nepal and IBSA, Energy Security Issues, Indian Nuclear Diplomacy, Indian Military Diplomacy and Joint Military Training will denote contribution of external elements of India's national security.

India's Global and Regional Policy

Over the years India's foreign policy has evolved as a strategy of engagement. Holistic engagement of continents, groupings and countries such as the United States (US), European Union (EU), Japan, Russia, Association of South East Asian Nations (ASEAN), China, Brazil, South Africa as well as continental nations of Africa based on balance of reciprocal interests rather than balance of power is now the prime driver.

This does not necessarily imply that there will be bonhomie with all states in the days ahead, but relations will be based on a spirit of accommodation to achieve core national interests of growth and development. The basic foreign policy challenge faced by India is, however relations with its South Asian neighbours. Reducing hostility of Pakistan and Bangladesh and ability to influence the situation in Sri Lanka to stop the mindless violence in the Island remains a priority for the country. The broad contours of policy of engagement evident during the year are covered in the succeeding paragraphs.

The Indian government's perspective on globalization was evident in the speech of the Prime Minister Manmohan Singh at the NAM summit in Havana in September.[1] The main path denoted greater involvement in Africa, energy security and developments within WTO. Point wise key political and economic issues covered were as follows:

Political

(a) Permanent representation in the UNO for developing World.

(b) Inclusive Globalization.

(c) West Asian crisis resolution. Form a group for promoting understanding and building confidence.

(d) Promoting dialogue on terrorism between civilizations, control the forces of intolerance and extremism so as to focus attention on poverty, ignorance and disease.

(e) Nuclear Disarmament.

Economic

(a) Development oriented outcome in multilateral trade agreements—WTO.

(b) NAM Working Group on Energy Security to be constituted which could be coordinated by India to enable:

  (i) Drawing up a NAM Action Plan for Energy Security based on a shift from fossil fuels to non-fossil fuels; and from non-renewable sources to renewable sources of energy.

(ii) Create a NAM-wide network for sharing best practices in energy efficiency and conservation, in order to substantially reduce energy intensity of GDP growth.

(iii) Establish a network of institutes to engage in research in developing new and clean sources of energy such as solar energy, wind energy, hydrogen fuel cells and bio-fuels, including bio-mass and bio-diesel.

(c) Human resource and agricultural development in Africa.

While these are substantial issues, measures to implement policy through greater economic and political engagement in specific fields of interest and countries were not evident. For instance unlike China which now has a major presence in Africa, India's potential determined by historical social and cultural ties with Africa remains largely untapped. Relations with the US and EU improved, but have yet to achieve the momentum essential to take the nation on an accelerated growth chart.

India's security policy was denoted by then Defence Minister Pranab Mukherjee in his address to the Combined Commanders Conference on 17 May 2006. Some excerpts culled from the Ministry of Defence Press Release are as given below:

(a) *Full Spectrum Security*. There is increased recognition of the need for full spectrum security covering "*spheres such as political, economic, social, diplomatic, and many more.*" The shift to asymmetric warfare due to expensive nature of wars was acknowledged. Thus, the need was for an, "*integrated, flexible, innovative and in real time*" strategy.

(b) *Joint Commands*. The Governments aim to create joint commands was highlighted thus, "*There is a need to evolve a road map towards furthering the process of joint commands so as to make resources available for modernization*". While functional joint commands are being created the test of the Government resolve will be seen when attempts are made to establish joint theatre commands.

(c) *Pakistan.* Some hopes of improvement of relations with Pakistan were indicated. However the bogey of terrorism continues thus, "*The decline in terrorism in the Valley is on account of sustained efforts by Indian Army and paramilitary forces. No evidence is available to suggest that Pakistan has taken measures to completely dismantle the terrorist infrastructure within Pakistan and Pakistan Occupied Kashmir. Therefore, while it is necessary that we continue with all sincerity our dialogue process, we cannot afford to become complacent in this regard.*" But overall the mood was of hope as indicated by, "*Though terrorism from across the border continues to strike at regular intervals, and across the length and breadth of the country, the overall situation is more positive than a year ago. India-Pakistan relations have witnessed notable progress in the two rounds of composite dialogue and third round currently underway. It is significant that people to people exchanges are taking place in large numbers.*"

(d) *China.* India and China are developing a comprehensive relationship transcending differences over the border dispute. Thus, the Defence Minister stated, "*We seek friendly, cooperative, good neighbourly and mutually beneficial relations with China. At the same time, we are also seeking to address our differences, including the border issue, through peaceful dialogue, without allowing them to affect the comprehensive development of our relationship.*" There are a number of new stresses which are likely to come up with China such as water, trade and competition for resources which will have to be addressed in the years ahead.

(e) *Afghanistan.* The Defence Minister emphasized that security concerns of Indians working in Afghanistan are being addressed in consultation with the Government of Afghanistan. India's commitment to rebuilding the country with $ 750 million aid for reconstruction and capacity building was also highlighted.

(f) *Nepal*. The resolution of the political situation through a process of constructive dialogue and restoration was highlighted. There appeared to be some measure of support for the rapprochement between the Seven-Party Political Alliance and the Maoists.

(g) *Bangladesh and Myanmar*. Efforts to deter terrorist activities that have easy access into India through these countries were to be made. There was considerable follow up with Myanmar; however no breakthrough could be made with Bangladesh given the consistently anti-Indian policies of the former Bangladesh Nationalist Party government in Dacca.

(h) *Sri Lanka*. While the Defence Minister indicated that "*We have urged for a return of peace and for the peaceful resolution of all issues while maintaining the integrity of the nation*", there was lack of forceful follow up as the fratricide in the Island state continued to increase during the year.

SAARC Diplomacy. United States and South Korea were granted observer status in SAARC. China and Japan have been made observers in 2005. These nations are expected to add much needed impetus to the SAARC forum. Outside influence sometimes acts as a better coagulant than internal interests. Afghanistan is also being inducted as a member of SAARC. This should considerably increase regional cooperation between South Asian countries in the year ahead especially since India is actively enlarging its role in the region.

Indo-US Relations

The seminal events in Indo-US relations during the year were signing of the Henry Hyde Act which paved the way for removal of sanctions against India and granted New Delhi entry into the exclusive nuclear club. The second occasion was visit by US President George W Bush to New Delhi in March. These activities considerably strengthened US-India relations placing these at an even keel after many years of serrated exchanges.

There are expectations of enhanced cooperation in all sectors of economy including nuclear energy and defence.

March was a momentous month for South Asian security. It commenced with the visit of President of the United States, George W Bush to India, Pakistan and Afghanistan. The visit was preceded by a talk by the US President at Asiatic Society in Washington on 22 February. The speech clearly outlined the agenda of Indo-US engagement based on common interests between two democracies, combating terrorism, free trade, outsourcing jobs, improving health and environment and meeting India's energy needs through joint initiatives. This was a symbolic visit signifying strategic realignment of India into the US orbit, with some political scientists propagating India band wagoning rather than balancing with the USA in the future.

Indian interests however are centred on sourcing nuclear fuel. The Indo-US Civil Nuclear Separation Plan inked on 2 March 2006, entailed placing 14 of the 22 nuclear facilities under International Atomic Energy Agency (IAEA) scrutiny. The underlying strategic bargain appears a minor sacrifice for India grossly deficient of fuel to run its nuclear power plants. Domestic opposition cried hoarse over abrogation of strategic autonomy ignoring the fact that inter-dependence is the reality of a globalized World. While much work lies ahead to gain approval of the US Congress, the first hurdle has been successfully crossed and it is expected that with consistent lobbying, Congress approval should be forthcoming. Preliminary indications were not very encouraging with US congressmen incensed with India's links with Iran including port call by two Iranian naval ships to Kochi. Indian diplomacy was thus in for a tight rope walk, with two of its strategic partners at loggerheads, the United States and Iran, none of whom it can shed, but may be it can temporarily annoy Iran, the current American, "hot button". However, sustained pressure from both India and the United States government finally secured the Bill by the end of the year.

The expectations over a new era in Indo-US relations generated with the Bush visit were fulfilled with signing of the Henry Hyde United States-India Peaceful Atomic Energy

Cooperation Act in December. This was a landmark event in many ways. Nuclear non-proliferation has been one of the steadfast foreign policy objectives of America. Restricting access to nuclear technology leading to weaponisation is the primary means to achieve this goal. For the first time the United States was placing its relationship with India above its concerns over nuclear non-proliferation. By allowing nuclear energy goods exchange with India which is not a signatory of the Nuclear Non-Proliferation Treaty, the United States showed flexibility in approach to non-proliferation based on ground realities.

The truths are quite obvious. First and foremost is an emerging consensus within the United States that India has responsible nuclear governance which understands complexities of management of atomic weapons and would thus ensure that these are not used to pursue tangential goals. This conclusion would have come after a reasoned analysis of the Indian political spectrum as well as stability of governance in the country. The US administration is thus fully confident that whatever the political dispensation in New Delhi, there is no scope of unrestricted proliferation beyond reasonable security needs of the country and that India's nuclear armoury will always remain in safe hands.

The emerging economic importance of India is another issue of consequence which needed consideration. The United States has had to subordinate its concerns on nuclear proliferation by a responsible state due to emerging opportunities in economic relations with one of the largest markets in the world, second only to China. While China's growth appears to be reaching its apogee, India has just about started to chart its trajectory on the J curve. The United States would not want American industry including defence and armament to be denied an entry in what is today one of the largest strategic markets in the world. The Hyde Act thus provides an ideal inflection point for White House to work out a partnership which has been in the offing over the years.

India's growing political importance in the Asian region is also evident as it has successfully managed its internal complexities and is now looking outwards. This externally driven approach of the country will engage many nations in its path and thus the US initiative was more than expected. That such a concession is not being given to any other state is also worth noting. Critics within the US establishment are, however, sceptical of the impact this move will have on negotiations with other nuclear aspirants as Iran and North Korea.

The next stage in fructification of the Deal would be the 123 Agreement between the two countries which will have to take into account the many apprehensions expressed in Indian political circles about the Act including its impact on India's sovereignty. But the momentum of greater economic engagement is already evident with a green signal given to American industry. The key beneficiaries are likely to be companies as General Electric, Boeing, Northrop Grumman and Pratt and Whitney which will be competing with European and Russian firms for the large nuclear energy, aerospace and defence market in India. Other large conglomerates as Wal-Mart are also foraying in partnership with Indian companies as Bharti Telecom which has a large retail footprint in the mobile telecom sector in India. The era of a golden phase in Indo-US relations is just beginning given that the Act is against the backdrop of a government in India which is supported by the Left parties traditionally antagonist towards America.

The passage of the Bill, however, entailed sustained negotiations between India and the United States in addition to debate over the issue in the Indian Parliament as well as the US Senate and Congress. The Indo-US Civil Nuclear Agreement cleared the first hurdle in the US Congress with overwhelming approval of the legislation, HR 5682—India-US Nuclear Cooperation Promotion Act of 2006, by a majority of 350 to 68 votes in June 2006. The Bill could be cleared by the US Senate in November 2006, thereafter which amalgamation of the versions passed by the Congress and the Senate was undertaken till the unified Bill was passed.

Indian political landscape remained a minefield of opposition of all hues, to the Deal which changed colours based on opportunism of public opinion. The ideological stasis of the Left was another impediment. The country's atomic energy establishment was also up in arms against nuclear glasnost. The Prime Minister Manmohan Singh silenced critics for the time being with a spirited response in the Parliament.

The writing is on the wall. Civilian nuclear establishments other than the Fast Breeder programme and the Rare Earths facility in Mysore will have to come under the IAEA scanner. The harsh reality is that India needs Uranium supplies to run its nuclear establishments, without the Indo-US Civil Nuclear Agreement, the sanctions will not be lifted. Once the sanctions are lifted, 16 of India's 22 nuclear establishments will be under IAEA inspections, paving the way for supply of fuel by the Nuclear Suppliers Group (NSG). The country can exercise its flexibility within this paradigm.

US-India Bilateral Trade

India is the 12th largest economy in the world and fourth largest in terms of purchasing power parity. Thus trade with India has occupied the attention of all major countries particularly the USA and China. US India Bilateral trade in 2005 was $ 26.77 billion with US exports to India at $ 7.96 billion and US imports from India at $ 18.81 billion. Key areas of interest denoted by Americans in India are airport and ground handling, computers and peripherals, education services, power generation, distribution, transmission and equipment, food processing, cold storage equipment, machine tools, medical equipment, mining and mineral processing equipment, oil and gas field machinery, pollution control equipment, security equipment, telecommunications, textile machinery, water. The Henry Hyde Act will enable a large number of US firms to participate in commerce with India.

SINO-INDIAN RELATIONS

2006 was the Year of India-China Friendship. This was also marked by a visit by the Chinese President Hu Jintao to India in November and a number of initiatives taken in varied spheres including the border issue. The latter, however, does not evoke confidence of resolution in the near future. But the positive development is both countries deciding to progress beyond the vexed boundary issue. An indication of this resolve was evident with opening of the Nathu La trade route in Sikkim during the year.

There is growing belief in China that a conflict with India should not and will never happen again not at least in the mid-term future. The boundary question is not a priority and hence can be resolved in good time. Other important issues of concern should thus be taken up first. China is an observer in the SAARC group and India has been granted the same status in the Shanghai Cooperation Organization (SCO) and has also participated in the East Asia Summit.

China has accepted Indo-US Nuclear agreement with equanimity. This demonstrates a growing confidence in Beijing as it no longer feels constrained by any power in the world or even an axis of powers. China is also aware that in the global environment, bilateral and multi-lateral interaction can be conducted simultaneously. Chinese diplomats are also seen to be better placed to respond to questions of democracy in the country. The Chinese are evolving a concept of cooperative democracy which is unique and far removed from the Western either/or concept. Thus, there are said to be one ruling and eight cooperating parties in China rather than opposing parties. Democracy is seen as a means for good governance and not competitive politics, a concept which needs to be examined by India. There is thus growing convergence of political interests between the two countries.

Activities related to Year of Friendship—2006 commenced with Chinese cultural ambassador being felicitated in April as one of the key diplomats in the capital. The programme included establishment of temples, a Confucius centre in Jawaharlal Nehru University and a Hindi Centre in Beijing University apart from other cultural exchanges.[2]

Sino-Indian trade is also due to gain considerably with 160 Indian companies operating in China at present and 50 to 60 Chinese companies in India. The trade targets could be as high as $ 30 billion by 2008 and $ 50 billion by 2010. Sino-Indian cooperation in energy is another key area and this is likely to be taken forward in a significant manner.

There is substantial activity in the defence field as well with a number of Chinese defence officers visiting India, joint exercises on sea rescue held and more slated on anti-terrorism and anti-piracy operations. Increased interaction between the border guards and visit of Chinese naval ship to Cochin are some of the other areas of interest. The Defence Minister Pranab Mukherjee also visited China in May 2006.

A point which needs consideration is the manner in which the US and China are structuring their relationships with each other as well as with other allies. These are totally independent of each other and removed from the either or paradigm of the Cold War. For China, economy and energy are the key issues. In economy, information technology assumes maximum significance; hence President Hu started the visit to America from Microsoft headquarters. He also proclaimed that China was adopting a path of "peaceful development". The United States too adopts a parallel rather than an intersecting approach in relationships. The Indian Prime Minister placed the issue in perspective when he said that there is no balancing required in developing relationship between India and the US *vis-à-vis* China as both can be developed simultaneously. However public proclamations apart, the intelligence and security infrastructure in states denote a confrontational trajectory. Realism decrees that the two paths, cooperation and covert confrontation progress simultaneously.

President Hu's Visit to India

The visit of President Hu Jin Tao to India reaffirmed Sino-Indian commitment to a strategic partnership with a "collective political will to enrich and reinforce our strategic and cooperative partnership for peace and prosperity and to resolve outstanding issues in a focused, sincere and problem-solving manner". At the global level a common platform for, "sustainable and equitable development, energy security, peace and prosperity in Asia and in the world, environment protection and the fight against terrorism and cross border crimes" was envisaged. Hu considered Sino-Indian relationship as a "long-term and strategic view". The Chinese President placed five priorities for strategic relationship with India. These include increase in mutual political trust to consolidate the relationship, enhance business cooperation, enlarge public support to China-India relationship, accelerate efforts for early settlement of boundary issue and develop multi-lateral cooperation to jointly uphold legitimate rights and interests of developing countries.

In concrete terms the visit achieved the following:

(a) Opening of additional consulates in Kolkata and Guangzhou, for furthering growth of trade and tourism. The dispute over property of Indian Consulate in Shanghai has also been resolved.

(b) Strive to increase volume of bilateral trade to US$ 40 billion by 2010 and encourage two-way investment flows.

(c) Joint Task Force established to expedite study of feasibility and benefits of the India-China Regional Trading Arrangement and submit its report by October 2007.

(d) Enhance trans-border connectivity and cooperation.

(e) A major initiative on science and technology, which will involve launching of several joint projects.

(f) Cooperation in the field of civilian nuclear energy.

(g) People to people contacts and cultural ties.

(h) 'India-China Year of Friendship through Tourism' in 2007

(j) Five-year programme for exchange of youth delegations.

(k) Acceleration of efforts of Special Representatives on the boundary question on the basis of the Agreement on Political Parameters and Guiding Principles signed in April 2005.

(l) An expert-level mechanism to discuss interaction and cooperation on the provision of flood season hydrological data, emergency management and other issues regarding trans-border rivers. This should address India's concerns on diversion of waters of the Satluj and the Brahmaputra.

(m) Bilateral Investment Promotion and Protection Agreement, fixing of trade target of US$ 40 billion by 2010 and mandating the Joint Task Force already established by the two countries to complete its study on the feasibility and benefits of India-China Regional Trading Arrangement by October 2007.

(n) Expansion of border trade and greater facilitation of Kailash-Mansarovar Yatra.

(o) Furtherance of Memorandum of Understanding for Exchanges and Cooperation in the field of Defence signed on May 29, 2006, which provides a sound foundation and institutional framework.

Sino-Indian Border Opens at Nathu La

The Sino-Indian border outpost opened for trade at Nathu La on 6 July 2006. This will enable traders to move between Serethang to Renqinggang a distance of 7 to 8 kms for four months in a year from 1 June to 30 September from Monday to Thursday from 7.30 AM to 3.30 PM. Twenty-nine items for export from India and 15 items from China have been earmarked. This will give a boost to the economy of Sikkim where 5,000 additional jobs are expected bringing Lhasa, 1,000 kms from Kolkata, a port for Chinese goods from the western and the south western provinces.[3] The Chinese have undertaken extensive development of infrastructure on their side of the border and the delay in opening of the pass has been attributed to delay in developing the same. The Indian infrastructure is, however, not developed as India feels that the route should be restricted to border trade and does not foresee a chance of the Chinese trading globally through Kolkata. This appears to be a retrograde step as Tibet is reported to have an annual trade of $ 200 million. The rights of passage through Sikkim to Kolkata would considerably benefit the economy of West Bengal and Sikkim.

Sino-Indian Border Talks June 2006

The Eighth round of talks between the Special Representatives of India and China, M.K. Narayanan and Dai Bingguo, Vice Foreign Minister on the India China Boundary Question concluded on 27 June 2006. Discussions of an agreed framework for the boundary settlement on the basis of the Agreement on Political Parameters and Guiding Principles for Settlement of India-China Boundary Question were held.[4] The Sino-Indian peace talks are being held with the premise that there would be constant political involvement and that these will in no way affect the progress of dialogue in other areas of mutual interest.

The bottom line appears to be a cartographic adjustment which should come about to cater for settled populations on both sides of the border. The ongoing talks may result in a possible framework being evolved over the next two to three rounds that would take us to the end of 2006 and beyond. Thereafter, the key issues will be discussed and thus a time frame of three to five years seems to be more realistic to evolve a solution to this long-standing issue. However, both China and India having agreed to continue negotiations in other spheres without awaiting resolution of the boundary issue is a positive step, particularly in trade and civil technology sharing.

The Chinese have been generally following the practice of making official statements on Arunachal Pradesh just before important visits of leaders to each others countries as indicated by D.S. Rajan, former Director in the Cabinet Secretariat, Government of India. This trend has been noticed after Indian Prime Minister Vajpayee's visit to China (June 22-27, 2003), Ambassador Sun's statement a week prior to Premier Wen Jiabao's visit to India (April 9-12, 2005) and most recently prior to visit of President Hu. The aim of these pronouncements is to lay at rest any inclination to discuss the Border issue. There is some improvement in the Chinese approach over the years, while earlier, the Chinese used to precede such visits by physical intrusions as seen in Himachal Pradesh in February 1997, after former PRC President Jiang Zemin's visit to India in December 1996. A Chinese patrol even reportedly entered the Line of Actual Control (LAC) in Asaphila in Upper Subansiri, Arunachal Pradesh on June 26, 2003 when the Indian Prime Minister was visiting China with a similar intrusion in May 2005, one month after Premier Wen Jiabao visited India.[5]

The Sino-Indian border bonhomie has been recently extended to the Lohit Valley with reports that a meeting was held between the Indian delegation led by Brig A.K. Bardalai and Chinese Col Li Shi Zhong with six officers at Kibithu in Anjaw district of Arunachal Pradesh on 18 November 2006. This opened a fourth point of military to military exchange after Chushul in Ladakh, Nathu La in Sikkim and Bumla in the Kameng district of Arunachal Pradesh as per the Indian Ministry of Defence press release. Thus a concurrent blow hot and blow cold could be anticipated in the future, till China is able to convince its leadership back home, that a border solution with India is in its interest.

Sino-Indian Defence Cooperation

The visit of the Defence Minister Pranab Mukherjee to China resulted in signing of a historic Memorandum of Understanding (MOU) on Exchange and Cooperation in the Field of defence between India and China. Gen Cao Gangchuan, Minister of National Defence of the People's Republic of China represented the Chinese side. The MOU established the formal basis for defence and military exchanges between the two countries. The key facets of this understanding were as follows[6]:

(a) Exchange between leaders and high level functionaries of the Defence Ministries and Armed Forces of the two countries based on an annual programme.

(b) An annual defence dialogue to be hosted alternately to review the progress, make suggestions for the future and exchange views on international, security and strategic issues.

(c) Joint military exercises and training programmes for search and rescue, anti-piracy, counter terrorism and other areas of mutual interest. Exchange of senior military officers for designated exercises is also relevant.

(d) Participation in seminars and discussions.

The MOU is a significant step which has placed relations between the two countries on a new footing. The ides of 1962 and Somdurong Chu are well past and a new era of cooperative security seems to be emerging. The key security issues are those related to state versus non-state players thus covering search and rescue, anti-piracy and counter-terrorism. Such an understanding acts as a deterrent for terrorists and criminals in respective countries and thus needs to be encouraged with other nations as well.

The visit of the Defence Minister included a trip to the Lanzhou Military Command which is responsible for areas adjacent to Sino-Indian border in Himachal Pradesh and Ladakh. This was perhaps the closest the Chinese would have possibly taken an Indian Minister to the Chengdu Military Command which controls the Tibetan Autonomous Region. The significance of the Lanzhou Military Command is also indicated by its bordering the Great Game area of Central Asia, Afghanistan, Tajikistan, Kyrgyzstan and Kazakhstan apart from the sensitive Xingjian province. An interactive discussion is reported to have been held on issues such as anti-terrorism, disaster management, training of military personnel, handling internal conflict situations and information warfare. These are the possible areas of cooperation in future.[7] As the final event of the trip to China, the Defence Minister also visited the Shanghai Naval Base and was shown a missile frigate, possibly a X 12 (capacity 2,066 tons, maximum speed 27 nautical miles).[8]

Sino-Indian Trade August 2006

Sino-Indian Trade will see a quantum jump over the next two years and is slated to reach US$ 20 billion by the end of financial year 2008 with a growth rate of 37.34 per cent. A Joint Task Force to study the feasibility of enhancing trade has also been set up which will work out a China-India Regional Trading Arrangement which will be highly conducive to increase in trade of goods, services and investments by the Chinese. The surging Sino-Indian trade is set to receive further impetus with the likelihood of opening of the Indo-Nepal-Tibet route for trade, which would have the benefit of being open throughout the year. The Indo-Nepal Inter Governmental Committee (IGC) on trade and transit cooperation which has resumed talks after return of popular governance in Nepal has agreed on exploring this possibility, which would also require acceptance by China.

Knowing Chinese proactive conduct of trade dialogue and measures, there is all possibility that such a move will find favour with Beijing. China is gradually emerging as India's largest trading partner and will in all likelihood replace the USA shortly. Such an arrangement will also be beneficial to Nepal providing advantage to the services industry in the country apart from a boost to trade. News reports also indicated an offer from China to extend the Lhasa rail line to the Nepal border with the first extension being planned to Xigaze, which is the largest city closest to the Nepal border.[9]

Water Stress—Need for Bilateral Agreement

Water stress is likely to be a cause of concern between India and China over the next few decades. India being a lower riparian state *vis-à-vis* China would be subject to manipulation of the water flow by the Chinese in major rivers which are emanating from Tibet such as the Brahmaputra and Sutlej. Reports in the *Hindustan Times* indicate that the Chinese have built a barrage near Zada in west Tibet on the Sutluj. This is likely to facilitate the Chinese in control of the river and will affect the quantum of water available to India.[10] The dangers of flash floods in India which resulted from the Parichu lake out break in 2004 cannot be ruled out.

The Spiti and Sutlej are the most vulnerable valleys which need continuous monitoring. While a Memorandum of Understanding on sharing of hydrological information of the Sutlej or the Langqen Tsangbo (Chinese name for Sutlej) has been concluded in 2005, it may not be adequate to ensure proper water sharing arrangements including control of flooding.[11] Chinese have undertaken development of the Tibetan plateau and over the years a number of settlements are coming up in the area. This will necessitate development of infrastructure with power being the key resource. Tapping hydel power is the easiest and most cost effective option. In the long-term interest of both the countries, there is a need for a treaty on water sharing between India and China on the lines of the Indus Water Treaty to avoid future conflict due to water stress as well as disasters due to barrage breach.

INDO-PAKISTAN RELATIONS

Indo-Pakistan relations flowed at an even temper during the year though with some hiccups. The main one occurred in July when Pakistan was overtly accused by the Indian leadership of sponsoring terrorism in the hinterland, direct manifestation of which was seen in Mumbai local train blasts which had led to 187 deaths and many injured. However, considerable ground was retrieved with the Havana Declaration by the Prime Minister of India and President of Pakistan in September resuming the process of dialogue. The processes are quite complex, apprehensions abound and number of issues so varied and deep-rooted in mutual antagonism that successful rapprochement will take much time and requires boundless energy. A detailed review of all these issues is being undertaken in succeeding paragraphs.

Indo-Pakistan—Joint Terrorism Mechanism

The Indian Prime Minister and President of Pakistan met at Havana against the backdrop of the NAM Summit and renewed the strategic peace agreement between the two countries. Considerable debate has been going on in India over the joint statement issued after the meeting. The statement and comments are as given herein.

"President General Pervez Musharraf and Prime Minister Manmohan Singh had a cordial, frank and detailed exchange of views on all aspects of India-Pakistan relations. Desirous of carrying forward the dialogue process, the leaders reiterated their commitments and determination to implement the joint statements of January 6, 2004, September 24, 2004, April 18, 2005 and September 14, 2005.

The leaders agreed that the peace process must be maintained and its success was important for both countries and the future of the entire region. In this context, they directed their Foreign Secretaries to resume the composite dialogue at the earliest possible.

The two leaders met in the aftermath of the Mumbai blasts. They strongly condemned all acts of terrorism and agreed that terrorism is a scourge that needs to be effectively dealt with.

They decided to put in place an India-Pakistan anti-terrorism institutional mechanism to identify and implement counter-terrorism initiatives and investigations.

The leaders decided to continue the joint search for mutually acceptable options for a peaceful negotiated settlement of all issues between India and Pakistan, including the issue of Jammu and Kashmir, in a sincere and purposeful manner. On the Jammu and Kashmir issue, there have been useful discussions. There is a need to build on convergences and narrow down divergences.

The two leaders also directed the Foreign Secretaries on the following:

(a) The Foreign Secretaries should meet shortly in New Delhi to continue the composite dialogue.

(b) To arrange consultations for early solution of the Siachen issue.

(c) Experts should meet immediately to agree on coordinates for joint survey of Sir Creek and adjoining area, without prejudice to each other's position on the issue. The Survey should commence in November 2006. The experts should start-discussions on the maritime boundary.

The two sides will facilitate implementation of agreements and understandings already reached on LOC-related CBMs, including bus services, crossing points and truck service."

Comments—Havana Joint Statement

There are four basic issues highlighted by the Joint Statement as follows:

(a) Resumption of the process of composite dialogue. Suspended after the Mumbai train blasts.

(b) Resolution of the Siachen issue.

(c) Resolution of maritime boundary at Sir Creek.

(d) Joint mechanism for countering terrorism, "to put in place an India-Pakistan anti-terrorism institutional mechanism to identify and implement counter-terrorism initiatives and investigations".

Of these the first three issues are a continuation of past positions, hence have not invited any comments or criticism in India. The last point on Joint Mechanism for Counter-Terrorism however, has been stiffly opposed by security analysts as well as political parties in New Delhi as it is perceived to equate terrorism in India and Pakistan, wherein the latter is seen by many as the chief sponsor of terror in Kashmir. Lack of *a priori* debate on the issue has also rankled many particularly those in the intelligence community. The alleged involvement of Pakistan in 7/11 Mumbai blasts, dramatically announced by Mumbai Police Commissioner has provided critics with strong fuel for their arguments.

The view of the Indian government appears to be that it is better to actively engage Pakistan on all issues even those which are as acrimonious as terrorism. This is perhaps the first time an attempt is being made to address the core issue of terrorism from Indian side by suggesting specific measures towards an achievable goal. The exact mechanics of the joint terrorism mechanism may take some time to evolve, but the proposal on the whole needs to be commended. India's new foreign secretary Shiv Shankar Menon is perhaps well suited to play a big role of coordinator, having just returned from Islamabad where he was the Indian High Commissioner. He should have good links on both sides of the Line of Control to carry forward the government's agenda. If the end game as seen by India is control of Pakistan ubiquitous intelligence agency Inter Services Intelligence, then it would be a fair deal. However, if it is to be another talking shop, then terrorism across the border will continue.

As far as the other issues of Sir Creek and Siachen are concerned, it is more than obvious that an agreement on both will be arrived at in the near future. The waters of the Sir Creek will be internationalized, in case India and Pakistan do not arrive at an agreement by 2009, while the Indian government is attempting to overcome the resistance of the Army on disengagement in Siachen.

Progress of Indo-Pakistan Talks During the Year

The Third round of the Composite Dialogue held during January 2006 for instance focused on Pakistan's proposal for self-governance in Kashmir which was countered by the Indian Foreign Secretary stating that institutions like representative legislative assemblies were functioning in Kashmir but the same were absent in Muzaffarabad, Gilgit and Baltistan. On the proposal of demilitarization the Indian Foreign Secretary pointed out that this is possible only if violence is eliminated and clearly linked terrorism across the border with demilitarization. India provided information of 15 terrorist training camps to Pakistan with satellite photographs and other details as proof. Pakistan countered with Indian interference in Balochistan. India also proposed an Extradition Treaty and a Mutual Legal Assistance Treaty (MLAT) to ensure that terrorists and criminals on both sides are brought to book. This had a tepid response from Pakistan. India also proposed some concrete measures as holding Flag meetings at the level of brigade commanders and ban on rebuilding and reconstruction on the Line of Control. Pakistan is reportedly not willing to turn off the terror tap as it is a powerful bargaining chip which it feels has brought India to the negotiating table.

In March, Confidence Building Measures (CBMs) with Pakistan were taken to a new level by the Indian Prime Minister Manmohan Singh. A Treaty of Peace, Friendship and Security was offered to Pakistan, to include development of cross border links between two parts of Jammu and Kashmir, improve quality of governance and provide dignity and self-respect to the people of the state. He also announced that the Line of Control should be made irrelevant and marginal issues as Siachen, Sir Creek and Baglihar should be resolved speedily. These initiatives should receive a favourable response from across the border as it is in the interest of both, India and Pakistan to focus on economy rather than security issues. The greatest contribution to both economies would be reduction in manned surveillance of the borders in areas such as Siachen which can, however, come about only with trust and credibility.

An indication of the smooth flow of peace trajectory was Munna Bao-Khokrapar Thar Express which was flagged off by India's Railway Minister, Lalu Prasad Yadav on 18 February. This was followed by commencement of Amritsar-Nankana Sahib bus service inaugurated by Manmohan Singh on 24 March 2006 and resumption of the Uri-Muzaffarabad bus after reopening of the road from Uri to Muzaffarabad on 31 March 2006. After the initial euphoria, not many takers have been reported for travel to Pakistan Occupied Kashmir.

There are also indications of Pakistan increasingly amenable to inter people talks of diverse nature. One such meeting held under the Pugwash initiative saw heated exchange between Omar Abdullah, National Conference leader and a group of Pakistani journalists when Abdullah castigated the role of foreign militants in the Kashmir struggle. The journalists were incensed and referred to terrorists as martyrs.[12] Till the role of violence continues to be eulogized in any Indo-Pakistan dialogue, the relationship cannot be placed on an even keel.

Nuclear CBMs. The Fourth Round of Expert level Dialogue on Nuclear Confidence Building Measures (CBMs) India-Pakistan was held in Islamabad on 25 and 26 April 2006. A draft agreement was finalized for reducing the risk from accidents relating to nuclear weapons through radiological leakages by the end of the next round of negotiations. Development of security concepts and nuclear doctrines to improve confidence building measures continue. The talks on nuclear risk reduction as far as India is concerned are from accidents and not actual use as India has already given up the right for first use as also to strike a non-nuclear state. Nuclear hawks in the Indian security establishment are, however, concerned of continued collusion between Pakistan and China and development of missile technology by Pakistan which in some areas is said to be ahead of the Indian capabilities. However, a two track policy may have to be continued, which will comprise of simultaneous peace and arms build up till the relationship matures into that of sustained peace building.

Conventional CBMs. The Third round of dialogue of experts on Conventional CBMs has agreed to work on the ground rules for implementation along the international border, holding quarterly flag meetings and speedy return of person's crossing over inadvertently. The agreement on non-development of new posts and defence works was also carried forward to include non-fortification of existing defence works. Pakistan proposed demilitarization in a different form. This was redeployment of artillery guns and offensive formations from Jammu and Kashmir. The Indian side obviously rejected the proposal and noted that this violated sovereign rights of a state to deploy forces within its own borders. Outwardly this may appear an innocuous proposal but in relation to the terror campaign launched from Pakistan, it has significant implications as it would imply a reduction of density of ground troops in Jammu and Kashmir which if it falls below the optimum levels will facilitate operations by terrorists.

A major breakthrough seen was commencement of screening of Indian films in Pakistan. This will facilitate other forms of trade as the Pakistani business lobby has maximum resistance to induction of Indian goods including films. Thus, this entrenched bureaucracy in Pakistan having been marginalized, greater impetus in trade ties including the most favoured nation status can be expected in a few years ahead.

As a part of the Confidence Building Measures (CBMs), talks were held between the Home Secretaries of India and Pakistan in Islamabad on 30 and 31 May 2006. Considerable headway has been made in inking an agreement on notification of prisoners and their early release. This will particularly benefit the large number of fishermen who inadvertently trespass national waters. A Memorandum of Understanding on narcotics control was also discussed. A list of wanted persons, 35 by India and 58 by Pakistan was exchanged. The Indian list included the notorious criminal recently outlawed by the United States, Dawood Ibrahim, Anees Ibrahim (brother of Dawood), Hafeez Saeed (Chief Terror Coordinator of Lashkar-e-Taiba), Masood Azhar (chief terror coordinator of Jaish-e-Mohammed), Syed Salahuddin (Chief terror coordinator United Jihad Council), Salim Haji Ibrahim, accused in the Godhra fire incident reportedly in hiding in Karachi, hijackers of the IC 814 flight, Athar

Ibrahim, Zahoor Ibrahim Mistri, Shahid Akhtar, Shakir Mohammed and Azhar Yusuf. The basis of this list is apparently issue of red corner notice by the Interpol.[13]

Indo-Pakistan relations received a fillip with relaxation of visa policy by Pakistan in June. Group tourists with designated tour operators will be provided with a 30 days visa instead of 14 days earlier, Indian pilgrims 15 days rather than a shrine specific visa and in the business visa category a six-month triple entry visa with a maximum stay of 30 days has been allowed each time. Persons in the civil society category, senior citizens, widows and divorcees will get visas for up to two years.[14] This will be a boon to the large group of migrants from the areas which are now part of Pakistan, who would like to relive memories of the past. This will also provide a considerable boost to Indo-Pak tourism.

Pakistan allowed transit of Indian trucks to Afghanistan. 240 trucks were donated by India to Afghanistan which are now being driven through the Wagah border. This request has been long outstanding and Pakistan's' insecurities of increased Indian role in Afghanistan had prevented from flow of Indian aid through the land route to the country. The Punch-Rawalakot bus was flagged off by Sonia Gandhi on 20 June 2006, another crossing place softening the Jammu border.

The Third Round of the Indo-Pak composite dialogue process came to an end with the last of the eight part talks, the Tulbul-Wular barrage on 23 June 2006, without any progress. Reconciliation of differences over the concept of the barrage as a reservoir *vis-à-vis* a diversionary channel was not feasible.

Indo-Pakistan relations received a significant boost with signing of a Memorandum of Understanding (MoU) for sharing and learning from each others experiences in devolution of power to the grass-roots. A Joint Working Group is being established to foster relations between the two countries in Panchayati Raj institutions. This is not part of the Confidence Building Measures (CBMs) but needs to be considered as an effective mechanism to develop linkages and, therefore, enhance people to people relationship.

The Lows of Mumbai Blasts. Indo-Pakistan relations were at a new low after the Mumbai blasts on 11 July 2006 followed by Indian official statement in August chastising Pakistan for killing of Akbar Khan Bugti. There were veiled allusions in Pakistan of India being behind the uprising in Balochistan, allegations virtually unrestrained in the coffee table circuit. The speculation in the Indian media of a Indo-Pakistan border war, allegedly fed by intelligence agencies was a manifestation of this false supposition. The availability and deployment of Pakistani forces at present, the political situation in Pakistan and international pressures negated the possibility of a conflict. An Indian non-paper providing suggestions on resolution of the Kashmir issue is being debated within the Pakistani establishment. There may be some discussion on the same to provide a firm direction to Indo-Pak relations in the future, hostage to the many mishaps that have tempered it over the years.

Musharraf's Kashmir Formula

President Musharraf's four-point proposal for resolution of the Kashmir issue in an interview with the Indian news channel, NDTV included the following:

(a) Freedom of movement for the people of Kashmir thereby making the border irrelevant.

(b) Self-governance or autonomy but not independence for the state.

(c) Withdrawal of troops from the region in a staggered manner.

(d) Joint supervision mechanism for administration of the province.

The proposal was also accompanied by a caveat that only in case these proposals were accepted, Pakistan will give up its claim over Jammu and Kashmir and not press for a plebiscite. The Indian government was naturally reticent to respond to a proposal made to the media and awaited an official communication from Pakistan. Indian Prime Minister, however, clearly indicated that he was willing to examine such proposals with an open mind.

Pakistan's foreign office spokesman Tasnim Aslam surprised many observers by stating that Islamabad had never claimed Kashmir. This and other assertions by Pakistani leadership leads one to believe that the Pakistani elite appears to have reconciled to mediate on Kashmir and is probably focusing on its internal problems as well as development of economy. Whether this is a tactical trend or a permanent positional shift will need to be watched closely. On the other hand there were widespread protests by the Pakistani media over Tasnim's statement.

Other changes are also evident with the decision of the government to redefine the two nation theory by providing a more balanced view which could result in the government clashing with fundamentalist elements. The Pakistan media however, welcomed this view. The mainstream media was quick to emphasize that Pakistan's founder Jinnah had stated that creation of Pakistan was for the purpose of greater harmony between Hindus and Muslims. Jinnah was perhaps too idealist for human interaction thrives on emphasizing differences rather on similarities.

Siachen—Thaw?

Pakistan's Foreign Minister, Khurshid Kasuri set the ball rolling on Siachen by proclaiming that there could be a break-through on the issue which would pave the way for a substantial agreement at the time of visit of Manmohan Singh to Pakistan. The Indian Ministry of External Affairs, vehemently denied reports that any such agreement was in the offing. The official reaction by the Indian Armed Forces remained guarded. The Indian Army has through individual sacrifice, tactical dexterity and superior logistics occupied and maintained posts on the Saltoro Ridge, the highest battlefield of the World, over the past two decades or so. The Pakistan Army on the other hand has never accepted that it was not in a commanding position on the Saltoro Ridge to the Pakistani people. The issue is now authenticating the grid references and the "on ground" positions. If Pakistani Army accepts Indian positions on the Saltoro, it will permanently sully its reputation at home, losing political clout at a time when its credibility is increasingly being questioned. With elections slated in Pakistan in 2007, if the Army wants its candidates to win, it cannot accept back tracking on Siachen.

The Indian Army's apprehensions are based on its experience in Kargil in 1999 when Pakistan blatantly violated the Line of Control, upturning the Shimla Agreement of 1972. In case Pakistan undertakes a similar manoeuvre in the Glacier after both sides have withdrawn, which is tactically possible given the ease of approach from its side, Indians will find it virtually impossible to reoccupy the Glacier. The human and material costs of having occupied the Glacier have been quite heavy for both sides. The daily costs are also said to be over Rs. 4 Crore for India and a relatively lower Rs 1.5 Crore for Pakistan. The Prime Minister Manmohan Singh had been the original votary of the proposal for conversion of Siachen into a peace park.

Pull back from Siachen means a peace dividend of Rs. 1000 Crore a year and a new lease of life to the many brides in waiting in Jhunjhunu and Guntur or Multan and Faislabad, for the toll on lives from weather and terrain hazards has also been very heavy. The Prime Minister will have to finally over rule the nay sayers and restore sanity to the conflict matrix in the Subcontinent.

Technology can provide an answer to all fears. Satellite imaging can detect build up and movements in real time and these techniques are available even in the civilian domain today. Ground surveillance equipment can be deployed which can be monitored regularly to detect violations. An integrated surveillance plan including UAVs and the proverbial foot patrols is quite viable provided it is carried out with due rigor. Innovation and imagination is thus the key to Siachen and not boots on the ground.

However, the final word perhaps should be taken from the man on the ground. As per a report in the website www.defencetalk.com which has quoted the Press Trust of India, Brigadier Om Prakash the Commander of the Siachen Brigade had said that, "If we vacate the glacier, it will weaken our position." Thus not much progress could be expected with the Army taking an intractable stand on the issue.

Sir Creek Towards a Resolution

A joint review by Indian and Pakistan surveyors of the Sir Creek was held from 15 January 2007 leading to likely resolution of the long-standing maritime boundary dispute between both the countries. The Indian stand is that the border should be in the middle of the 100 kms Estuary while Pakistan wants it to run on the south-eastern side towards India. The United Nations Convention on the Law of the Sea (UNCLOS) states that the deepest point in a marshy land is to be the centre point for marking a boundary. The urgency of settlement is highlighted by the need to submit a demarcated maritime boundary to the United Nations by 2009 as else the waters would be converted into international territory.

Baglihar Water Dispute

Arbitration over the Baglihar Dam in Doda district of Jammu achieved a solution to the dispute over construction of the barrage over Chenab River. Pakistan protested over reports which appeared in Indian media on independent Swiss experts accepting India's claims over the Baglihar dam dispute. The Pakistani side claimed that these reports were misleading and broke the code of confidentiality.

The Baglihar dispute had been raised by Pakistan over unilateral increase in the height of the dam and also the need to construct sluice gates beneath the pondage. The design of the dam was also questioned by Pakistan. The arbitration held under the aegis of the World Bank which is financing the project has since been completed and the issue has been successfully resolved. Professor Lafitte is the World Bank nominated expert for arbitration. The Baglihar project presents an opportunity to develop the region of Doda in Jammu area of the state which had been languishing over the years.

Indo-Pakistan Relations—Activating SAFTA

The South Asia Free Trade Agreement (SAFTA), signed by the member states of SAARC during 12th Summit in Islamabad in January, 2004 came into force from 1 January 2006. Under this agreement, SAARC member countries are to implement the trade liberalization programme as per Article 7 from 1 July

2006. India has accordingly notified the reduction of tariffs as per Article 7 of SAFTA Agreement on 1 July 2006. The notification (SRO No. 695(I)/2006) issued by the government of Pakistan on 1 July 2006 has notified tariff concessions on import of 4872 items from SAARC member countries. However, according to this notification, imports from India would be subject to Pakistan import policy order of July 2005 which restricts goods from India or goods of Indian origin to a positive list of only 773 items.[15]

Kamal Nath, Union Minister of Commerce and Industry, took up the issue of restricted import of goods under the SAARC Free Trade Agreement (SAFTA) from India by Pakistan with the SAARC Secretariat. The Minister indicated that notification by the government of Pakistan dated 1 July 2006 is against the letter and spirit of SAFTA. "I am sure you would agree with me that SAFTA has little operational meaning if Pakistan does not apply SAFTA to all items, except those tariff lines in the sensitive list, to all member countries", Kamal Nath has said in a letter to the Secretary General of SAARC. The letter also recalls that the government of Pakistan had earlier ratified SAFTA without any reservation.

India also attempted to hold bilateral dialogue with Pakistan on SAFTA but failed to make headway as Pakistan remained determined to deny India tariff concessions. Pakistan's trade lobby has been pressuring the government to deny entry to more Indian goods as they are fearful of an Indian sweep of the markets. There is sound reason to believe that this is not in the overall interest of Pakistani commerce, as empirical evidence from other examples including the threat of flooding of Chinese goods of Indian markets in 2000 has conclusively proved that private industry adjusts to competition much more easily and can diversify in areas which are to its advantage. Thus, Indo-China trade is now slated to cross the $ 20 billion mark over the next few years.

The Bank of Pakistan has also been a very strong proponent of Indo-Pakistan trade.[16] With firming of this relationship in the field of economy and trade, political relations are also set to improve though at a much gradual pace. The hidden Indo-

Pakistan economy is said to be almost at par with the official trade as black market profiteers have ingenuous means to circumvent the white routes for profit. However, these channels were also hindered by lack of direct cargo traffic between the two countries. Open channel trade will considerably reduce black markets in goods between the two countries and will prove of benefit to both, particularly Pakistan just as has Bangladesh, Sri Lanka and of course Nepal.

Pakistan finally extended the restricted list of imports from India to 1000, setting the stage for broadening the economic relationship with its eastern neighbour and perhaps for the first time not punctuating it with Kashmir. Pakistan has finally recognized rather late that a positive trade rapport with India will enable it to partake of substantial 9 per cent growth that is being experienced in New Delhi. Other SAARC countries as Sri Lanka, Nepal and Bhutan have been benefiting from SAFTA. Pakistan has much greater potential than these states and this belated decision would provide impetus for furthering Pakistan's economy.

Indo-Pakistan Shipping Protocol

A new Indo-Pakistan shipping protocol will allow Indian and Pakistani ships to lift third country cargo from each others ports and will increase trade between the two countries. Presently ships had to wait for adequate tonnages for transportation as only intra-country lifting of cargo was permitted. The volume of cargo between India and Pakistan is reported to be exports at Rs. 22.88 billion and imports at Rs. 4.70 billion in 2004-05.[17]

Review of Indo-Pakistan Relations in 2006

Manmohan Singh India's Prime Minister articulated his vision of Indo-Pakistan relations based on a Treaty of Peace, Security and Friendship which can come about only by building an atmosphere of trust between the two countries. This Treaty will be as per the Prime Minister harness the collective destiny of the two nations. The vision is certainly noble but at present may appear too far in the future as both India and Pakistan have to resolve internal complexities while coming to grips with the neighbourhood. As things stand it appears, that Pakistan is likely to face major challenges in the coming decade as past indulgences with the Taliban in Afghanistan, insecurities on the Western border in Federally Administered Tribal Areas and the North West Frontier Province come into play. As the forces of modernization clash with tribalism and fundamentalism in these areas, Pakistan will have to bear tectonic shocks. India has managed to cross this hump on its eastern peripheral states of Nagaland, Manipur and Mizoram which are well on their way into assimilation in the Indian nation state, though minor problems continue. Pakistan is just about starting to meet these challenges. The resolve of the Pakistan Army alone will ensure that the nation prospers if not actually survives.

Indo-Pakistan relationship can be expected to be punctuated by terrorist strikes within India including Jammu and Kashmir. The spread of the jihad network is evident not only with incidents of blasts in the country during the year but also the large number of apprehensions of suspected terrorists including Pakistani nationals made in cities as Mysore. It is also evident that external groups such as Lashkar-e-Taiyyaba and Jaish-e-Mohammad both based in Pakistan have developed a network with activists of the banned indigenous organization, Students Islamic Movement of India or SIMI and its smaller satellites. This network will continue to be sustained over the next few years. Moreover, the root cause of growth of SIMI and its allies is disaffection amongst large number of Muslim youth due to alleged pogroms as in Gujarat and most recently in Mangalore during the year. This creates a *casus belli* for the rebels to exploit.

The key issues with Pakistan will be resolution of the Sir Creek and Siachen dispute in 2007. Establishing a Joint Counter Terror Mechanism is laudable, however, there is unlikely to be much optimism given that Pakistan has sought evidence which can be produced in court to prove any of its citizens indulging in terrorist acts. Such evidence is not likely to be obtainable given the nature of the acts and the shady credentials of most of those who commit the same. The presentation of specific evidence and its acceptance by the other side will facilitate effective functioning of the joint counter-terror mechanism. Thus joint interrogation, alibis, suspect apprehension and questionnaire are some of the issues which may be discussed by such a mechanism.

A settlement of Jammu and Kashmir problem is not likely in the near future, but what may be expected is a reduction in level of violence leading to a possible ceasefire in the Valley, which again will see intermittent interruptions for there is no mechanism which can control terrorists from conducting isolated attacks as a large number of these outfits operate virtually independently.

DIALOGUE – INDIA AND OTHER COUNTRIES

Indo-Australian Relations

The Australian Prime Minister, John Howard visited the country in March 2006 in the wake of President Bush. Australia is an important player in the nuclear fuel segment holding 60 per cent Uranium reserves of the world. Howard, however, preferred to await excision of sanctions by the United States and a green signal from the Nuclear Suppliers Group before making any commitments.[18]

Indo-German Relations

The momentum of Indian diplomacy saw the Prime Minister visit two crucial states, Germany and Uzbekistan in April 2006. The former is a technology and manufacturing giant while the latter has large oil and gas reserves. The joint statement by the Prime Minister and Chancellor Merkel stressed a number of facets of bilateral interest, such as defence cooperation, trade, investment, technological collaboration, infrastructure, energy and space. Indian participation as Partner Country in Hanover Messe acknowledges the growth of manufacturing sector in the country. This appears to be the beginning of a sustained collaboration as India is invited as the Guest of Honour Country for the Frankfurt Book fair and Indian Council for Cultural Relations is setting up five rotating Chairs on Contemporary Indian Studies in German universities.

Indo-Uzbek Relations

The strategic partnership with Uzbekistan based on long-standing bonds of friendship will prove beneficial to India in terms of its energy security. Uzbekistan can act as a hub for sourcing natural resources particularly oil and natural gas from Central Asia. The information technology and management resources can be the key drivers from the Indian side. Thus, a Jawaharlal Nehru India Uzbekistan Centre for Information Technology was inaugurated and an Entrepreneurship Development Centre is being set up in Tashkent. Satellite based tele-education and tele-medicine connectivity between India and Uzbekistan is also being provided.

Indo-Myanmar Relations

Indo-Myanmar relations received a fillip with the visit by Indian President Kalam to Yangon in March 2006.[19] Though the country is ruled by a military junta, Myanmar is being viewed from an economic perspective by India as a bridge to South East Asia ignoring its poor record on human rights, particularly incarceration of the fragile Aung Suu Kyi. Myanmar is also important due to its gas reserves and possibilities of an oil and gas conduit. The operations launched by Myanmar's Army on the Indo-Myanmar border against Khaplang faction of the NSCN last year also proved of utility to keep the militants under check.

Indo-Myanmar Talks at the level of Home Secretaries were held on 16 September 2006 at New Delhi. The Indian government provided to the Myanmar representative a list of 15 Camps in which cadres of various terrorist outfits of the North East the ULFA, PLA, UNLF and the NSCN Khaplang as well as the Isaac Muivah are undergoing training. Standard protocols on intelligence sharing, drug trafficking, arms smuggling and militant activities were exchanged. A detailed mechanism for greater interaction is important and was proposed to be drawn up shortly. These talks were followed up by a meeting of the Home Ministers of India, Shivraj Patil and Myanmar, Major General Maung Oo in December to discuss issues such as drug trafficking, security and border management. The Indian government offered training and capacity building for Myanmar's officials who also visited Indian Space Research Organization (ISRO) and Hindustan Aeronautics (HAL). The issue of operations against terrorists of the North East lodged in camps in Myanmar was also discussed. Myanmar's officials are reported to have confirmed that action will be taken shortly.

India continued to enlarge its strategic relationship with Myanmar with offer of upgradation of fighter aircraft, sale of Advanced Light Helicopters (ALH) built by Hindustan Aeronautics Ltd. (HAL), Bharat Electronics Radars, airborne radio equipment and surveillance electronics. Provision of arms and ammunition and construction of frigates were also considered during the visit of Air Chief Marshal S.P. Tyagi over three days to Myanmar during November.

The Indo-Myanmar Gas pipeline is another issue which is crucial to the relationship. A pipeline was proposed by Gas Authority of India Ltd. (GAIL) for importing gas from Myanmar which will be through the North Eastern states of Mizoram, Assam and West Bengal to Gaya in Bihar. The total distance is 1573 kms and the cost Rs. 8500 crore. A pipeline through Bangladesh was also considered but plans for the same had to be abandoned due to uncertain political trends in that country. However, Myanmar has not been forthcoming on gas deals as apparently it is attempting to gain maximum advantage from this critical resource by bargaining with a number of countries including India and China.

India's policy of negotiating with the military regime with Myanmar has been dictated by real politic rather than idealism. China has developed a strategic relationship with Myanmar which has seen it gaining a base in the country as well as oil and gas resources. India's Oil and Natural Gas Corporation (ONGC) was surprised recently when the Myanmarese made an agreement with a Chinese company for supply of gas without its information though it has a proportionate stake in a joint venture. The border areas of Myanmar are also seen as a major base for Indian militant organizations particularly the NSCN (Khaplang) faction. A joint operation with the Myanmarese forces is thus seen to provide considerable benefits to the Army in its control of insurgency in the North East.

Reports in sair.org indicate that there is a nexus between the Myanmarese army and various terrorist organizations of the North East who are running profitable business on the other side of the border. Availability of adequate funds with these organizations reported to be Rs. 4 million in Manipur through extortion in 2005 alone has led to an increase in transborder activities. The length of the border and the difficult terrain limits the ability to plug the gaps in any substantial way. In 2005, there were reports of raids on the NSCN Khaplang camps in Myanmar, however the impact and results achieved of these raids is not known. It appears that there is a live and let live atmosphere in cross-border activities of the terrorists as well as the Myanmarese Army on both sides.

IBSA—Strategic Alliance

The India Brazil South Africa (IBSA) initiative received a boost with the Indian Prime Minister visiting both Brazil and South Africa during September. Extensive cooperation between the three continental giants is in the offing providing synergies in development and exchange of best practices. Apart from increased political and economic say in global affairs, the IBSA will also provide India with considerable trade leverages. It is also hopeful of getting Uranium from South Africa, an essential prerequisite for nuclear energy for the country apart from support in the crucial negotiations in the Nuclear Suppliers Group. The recent joint initiatives by IBSA in WTO were the first indication of growing significance of the movement.

Evacuating Indians from Lebanon, June 2006

Indian Navy undertook a massive relief and rescue effort to evacuate Indian citizens from Lebanon. Four Indian Naval ships on port of calls in Turkey and Libya were diverted to Lebanon to undertake the operation of evacuation of Indian citizens which was carried out successfully over a period of four days. A large quantum of relief material was also transported from Cyprus to Lebanon during the period.

Indo-Nepal Relations

Indo-Nepal relations were placed on an even keel with the Seven-Party Alliance and the Maoists reconciling with New Delhi on various issues including release of Maoist leaders in Indian jails. India underlined its commitment to Nepal during the visit of the Nepalese Prime Minister, the ageing G.P. Koirala in June 2006. The emphasis during the visit was on an economic package for recovery to include grants, credit, soft loans and new projects including rescheduling of loans. Military aid did not appear on the overt agenda. Works on 137 small and big projects in Nepal with Indian assistance is to be speeded up. India has reportedly recommended disarming Maoists as a precursor to holding elections which is under way.

A package of Rs. 8.5 billion has also been offered to Nepal for infrastructure development in the Terai region. This will supplement the Rs. (Nepal) 1,500 crores aid announced during the visit of the Nepali Prime Minister to India. India's total aid to Nepal was Rs. (Nepal) 1,800 crores in 139 projects at various stages of implementation in the fields of health, education and infrastructure.

ENERGY SECURITY ISSUES

Indo-Russian Energy Cooperation

India's immediate requirements for nuclear fuel were resolved with assistance from Russia. Russia agreed to supply 60 tonnes for the two reactors at Tarapur starved of Uranium 135, under the safety exception clause of Nuclear Supplier Group guidelines. The replacement was slated in 2001 and is overdue by five years. Russia's atomic energy agency, Rosatom will supply the fuel.[20]

India is in the process of engaging Russia extensively in the field of energy with the Minister of Petroleum, Murli Deora having a number of successive meetings with the Russians during the year including one with Russian President Vladimir Putin. Russia has also offered India participation for prospecting in Timan-Pechora oil fields in East Siberia and the Far East as well as West Siberia, Barents and Okhotsk Seas. India is already a partner in the Sakhalin 1 project.

There is a need for exercising caution in oil projects with Russia due to a number of factors. The environment in the oil and gas sector in Russia is quite unstable, hence there is constant uncertainty in terms of policies, leadership as well as investments. The environment protection standards of Russians are also not effective. The final issue is that of security of personnel. The Russian oil and gas complexes are infamous for a number of killings and kidnappings even of high officials who are under heavy security.

The impasse on acquiring of gas from Iran appeared to be nearing resolution with India willing to pay a higher price of US$ 4.50 per million British thermal unit (BTU) for Iranian Liquefied Natural gas. The initial deal which was signed by Indian companies with Iran's National Iranian Gas Export Company in June 2005 for 5 million tons of LNG at a price of $ 2.9 per million BTU was reneged by the Iranians after oil prices touched a new high during the year. The high level of demand for LNG has led to Indian acquiescence to a higher price for gas by Iran.[21]

India is facing massive challenges in availability of natural gas. The three main pipeline projects, IPI, Iran-Pakistan-India TAPI Turkmenistan-Afghanistan-Pakistan-India and MBI Myanmar-Bangladesh-India are embroiled in political controversies and appear to be non-starters unless issues of multi-lateral cooperation are resolved in a much more proactive manner than being done so far. Moreover, security concerns in all these as well as intervening states such as Balochistan province of Pakistan, Bangladesh and Afghanistan are major hindrances in these projects.

INDIAN NUCLEAR DIPLOMACY

Proactively Engaging IAEA and NSG

In anticipation of the Indo-US Civil Nuclear Deal being accepted by US legislators, Indian diplomat's commenced interaction with the IAEA as well as members of the NSG, the next two stages of clearance required for supply of nuclear fuel for the strategic nuclear power sector. Brazil, South Africa, Germany and France were approached during the visit of the

Prime Minister, Manmohan Singh and Defence Minister Pranab Mukherjee. These nations sounded positive in supporting India's case in these international nuclear institutions.

Discussions with the IAEA officials in New Delhi on a proposed India specific safeguards agreement as required under the Indo-US Civil Nuclear Agreement were also held. India specific Safeguards Agreement will denote the level of supervision of India's nuclear facilities by the IAEA as per a Press Trust of India report. Simultaneous conclusion of the Indo-US Civil Nuclear Agreement and the safeguards agreement with the IAEA will leave approval by the NSG as the last hurdle for India to de facto join the elite nuclear weapons club and also receive assistance to support its nuclear energy programme. In the NSG, India is assured of support by the USA and the Western bloc, particularly those countries seeking nuclear trade with India. China and other non-proliferation activist nations are expected to raise a number of issues for clearance of India by the NSG.

Members of the Nuclear Supplier's Group (NSG) in Vienna were given a presentation by Indian officials for exemption from NSG guidelines. Support requested by the Prime Minister Manmohan Singh personally from various countries including Finland, South Africa and Brazil paid rich dividends. India now needs to seek support of China and Ireland. The latter has opposed the proposal of exemption of India from NSG guidelines as it is a non-signatory of the NPT. China is continuing to be ambiguous.[22] India is optimistic of supply of fuel by 2008. This is due to slow pace of multi-national negotiations and apprehensions of states after North Korea's nuclear test in October 2006.

The relevance of being a Permanent member of the UN Security Council is highlighted. It places a nation in the forefront of international relations as a global policy maker rather than being a marginal commentator. In the recent past major decisions were taken by the UN Security Council related to nuclear proliferation by Iran and sanctions against North Korea. In case India had been a Permanent member of the UN

Security Council, it would have provided the country excellent leverages of control.

International Thermonuclear Experimental Reactor Project (ITER)

India was formally admitted to the ITER in May 2006. The programme for building a reactor with hot fusion is conceived jointly by the United States, Russia, China, Japan, Korea and the European Union. The large hardon collider project is being built by the European Organization for Nuclear Research or CERN at a project cost of $ 10 billion. ITER is to provide unlimited, clean and cheap energy wherein one kg of fusion fuel would be able to produce the same amount of energy as 10 million kg of fossil fuels. The reactor is expected to be built by 2016.[23] This will provide substantial boost to energy supply in the country once this project fructifies contributing to India's ambitious target for nuclear energy of 40,000 MW by 2030.

Nuclear Non-Proliferation of Technology to Terrorists

India made a significant plea in the United Nations for prevention of access of radiological materials and technology to terrorists. The Indian representative in the United Nations, former Jammu and Kashmir Chief Minister, Mufti Mohammed Sayeed, also called for priority in creating a global security culture and offered India's assistance towards this effort including peaceful uses of nuclear energy. The closed fuel cycle which is being developed by India through the Thorium route was indicated as a possible option. He had also predicted a growth in demand of nuclear energy in the future and posited that Thorium offered much lower scope for proliferation than plutonium.[24]

India's call for a Thorium based nuclear fuel cycle is in line with the country's nuclear energy policy based on the large scale of Thorium reserves available indigenously. This will reduce its dependence on Uranium. However, effective operationalising of the Thorium fuel cycle has not been achieved so far and is expected to be many years away.

INDIAN MILITARY DIPLOMACY

Indo-Japan Defence Cooperation

Indian military diplomacy appeared to be in an overdrive in 2006. India actively engaged China, Japan, Germany and Myanmar during the year.[25] The first major visit was by General Tsutomu Mori, Japanese Army Chief, who came to India on 6 March 2006 and was conducted around the Line of Control as well as observed special forces exercises in Agra, the two areas of interest apparently of all foreign military commanders visiting India.

The Joint Statement issued during the visit of the Defence Minister, Pranab Mukherjee to Japan indicated stepped up defence cooperation between the two nations. Goodwill exercises have been proposed between Indian Navy and the Japanese Self-Defence Force. Exchange of ships, invitations for witnessing designated military activities, frequent meetings between the two defence ministers, a Defence Policy Dialogue at Defence Secretary level, Comprehensive Security Dialogue and Military to Military Talks were other areas of mutual cooperation. A vacancy in the National Defence College was also offered by the Indian Defence Minster.[26]

The focus of Indo-Japanese engagement is, however, on maritime security. The Defence Minister's statement during the press conference placed the relationship in context thus, "...the security of maritime trade, security of sea lanes which carry major energy sources and the growing concentration of lethal weapons at the hands of non-state actors require the collective intervention of the world community who have interest in peace and stability of the world. Therefore, I do feel it is necessary to have defence cooperation among the peace loving countries all over the world including our region. Japan is an important collaborator of India in our economic and trade activities. Therefore, we do feel, in order to ensure the maritime security in the Indian Ocean, Malacca Straits cooperation between India and Japan will be helpful." A large proportion of Japan's energy requirements is being met by West Asian oil. India straddling the oil trade routes through the Arabian Sea and the Indian

Ocean is regarded as a significant player for maritime security by Japan, with increasing threat to shipping in these areas.

Indo-German Defence Cooperation June 2006

2006 has been declared as the Indo-German Friendship Year. A two-day Indo-German Colloquium was organized by Konrad Adenauer foundation on 'Responsibilities in International Relations and Opportunities of Bilateral Cooperation' in Stuttgart, Germany. The Minister of State for Defence M. Pallam Raju called for an upgradation of defence ties with Germany. The present defence cooperation between India and Germany is limited to availing courses, staff talks and procurement of spares. Indian interest in German EW systems, radars, electro-optic devices and recovery vehicles was indicated. Indo-German defence cooperation has largely been dominated by equipment acquisition. As such, there is a need to move towards joint development ventures or technology transfers through which long-term self-reliance with respect to maintenance product support could be achieved.

An important area of convergence between India and Germany in today's globalizing world was identified as promotion of comprehensive reform of the United Nations system. Today's political realities, including the unvarying support and participation in the UN and its programme by countries such as Germany and India must be reflected in a reformed UN.

India's Defence Minister Pranab Mukherjee and German Defence Minister Franz Josef Jung signed a military partnership agreement in September 2006. An India-Germany High Defence Committee (HDC), was formed which is to meet once a year, alternately, in India and Germany. In these three sub-groups on Strategic Defence Cooperation, Defence Technical Cooperation and Military to Military Cooperation have been formed.

- The Strategic Defence Cooperation sub-group will be headed by officials at the Joint Secretary level and will cover areas as, security and defence policy, leadership concepts, disaster relief and humanitarian assistance.
- The Defence Technical Cooperation sub-group will cover defence technology cooperation, defence business

cooperation, exchange of information on armament procurement projects, including project related development and exchange of information on defence technological research and technology in both countries.

- The Military-to-military cooperation sub-group will deal with issues such as standard and advanced training of military and civilian members of the armed forces, organizational structure of the armed forces, maintenance of armed forces in peace time, military medicine, military geo-information affairs, environmental protection in the armed forces, deployment of the armed forces within the UN Framework, disaster relief and humanitarian assistance. The co-chairs of the three sub-groups will report to the HDC on their deliberations and bilateral work programme for approval.[27]

INDO-MOZAMBIQUE DEFENCE CO-OPERATION

A defence pact was also concluded with Mozambique inked by India's defence minister and his counterpart, Tobias Joaquim Dai, to cover military technical cooperation, logistics support and training. Joint patrolling of Madagascar channel was also discussed along with fast attack craft for Mozambique and assistance in research.[28]

JOINT MILITARY TRAINING

Joint training is emerging as a key area of mutual confidence building in the region as well as globally. This results in greater transparency and effective military to military engagement reducing the scope of conflict. The Indian Army's saga of joint training with foreign armies continued during the year. The first event was an Indo-US exercise held in the mountainous region of Kumaon Hills. India also provided training facilities to personnel of the Singapore Army in Babina in Central India. Joint air, naval and army exercises were held with a number of Western armed forces in all the dimensions, sea, land and air and are outlined in subsequent paragraphs.

Indo-French Joint Naval Exercises—Varuṇa II

Varuna II, Indo-French joint exercises were held off the coast of Goa in the first week of April 2006. The Indian Air Force was also a part of this exercise. These were focused on training with aircraft carriers, Charles De Gaulle and INS Viraat. Submarines and destroyers also participated. There were joint landings by aircraft on the carriers and other maneuvers to improve technical and communication compatibilities.

Ex Konkan Indian and Royal Navy Manoeuvres—Western Seas

Exercise Konkan II a joint sea manoeuvre between the Indian Navy and the Royal (British) Navy was conducted in May 2006. Four surface combatants, one submarine, and a variety of shore-based fixed-wing and ship borne rotary-wing aircraft from the Indian side under the tactical command of the FOCWF (Flag Officer Commanding Western Fleet), Rear Admiral Anup Singh participated. The Royal Navy forces were commanded by Rear Admiral Neil Morisetti. The Indian Naval ships included guided-missile destroyer Mumbai, the guided-missile frigates Ganga and Brahmaputra, the fleet replenishment tanker Shakti, and the submarine Shankush. The Royal Navy task force comprised of aircraft carrier Illustrious (with her own air group), the guided-missile destroyer Gloucester, the fleet replenishment tanker Fort Victoria, and the submarine support ship Diligence and the nuclear-powered submarine (SSN) Sovereign. In addition it had one French frigate, FNS Surcouf.

The exercises included, 'DACT' (Dissimilar Air Combat) and 'COMAO' (Combined Maritime Air Operations) between the Indian Navy's Sea Harrier aircraft operating ex-Goa and the Harrier GR 7A off the Illustrious. Some of the 'firsts' of this exercise include combined maritime air operations by Indian Navy Sea Harrier aircraft and Royal Navy's Harrier GR 7A, cross-deck operations by Indian jump jets from the deck of Illustrious and flying demonstration by the Red Arrows. Immediate and advanced ASW (Anti-Submarine Warfare), MIO (Maritime Interdiction Operations), VBSS (Visit, Board, Search

& Seizure) procedures, NGS (Naval Gunfire Support), and tactical manoeuvre were also practiced. Admiral Sir Jonathon Band, first Sea Lord and Chief of the Naval Staff Royal Navy, also visited the exercises from 27 May to 01 Jun.[29]

Indo-British Joint Air Exercise Agra-Gwalior

An Indo-British joint air exercise was held in Agra and Gwalior from 13 to 20 October 2006. Hundred officers from each air force participated in the same. The British contingent took part with Tornadoes and in flight refuelers. This was one amongst the many joint air exercises undertaken by the IAF with other Air Forces of the World recently. In addition a number of joint para troop exercises have also been carried out in the past with Russian and the US forces.

Ex Shatrujeet—Indian Army and US Marines Joint Tactical Exercise

The Indian Army and the US Marine Corps conducted a joint exercise code named Shatrujeet in the beginning of November 2006. A company each of 21 PUNJAB and a company of the United States Marine Corps ex 2/4 Marine Expeditionary Units MARFORPAC participated in the same. The aim was to share experiences in joint counter-terrorism operations in semi-urban terrain, enhance functional interoperability in OOTW (Operations Other Than War). Tactical level intelligence, communications, weapons and equipment along with use of minimum force to achieve desired military objectives was practiced. Emphasis was on reducing collateral damage and achieving the mission with minimum casualties. A validation exercise was held in Cordon and Search operations as a culmination.[30]

Successful sharing of experience in counter-terrorism operations by the Indian Army and the US Marines both having a rich legacy in the same is of significance. However, whereas Indian forces emphasize on use of minimum force, non-employment of fire power such as artillery, the US Armed Forces have not hesitated in using helicopter, artillery as well as multi barrel rockets against insurgents in Iraq and Afghanistan. Though the situations obtained are quite at variance, the adoption of Indian model would pay the US rich dividends in winning the hearts and minds battle in Iraq, now that the Afghanistan front is under NATO.

SINDEX—Indo-Singapore Joint Exercise

A joint exercise was conducted in November between the Indian Air Force and the Singapore Air Force, the third in the series of bilateral exercises. Code named SINDEX, the exercises were conducted in the Air Force base at Kalaikunda, West Bengal which has emerged as a major training facility for joint air force training.[31] In 2005 a major Indo-US joint air exercise was also conducted in the area which had seen protests by the locals.

Singapore Air Force is one of the leading air forces in South East Asia with a fleet of F 16 fighters and reported plans of participation in the Joint Strike Fighter programme with Western nations. The exercise involved tactical control of aircraft as well as interaction between flight and air traffic controllers as well as radar system operators. The integration of engineering, logistics and administrative staff also contributed to the exercise goals.

Budgetary Constraints—Joint Exercises

The plans of the Indian Air Force for joint exercises were severely affected by the budgetary cuts imposed on non-tangible defence related activities. The Indian Armed Forces are said to have conducted 30 exercises with the United States in the last four years. Other countries as France, Russia and Singapore were also involved in joint exercises. Only two joint exercises per year are to be held in future, one at home and the other abroad. Indo-US fighter exercises will be held once in three years. Multilateral exercises are being discouraged as pilots use different languages, tactics and processes. Flight safety is another issue of concern when a large number of countries are participating. The IAF has probably assessed its potential after too many exercises and now wants to bench mark less frequently.

Restrictions due to budgetary cuts were anticipated as the initial euphoria of glasnost in training with joint forces has tapered off. The Armed Forces need to draw up a policy for such training activities factoring in budgetary requirements and spin offs. This can then be approved at the appropriate level and a programme of periodic conduct institutionalized. For instance a Times of India report has indicated that the Cope India exercises held at Kalaikunda air force base in November 2005, cost the IAF Rs. 21.20 lakhs with an infrastructure investment of Rs. 12.16 crores. The financial constraints can be overcome by making separate provisions in the defence budget for such events which are important facet of national security.

REFERENCES

1. South Asia Security Trends October 2006. Published online by Security-risks.com.
2. South Asia Security Trends May 2006. Published online by Security-risks.com.
3. Report in The Hindu. *The Hindu.* 30 June 2006. p. 13.
4. MEA India press release. 28 June 2006. Accessed on the web, meaindia.nic.in.
5. Based on inputs from D.S. Rajan at www.whatisindia.com. rajan@whatisindia.com.
6. Based on MOD India Press Release 29 May 2006. Accessed online. Mod.nic.in.
7. Based on Ministry of Defence Press Release. 1 June 2006. Accessed online. Mod.nic.in.
8. Based on Ministry of Defence Press Release. 2 June 2006. Accessed online. Mod.nic.in.
9. Hindustan Times Report. *The Hindustan Times.* 29 August 2006. New Delhi Edition.
10. Hindustan Times Report. *The Hindustan Times.* 30 June 06. New Delhi. p. 1.
11. Hindustan Times Report. *The Hindustan Times.* 30 June 06. New Delhi. p. 1.
12. Reddy, B. Murlidhar. "Foreign militant's... ". *The Hindu.* 12 March 2006. New Delhi. p. 12.
13. The Times of India Report. *The Times of India.* 1 June 2006. p. 12.
14. South Asia Security Trends July 2006. Published online by Security-risks.com.
15. Based on Ministry of Commerce and Industry Press Release 6 July 2006.

16. South Asia Security Trends December 2006. Published online by Security-risks.com.
17. Hindustan Times Report. *The Hindustan Times*. 27 October 2006.
18. South Asia Security Trends April 2006. Published online by Security-risks.com.
19. South Asia Security Trends April 2006. Published online by Security-risks.com.
20. Radyuhin, Vladimir. "60 tonnes of Russian fuel...". *The Hindu*. 1 April 2006. New Delhi. p. 12.
21. Based on inputs from www.whatisindia.com.
22. Indian Express Report. Indian Express. 15 October 2006.
23. South Asia Security Trends June 2006. Published online by Security-risks.com.
24. Indian Express Report. *Indian Express*. 31 October 2006.
25. For Sino India military engagement, refer to chapter on China.
26. Based on MOD India Press Release. 25 May 2006. Accessed online. Mod.nic.in.
27. Based on MOD India Press Release. Accessed online. Mod.nic.in.
28. Indian Express Report. 7 March 2006. New Delhi. p. 5.
29. Based on Press Release Ministry of Defence. New Delhi. Accessed online. Mod.nic.in
30. South Asia Security Trends December 2006. Published online by Security-risks.com.
31. South Asia Security Trends December 2006. Published online by Security-risks.com.

China: Peaceful Rise of an Emerging Superpower

7

"We must comprehensively strengthen the modernization of our army and ensure that under any complicated situation our military is capable of effectively confronting crises, containing war and safeguarding peace."

China's Defence Minister Cao Gangchuan,
31 July 2006

"China pursues a national defense policy which is purely defensive in nature. China's national defense provides the guarantee for maintaining China's security and unity, and realizing the goal of building a moderately prosperous society in an all-round way. To build a powerful and fortified national defense is a strategic task of China's modernization drive."

China's National Defense in 2006—Defence White Paper

KEY TRENDS—2007

China Internal Polity

- Systematic, consistent, unitary focus on development of Comprehensive National Power.
- Central stability but local instability marks Chinese internal polity.

China International and Regional Polity

- Extensive global and regional engagement.
- Focus on Asia and Africa.

China Strategic Defence

- Strategic defence and technological development to include space and nuclear sciences.

- Securing a, 'String of Pearls' chain of bases in the Indian Ocean littoral for security of Sea Lines of Communications.
- Chinese land communication links to Tibet consolidated by the all weather Golmund-Lhasa railway line.
- Development of the PLA as a potent, modern, informationized force emerges as the focus of defence policy.

Chinese Goals for the PLA

- 2010—Lay foundations of a modern force.
- 2020—Emerge as a force of consequence.
- 2050—Develop capability to win informationized wars.

China—Internal Situation

The internal situation in China continued to be marred by a series of local uprisings the impact of which was not allowed to transmutate into national political space. Some reports indicate over 87,000 small local uprisings in China. Chinese leadership proudly quotes these figures to justify their claim that China is a democratic society where dissent is being expressed openly. This is frequently flaunted as typical indigenous Chinese democratic way of functioning. Lo behold however if any person or organization attempts dissent at the national level. The first signs of such a movement are immediately quelled with a heavy hand. Differences at the local level are skilfully used by the central leadership to exercise control over provincial leaders.

Chinese concerns over growth differential between the highly developed east and the underdeveloped south continued during the year and many incentives were provided to entrepreneurs to develop industry in the hinterland. The outcome however remained poor. Corruption was another critical internal issue. A massive crack down on corrupt officials resulted in many eloping to neighbouring countries such as Myanmar and Vietnam.

Development parameters remained extremely healthy as indicated by a year end survey published in People Daily Online and are reproduced below:[1]

- GDP up 10.7 per cent
- Grain output up 2.8 per cent
- Per capita net income of farmers up 7.4 per cent
- Total import/export volume up 23.8 per cent
- Foreign exchange reserves topped US$ 1 trillion. Energy consumption per unit of GDP dropped 1.23 per cent
- Funds for research and development equivalent to 1.41 per cent of GDP
- Urbanization rate hit 43.9 per cent
- Newly completed commercial buildings dropped 0.6 per cent
- Privately-owned cars topped 10 million

Disasters remained a major area of concern for China during the year. The country had to face a series of typhoons and floods. China was ravaged by floods with the southern areas experiencing rains triggered by the Tropical Storm Bill which killed 170 with over 150 reported missing. Twenty million people were also affected by torrential rains which hit Hunan, Guangdong and Fujian provinces.

Typhoon Saomai with wind speeds of 216 kms per hour brought heavy rains and storms in the country in August 2006. Over 1.5 million people were evacuated from vulnerable areas in east China's Zhejiang and Fujian provinces. Statistics given out by the Chinese Ministry of Civil Affairs as published by the Peoples Daily indicated that in 2006, 1,699 lives have been lost up to July with 415 missing and loss of property worth US$ 14.8 billion. These losses are said to be highest in the last five years. The Chinese government allocated 166 million Yuan (20.75 million U.S. dollars) to assist provinces in relief and rehabilitation. The provinces and regions that will receive assistance included Liaoning, Fujian, Jiangxi, Hunan, Guangdong, Guangxi and Hainan, which were hit by Typhoon

Kaemi and Typhoon Prapiroon, the fifth and sixth storms during the year followed by floods.

Estimates of people affected by disasters in China are around 200 million every year. In 2005, there were 2,475 deaths and losses worth $ 25.5 billion. To overcome this major deficiency, the Chinese are in the process of establishing a satellite based disaster monitoring scheme.[2] China planned to launch 3 satellites in 2007 specifically to monitor disasters. These will be first in a series of disaster monitoring network comprising of eight satellites. The remainder will be launched in 2010. A ground to air monitoring system is also planned to be made operative in 2010. Other countries in South Asia including India could also look towards such a satellite monitoring network, as the impact of disasters on the country is considerable.

Chinese—Engaging Asia and Africa

The focus of China's engagement during the year remained Asia and Africa. Chinese conduct diplomacy at a rapid pace as is evident by five substantial joint statements and 54 agreements concluded by the Chinese President Hu Jin Tao's visit to four Asian states including India and Pakistan during the month of November 2006.[3] A brief overview of President Hu's visit would indicate the manner in which the Chinese are engaging the regional periphery. Hu visited four countries of considerable importance to China: Vietnam, Laos, India and Pakistan. The itinerary of the President followed the logic of geography but was also carefully calibrated to convey the subtlety of power balance that China seeks to maintain with these four states. Vietnam and India are two states with which China has not settled its long standing boundary disputes and have the potential to challenge Chinese quest for dominance in Asia and also have a location advantage impinging on China's great power ambitions situated astride the all important Sea Lines of Communications (SLOCs) through which much of China's gigantic oil supplies pass each day. Vietnam also has the organizational, political and national confidence to challenge China's supremacy in the South East Asian region particularly the eastern seas in which China has considerable interests. Laos and Pakistan have been China's partners for many years. Pakistan and Laos are ideal foils against India and Vietnam respectively.

The Chinese however have taken a fresh view of their regional policy and are embarking on a cooperative engagement strategy with India and Vietnam. The visits to Pakistan and Laos were in the nature of balancing power in the region, to ensure that regional prodigies, India and Vietnam do not step out of line or just in case they do, are checkmated. This is the realist view of Chinese foreign policy which is still stuck in the static, balance of power rut and in the long run may cause it more harm than good.

The overt theme of Hu's visit was however economic cooperation. Thus with Vietnam it signed a number of cooperation agreements spread over the next 5 to 10 years to take forward the process of ASEAN free trade zone. With Laos the theme was again bilateral trade and cooperation to include investment, communications, transportation, infrastructure, energy and mining. The areas of interest with India were information and communication technology, energy, infrastructure, science and technology and agriculture. The trade target has been placed at $ 40 billion by 2010.[4] The relationship with Pakistan was most significant with a free trade agreement signed to triple bilateral trade from the current $ 4 billion to $ 15 billion in the next five years. Thus the volume of Sino-Pakistan trade will be larger than that of Pakistan and India despite having very limited land communications. A significant feature of the agreement with Pakistan is inclusion of transportation and finance, a feature which is not common to agreements with India and Vietnam, though China shares a common border with these states. This will provide focus to widening of the strategic Karakoram Highway.

Sino — Global Presence in Africa

Africa is emerging as a key region for the future, as a large number of countries including the United States and China are making a bee line for partaking abundant resources including oil in the continent. The United States is in the process of creating a new military command for the African region while Chad an oil rich nation finds itself in a controversy after expelling Chevron Corporation. It is being accused of creating conditions for entry of Chinese oil companies.[5] As the battle for resources in the World heightens, there are increasing qualms over the direction it takes. India needs to ensure that its interests are protected by an enlightened diplomacy tempered with rational security measures. China as usual is already ahead in the race for economic and diplomatic engagement of Africa.

China has been making major forays into Africa over the last few years. Chinese venture in the energy sector in Africa has led to the region providing 30 per cent of Beijing's crude oil requirements in 2005 to the tune of 38.34 million tons. China's investment in Africa is evident with 27 major oil and natural gas projects which have been undertaken in 14 countries including some which are having perennial security problems such as Sudan, Algeria, Angola and Nigeria. Of these Angola has been the second largest source of oil for China providing 17.46 tons, just behind Saudi Arabia at 22.18 tons. Congo, Sudan and Equatorial Guinea also figured in the top ten oil exporting countries to China. In 2005, the volume of China-Africa trade reached US$ 39.8 billion. It included US$ 21.1 billion in imports from Africa, which exceeded China's exports to Africa. A majority of these imports were obviously oil and natural gas.

China is also actively involved in road construction, bridging, hospitals and health facilities in Africa. The Chinese believe that this has been a mutually beneficial arrangement. China is also claiming to have developed capability to process oilfields with difficult geological conditions and with low and depleted yields.

Chinese initiative and long-term relationship with African countries transcend beyond that of oil and energy. The political and economic basis of the affiliation has been highlighted by the Chinese State Councilor Tang Jiaxuan in an interview with Xinhua News Agency. The principle issues stated are summarized as follows:

- Politically, China and Africa are seen as strategic partners who have developed trust and support. High-level exchanges and dialogue is being maintained with popular support at various levels. Coalition is strengthened internationally and joint promotion of democracy is the key.

- Economically, enhancing South-South co-operation and North-South dialogue and economic globalization to develop balanced, general and win-win benefits is the motive. Chinese government will attempt to encourage and assist Chinese companies to invest in Africa and provide reciprocal arrangements for African companies in China.
- Culturally, China and Africa form partners in advancing human civilization and building a harmonious world. Governance, cultural diversity, promotion of tolerance, dialogue and equality among different civilizations to draw upon each other's strength is the key for common prosperity as indicated in the interview by Tang.[6]

A Forum on China-Africa Co-operation (FOCAC) has been formed as the chief instrument for developing China-Africa friendship. A summit to promote Sino African understanding has been held. The theme of this Summit is "Friendship, Peace, Co-operation and Development". This is designed to forge the strategic partnership and sustain bilateral cooperation in various spheres.

Against the backdrop of these initiatives, China substantially increased its investments in Africa which reached US$ 6.27 billion. China has launched over 800 non-financial investment projects in 49 African countries, covering trade, manufacturing and processing, resource development, communications and agriculture. China has completed 720 major projects in 49 African countries and 58 projects have been launched in 26 African countries with preferential loans from China. China has exempted 10.9 billion Yuan (US$ 1.34 billion) in debts by 31 heavily indebted poor countries and least developed countries in Africa, and extends zero-tariff treatment to some imports from 28 least developed countries in Africa. China has also trained over 14,600 African personnel in various fields. Thus the Chinese cooperation with Africa in the field of trade, development, economic assistance and human resource development is well established.[7]

China is stated to double aid to Africa by 2009 as well as increase trade particularly with the least developed African countries. Three billion U.S. dollars are to be provided in preferential loans and 2 billion U.S. dollars in export credits till 2009. A special fund of 5 billion US dollars was established to encourage Chinese investment in Africa. The Chinese repeatedly reaffirmed that there was no intent on merely focusing on exploitation of resources in Africa.

The pillars of Sino African partnership was thus to build cooperation in the following fields:

(a) Increase high-level visits, conduct strategic dialogue and enhance mutual political trust.

(b) Deepen and broaden mutually beneficial co-operation and give top priority to co-operation in agriculture, infrastructure, industry, fishing, IT, public health and personnel training to draw on each other's strengths.

(c) Increase exchange of views on governance and development to learn from each other.

(d) Increase dialogue between different cultures and promote people-to-people exchanges, particularly those between the young people.

(e) Enhance international co-operation.

(f) Enhance the Forum on China-Africa Co-operation.

(g) Properly handle issues and challenges that may arise in the course of co-operation in keeping with China-Africa friendship and the long-term interests of the two sides.[8]

China-ASEAN Relations

China ASEAN relations reached a new high with a Free Trade Area proposed to be established by 2010 to liberalize goods and services between China and ASEAN countries. A joint agreement to the effect was signed during the China ASEAN dialogue in Nanning, the capital of South China's

Guangzi Zhuang region bordering ASEAN in October 2006. In the first phase China will have a FTA with the primary members, Singapore, Philippines, Brunei, Malaysia, Indonesia and Thailand and by 2015 with the other members Cambodia, Laos, Myanmar and Vietnam. A significant issue raised by Wen Jiabao, the Chinese Prime Minister was that of expansion of military dialogue, exchanges, cooperation and formalizing conduct of defence forces in the South China Sea.[9]

China has a number of disputes with South East Asian states particularly on possessions in the South China Sea. There are large number of people of Chinese origin in ASEAN who continue to look towards Beijing for moral and social support. The growth of Chinese power in the region will be a cause of concern for Japan as well as the USA. Japan has exclusive dependence on the waters in the area for smooth passage of the large quantum of oil that is transported to fulfil its primary energy needs. For the USA which has had traditionally strong relationship with some states such as Philippines and Thailand, the emergence of China could possibly imply reduction of its own influence in the region.

Sino-Japanese Relations

Apart from Africa and developing countries of Asia, China also undertook improvement of relations with Japan. There were signs of a major shift in China-Japan relations embedded in bilateral trade which is likely to touch $ 200 billion. The visit by Japanese Prime Minister, Shinzo Abe immediately on taking over the chair to Beijing set into motion thaw in the relationship which had suffered a setback due to former Japanese Prime Minister J. Koizumi's visit to the Japanese Yasukuni war shrine.[10] This was greatly resented in China as it reportedly contains the names of those accused of war crimes. Japan had been in occupation of large portions of China during the period of the Second World War and the Chinese particularly take exception to this period of Japanese incursion. However, Prime Minister Abe seems to have created a favourable impact and the relationship between these two Asian giants is likely to see further improvement in the years ahead.

Overall Contours of Chinese Foreign Policy

Based on the key facets of regional relations established by the Chinese during the period as indicated above, the overall contours of Chinese foreign policy during the year will be evident. Chinese policy analysts claimed that China's rising strength was intended to improve political trust between the people and with the foreign forces through joint military exercises and exchange. Citing historical proof, Qian Lihua, Deputy Director of Ministry of Foreign Affairs Office told in an interview to China Central Television that China has a defensive policy and will not be part of any military bloc.[11] Throughout its history, he stated that China had not stationed any military force overseas and thus there were no threats arising from Chinese military build up as indicated from time to time by the United States. He cited the proof of 23 US military delegations which had visited China in 2006 and 18 delegations that China had sent to the United States during the year. The Exercises conducted by China with the United States Navy in November were also cited as a major confidence building measure.

The Chinese have provided a new elucidation of their foreign policy calling it, "harmonious world-oriented" diplomacy. A noted Chinese scholar Yan Xuetong, Director General of the Institute of International Studies of prestigious Tsingha University in Beijing in an article in the Peoples Daily Online website indicated that this policy had been set into motion by President Hu Jintao in October 2005. The underpinnings of this new policy however are curiously denoted by the rise of Chinese economic and trade power, with a surfeit of foreign reserves, the largest in the World, and China's preeminent position in global trade in 2004. The deficiencies envisaged were in the military and the political field.

Chinese initiatives in Africa starting with the Beijing Summit & Third Conference of FOCAC have indicated a desire to make up for the political deficiencies with aid and humanitarian assistance. Closer home, China held the Shanghai Cooperation Organization (SCO) Summit for building long-term relationship with an axis of states extending into Central Asia while it has firmed up its relationship with ASEAN states through the

China-ASEAN Memorial Summit in October 2006. The summit of the Shanghai Cooperation Organization leaders was held in Beijing along with celebrations of the fifth anniversary of its formation. The regional grouping which comprises of Russia, China, Kazakhstan, Kyrgyzstan, Tajikistan and Uzbekistan, with India, Iran, Pakistan and Mongolia as observers is focused on energy and political coalition in Central Asia.

China considers itself as the chief enabler of the six nation dialogue with North Korea and has also egged on the Japanese for a rapprochement set into motion by the visit of the new Japanese Prime Minister Shinzo Abe, the first in the last five years. The visit of President Hu Jintao to Vietnam, Laos, India and Pakistan during November marked another landmark to firstly foster strategic relationship with old rivals and cement that with old friends as Pakistan.

China has build special relationship with Kazakhstan, Central Asia's largest, most prosperous and perhaps only stable country. The two states have reportedly signed 11 cooperation agreements in the field of trade, energy, science and technology, culture and education. These were signed during the visit of the Kazakh President Nursultan Nazarbayev to China. A13 page document on China-Kazakhstan Cooperation Strategy for the 21st century was also released in which bilateral cooperation in politics, economy, international relations, security, culture and other fields has been highlighted. China is also steadily building a counter terrorism partnership with Kazakhstan given its proximity to the Xingjian province, China's key trouble spot with Islamic fundamentalist strains. Energy is the other pillar of China-Kazakhstan partnership.[12]

The United States-China relationship is also said to be based on a sound understanding of the nuances of each side's sensitivities. Leadership contact, agreement on various international issues, mechanisms for continuing cooperation and dialogue, military exchanges and maneuvers form the key to improvement in relations between the two states.[13] On the other hand it is stated that key differences on Chinese involvement in Africa, Sudan and Venezuela remain along with apprehensions on trade deficit and currency disparity. Yuan Peng, deputy director and researcher at the Division for North and Latin American Studies at the China Institute of Contemporary International Relations has also expressed concern of the shift in US Congress where the Democratic Party has won a majority.[14] This is felt to have an unfavorable impact on Sino US dialogue punctuating it with allegations of human rights abuse. This development has not been viewed favorably by the Chinese establishment.

Chinese reactions to the Indo US nuclear deal were limited to the impact it would have on negotiation with Iran and North Korea. Chinese scholars particularly emphasized this aspect of the Deal and expressed fears that the cooperation will break the existing strategic balance in the region.

China—A Strategic Technology Upsurge

China's spending on Research and Development in 2006 is said to have been US$ 136 billion. This will be greater than Japan which spends US$ 130 billion and second only to the United States at $ 330 billion. Chinese official sources however disputed this estimate and indicated that the spending could be as low as $ 36 billion. The difference in the estimation is presumably due to real purchasing power of the Yuan within China due to disparity in the rate between the Yuan and the Dollar.[15] Chinese potential in research and development is also evident with the large base of researchers that it is having at 926,000. Chinese officials however indicate that there is a need for China to increase its spending in basic research which touches upon physics, chemistry and genome sequencing.

The key focus of Chinese technological growth is space and nuclear energy. These fields will also have spin offs in enhancing defence capabilities. Developments in the field of nuclear energy and space technology in China have been impressive. China's White Paper on space activities, entitled, "China's Space Activities in 2006", the second of its kind after the first one was published in 2000 has indicated the progress made by the Chinese in this field. Beijing is planning to increase carrying capacity of its near Earth orbit stations to 25 tons and geostationary orbit satellites to 14 tons. This along with the anti satellite capability being developed will make China a space power in the decades ahead.

The Chinese Space industry is also developing the potential of its Long March carrier rockets to a 120 ton thrust liquid-oxygen/kerosene engine and 50 ton thrust hydrogen-oxygen engine.[16] Chinese progress in space and rocket sciences is also obvious from its ability to launch two satellites on one rocket, Long March 4 B from the Taiyuan Satellite Launch center in North China's Shanxi province. The second satellite followed one minute after the first and both entered successfully into the preset orbit. The satellites are mainly designed for space exploration, radiation and parameters of physical environment in space. China is only the fourth country in the World to have launched two satellites with one rocket.

China has over a decade from end October 1996 to the end of 2005 launched 46 consecutive rockets with breakthroughs in key technologies over the years. It is also reported to have developed three launching sites at Jiuquan, Xichang and Taiyuan.[17]

In a related report Chinese officials also indicated that compared to NASA, China is spending only one tenth of the budget on space activities. This could possibly be to dissipate Western criticism of the rapid growth of Chinese space industry.

Chinese advances in space science are also indicated by building of the Global Satellite Navigation System. This will provide accurate positioning and time and will cover the entire Chinese territory as well as parts of neighboring countries by 2008 and then extend further into a global network. The initial phase involves launching two Compass navigation satellites in early 2007. Open and authorized services are planned. The open service will provide to users accuracy of 10 meters, .2 meters per second velocity and 50 nanoseconds timing precision. The level of accuracy and other parameters of the Authorized service have not been specified but are considered to be much, "safer". The Chinese presently have a three satellite Compass navigation system which is providing effective survey, telecommunications, transportation, meteorology, forest fire prevention, disaster forecast and public security.[18]

China's progress in the field of nuclear fusion is also very impressive. It has successfully conducted the first thermonuclear fusion reactor test recently at the Institute of Plasma Physics under the chinese Academy of Sciences in Hefei, capital of Anhui province in eastern China. The experiment involved fusion of deuterium and tritium atoms at a temperature of 100 million celsius. The test which lasted three seconds is reported to have generated a current of 200 kilo amperes and was conducted by using the Experimental Advanced Superconducting Tokamak (EAST) fusion reactor. This project has been ongoing simultaneously with that of the International Thermonuclear Reactor (ITER) by an international consortium for thermonuclear fusion. The route of thermonuclear fusion is said to be cheap and also environmentally safe with unlimited potential for generating energy. The lead taken by China demonstrates its continued progress in the field of strategic technologies including space sciences. China's progress in this sphere is commendable technologically and will also benefit it economically with a likely reduction in expenditure on oil with heavy consumption at 3.5 billion dollars per day in 2005.[19]

The most recent Chinese venture is launching of the one million kilowatt nuclear plant project in the eastern province of Zhejiang by the China National Nuclear Corporation (CNNC) as an extension of the Qinshan nuclear power plant. Experts are analyzing the feasibility of this project including its safety, environment and evaluation. The project design is likely to take about six years.[20] China has a goal of producing 40 million kilowatts of nuclear energy by 2020 and towards this the one million kilowatt nuclear plant project will be a major contributor.

Chinese Defence Capabilities

Defence White Paper

White papers are major instruments of transparency which comprehensively lay down the policies of governments on various issues. When published on defence these become foremost confidence building documents. However, in the case of China such reports are always viewed with suspicion. Thus, when China produced a White Paper at the end of 2006 a number of caustic comments were heard from analysts across the board and particularly in the United States which increasingly views

China as a future antagonist power. The fifth in the series since 1998, this is a biennial review which covers amongst other issues the state of the People's Liberation Army which at 2.3 million troops continues to be numerically potent. There was special emphasis on the defensive nature of Chinese defence policies and arms procurement, focus on Taiwan and Chinese strategic goals of growth and development of the PLA. The policy paper also indicated that it is likely to strengthen its capability to strike against Taiwan militarily, enhance capability to police borders and territorial waters and modernise its weapons systems. A survey of Chinese military activities would indicate that China has increased its commitment to the United Nations Peacekeeping Forces and also engaged in military exercises with a number of nations including India. The hold of the Communist Party on the PLA however continues reiterated thus, "China's armed forces are under the leadership of the Communist Party of China (CPC)."

A snippet analysis of select issues covered in the White Paper is as per succeeding paragraphs. Snippet analysis format is used to focus on the key determining facets of the White Paper as they affect the projected Chinese security inclinations and force development paradigm.[21]

The White paper reiterates China's commitment to, "peace, development and cooperation, China pursues a road of peaceful development, and endeavors to build, together with other countries, a harmonious world of enduring peace and common prosperity". The world is at a critical stage, moving toward multi-polarity. But, they also maintain coordination and practical cooperation in their mutual relationships, and draw on each other's strengths. Some major developing countries and regional groupings have grown in power, and the developing world as a whole is becoming stronger. This explains China's current over drive of engagement of wide range of countries including past and potential rivals India and Japan, ASEAN, nations beyond the immediate geographical periphery in Africa and traditional friends Pakistan and Russia.

The trend is further amplified by increased focus in China on creating and preferably heading regional alliances thus, "The international community is increasingly facing comprehensive, diverse and complex security threats. The world is not yet peaceful. Political, economic and security problems and geographical, ethnic and religious contradictions are interconnected and complex. The Shanghai Cooperation Organization (SCO) has entered a new stage of substantive growth, contributing to the establishment of a new mode of state-to-state relations. ASEAN has made steady progress in community-building and in talks on establishing free trade areas with other countries. East Asian cooperation, which is conducted mainly through the ASEAN plus China, Japan and the ROK (10+3) channel, has expanded in scope and its institutional building is improving constantly, continuing to play a major role in promoting peace, stability and prosperity in the Asia-Pacific region. The East Asia Summit has provided a new platform for East Asian cooperation. Moreover, significant progress has been made in South Asian regional cooperation. There is improvement in the relations between India and Pakistan." This possibly denotes China's area of influence and interest to include the SCO, ASEAN, East Asia and SAARC regions. China's interest in South Asian region is also evident from the comments. Observed from a perspective of balance of cooperation this could be seen as a need to ensure stability providing the Chinese freedom of trade through the Indian Ocean, while seen from the balance of power point of view, this may indicate a desire to maintain parity in the subcontinent.

The emphasis on technology as the keystone for modernization of the armed forces is indicated by the statement, "At the new stage in the new century, we will take the scientific development outlook as an important guiding principle for the building of national defense and military affairs, vigorously advance the revolution in military affairs with Chinese features, and strive to realize an all-round, coordinated and sustainable development."

Chinese Armed Forces are likely to modernize rapidly and by 2020 will pose a credible advanced information rich force. This is evident from the plan indicated in the White Paper thus, "China pursues a three-step development strategy in modernizing its national defense and armed forces, in accordance with the state's overall plan to realize modernization. The first step is to lay a solid foundation by 2010, the second is to make major progress around 2020, and the third is to basically reach the strategic goal of building informationized armed forces and being capable of winning informationized wars by the mid-21st century." The trend in modernization is denoted by the statement, "The Army is speeding up the upgrading and informationization of its active main battle equipment to build a new type of ground combat force which is lean, combined, agile and multi-functional. Priority is given to building Army aviation, light mechanized and information countermeasures units." China is already known to have information warfare units. The belief is to develop asymmetrical capabilities. This would provide the PLA the ability to defeat technologically superior forces. 2010 and 2020 are years to benchmark PLA's progress.

There is no change to China's nuclear policy as indicated thus, "China remains firmly committed to the policy of no first use of nuclear weapons at any time and under any circumstances. It unconditionally undertakes not to use or threaten to use nuclear weapons against non-nuclear-weapon states or nuclear-weapon-free zones, and stands for the comprehensive prohibition and complete elimination of nuclear weapons."

China is extremely sensitive to an intrusive survey of the defence budget. Thus elaborate details have been pictorially portrayed in the White Paper. The sum of it is, "From 1979 to 1989, the average annual increase of defense expenditure was 1.23 per cent. However, the defense expenditure actually registered an average annual decrease of 5.83 per cent, given the 7.49 per cent average annual increase of the consumer price index in the same period. From 1990 to 2005, the average annual increase in defense expenditure was 15.36 per cent. As the average annual increase of the consumer price index during the same period was 5.22 per cent, the actual average increase in defense expenditure was 9.64 per cent." Not many believe that this is the full story of China's defence spending. Perhaps rightly so, for to modernize a defence force which is twice the strength of the Indian Army and yet transform it into an information centric, RMA based power cannot be achieved in a budget which is just one and half times more than India's defence budget. While strategic systems are not part of this budget, even nominal accretion in capabilities will need a much larger outlay.

The above point is amplified by the next quote which states that, "Both the total amount and per-serviceman share of China's defense expenditure is low compared with those of some other countries, particularly major powers. In 2005, China's defense expenditure equaled 6.19 per cent of that of the United States, 52.95 per cent of that of the United Kingdom, 71.45 per cent of that of France and 67.52 per cent of that of Japan. China's defense expenses per serviceman averaged RMB107,607, amounting to 3.74 per cent of that of the United States and 7.07 per cent of that of Japan." So how does China get a modern armed force at such a low budgetary outlay per soldier. Either these figures are not telling the full story or PLA modernization will not be sustained to develop across the board capabilities. A more detailed review will reveal that the latter may be the actual story. Thus what we may see in 2020 is Chinese armed forces which has niche capabilities, strategic space and missiles, information and cyber warfare and at the same time flaunt a PLA soldier who can launch human wave attacks.

Military Modernization Programme

China's Defence Minister Cao Gangchuan speaking on the eve of the 79th Anniversary of the founding of the People's Liberation Army on 31 July declared that modernization remained the armed forces' priority. "The entire military must eye the historic destiny of China's military in the new century and new era and push forward the main line of a Chinese-style revolution in military affairs," as per Cao. "We must unswervingly fulfill our sacred duty to defend state sovereignty, territorial integrity and security and never tolerate Taiwan independence and never permit Taiwan independence forces under any name or under any circumstances or form to split Taiwan from the motherland."[22] A comprehensive modernization programme, providing the armed forces the latest in modern weaponry and information warfare was announced on the occasion. Cao said, "He insisted that China would be a force in maintaining world peace and would unswervingly strive for peaceful reunification of Taiwan."[23] The Chinese military modernization programme was translated in many forms during the year. Some of the key issues evident were building of infrastructure in Tibet, modernization of the PLA Navy, a series of joint exercises and upgradation of airborne forces denoting capacity building for projection of power. These are being covered in succeeding paragraphs.

Infrastructure Extension

Infrastructure was the first area of extension of Chinese programme of modernization which will have an impact on defence capabilities. The Chinese have considerably enhanced their mobilization and logistics build up capability in Tibet with opening of the Golmund (Qinghai)-Lhasa (Tibet) railway line. Commissioning of the Qinghai-Tibet Railway from Xining to Lhasa which is a journey of 48 hours has provided the Chinese enhanced capability for induction of troops into Tibet over the 1,956 kilometers stretch.[24] Though 960 kilometers of the railway is 4000 meters above sea level with the highest point at 5,072 meters, survivability during the first winters is expectedly good. This will provide Chinese forces the ability to induct over 30 to 35 Divisions into Tibet within one season with careful management of their transportation infrastructure thereby altering the entire context of a Sino-Indian armed confrontation in the future.

Chinese plans to extend communication links southwards were also highlighted with the launch of a daily flight from Lhasa to Kathmandu in the tourist season from July to October with four flights a week operating during the off season. Thus from a seasonal communication link this will be a perennial connection. Kathmandu will also have hopping connectivity with other cities in China to include Beijing, Shanghai, Chengdu, Guangzhou, Shenzhen, Qingdao. This will greatly enhance linkages between China and Nepal.

Capacity Building PLA Navy

China's naval resurgence continued apace with the Chinese President calling for a powerful Navy which would adapt to the "military's historical mission in this new century and at this new stage". The comment came on the occasion of his meeting with the delegates of the navy committee of the Communist Party.[25] Chinese naval build up is evident from large scale acquisitions being undertaken by the PLA Navy. There are also many accusations of corruption in high places, an inevitable result of any bureaucratic acquisition system.

The Chinese Navy acquired a modern, Sovremenny class destroyer built at Russia's St Petersburg shipyard for $ 1.5 billion. This is seen primarily to enhance China's potential against Taiwan and presence in the Pacific. The destroyer equipped with SS-N-22 Sunburn supersonic anti-ship missile is said to be devoid of any counter measures available with Taiwan as well as American forces. The ship also has the capability of striking with its Ka-28 helicopter armed with anti submarine torpedoes. Russo Chinese arms transfers have had a long history. Russia has already sold two ships of a similar class to China in the late 1990's. In addition it has also sold six Kilo class diesel electric submarines and six giant Hovercrafts useful for amphibious landings to China recently.

China is set to enhance its amphibious warfare capability, an ample warning to Taiwan by purchasing six heavy hovercrafts. These are 540 ton Zubr LCAC which has speed in excess of 60 knots, operating range of 300 nautical miles and can carry up to a battalion worth of troops capable of independent tactical missions or three 50 ton tanks denoting a troop. Six crafts will provide the PLA a capability to easily deliver a brigade worth combat power in an area of its choosing.[26]

China also established a blue water communication network for the navy based on use of satellite communications. One thousand six hundred remote units and large number of ships at sea will be covered by this project which is designed particularly for ships in the Paracel and Spratlys Island. The entire network will be digitized providing the PLA navy communications with all its ships across the globe. The network will also be used for gaining access to the political website of the PLA and conduct distance education for soldiers in Paracel and Spratlys.[27]

Airborne Forces—Capability Building

A report by Robert Fisher, Jr based on observations at the International Defense Exhibition Land Forces 2006 highlighted growing Sino Russian cooperation in the field of airborne warfare. Fisher reporting on the second International Defense Exhibition Land Force (IDELF) from 2 to 6 August 2006, indicated that this featured the *Vozdushno Desantniy Voisk* (VDV), or Russian Airborne Force in a major way. China's People's Liberation Army (PLA) is reported to have adopted the Russian model of mechanized airborne forces to perform offensive deep strike operations. The Chinese have purchased Russian equipment to build this capability and are also designing and manufacturing airborne mechanized fighting vehicle on the lines of the Russian BMD. PLA officers are also training in the Russian airborne training school, V.F. Margelov Higher Airborne Command School in Ryazan.[28]

There are some differences which have been noticed in para jumping techniques of the Chinese and the Russians. The Chinese surprisingly do not jump with their weapons which are in canisters. Thus till they retrieve their weapons, the troops will be vulnerable to enemy action. The Chinese have also shown interest in the heavy lift Mi 26 helicopter which will provide them with high level of mobility on the battlefield.[29] The acquisition of airborne and helicopter assets will provide the Chinese unprecedented power projection capability in the coming decades with the area of influence extending into the Persian Gulf and the Middle East.

Training for War?

A major exercise, "Queshan-2006" was conducted by a motorized division of the People's Liberation Army (PLA) in Zhengzhou, Henan province of Central China during October 2006. The exercise involved mobilization and move of the formation by rail and road at the end of which it undertook a motorized advance to the battle area. The division is said to have demonstrated capabilities to fight under electromagnetic conditions.

Xinhua also provided an account of the exercise debriefing stating rather candidly that a number of shortcomings were noticed in these maneuvers. Particular reference was made of the low accuracy of the missiles which was reported at 60 per cent and use of cell phones instead of military radios. The divisional commander was also criticized for postponing the attack thrice thereby exposing troops in forward areas for 50 minutes. On a request for fire support it was also stated that the precise timing and location was not indicated.[30]

This surprising admission of frailties in an operational exercise appears to be Chinese attempt at dispelling apprehensions of such maneuvers and is certainly not a glasnost in the PLA. Of consequence is the poor performance of the missiles and lack of readiness to function in the "electro magnetic" environment.

Sino-US Naval Exercise

A joint military exercise was held between the Chinese Navy and the US Pacific Fleet which involved search and rescue missions in November 2006. Two US amphibious vessels participated in the same. The aim of the maneuvers was said to be to coordinate disaster response and enhance regional security. The US purpose was also reportedly to assess at a very senior level through formal and informal interaction the level of morale, motivation and possible intent of the Chinese Navy, an element of the soft capability of the force as per Admiral Roughead, the commander of the US Pacific fleet.[31]

The exercises were held off the coast of Zhanjiang, a southwestern coastal city in southern China's Guangdong Province and east of South China's Hainan Island. The exercise is said to have enhanced transparency and build mutual trust between the two navies. The battle drills simulated were for procedures for assistance of vessels at sea and is a follow up of the first phase of the exercises conducted in September 2006 off the U.S. west coast between the Chinese destroyer Qingdao and the U.S. destroyer Shoup as indicated in the website of the U.S. Navy.

There was an increase in tensions between the US and Chinese navies particularly with reports that a Chinese submarine approached a US aircraft carrier Kitty Hawk in the Pacific Ocean in October 2006 within torpedo and missile firing range. These reports were denied by the Chinese Naval officials.[32]

Counter Terrorism Exercises

The Chinese held a major anti-terrorism exercise in the Inner Mongolia region involving over 2700 troops and policemen. Inner Mongolia is one of China's largest provinces in the north bordering Russia as well as Mongolia. These exercises conducted over three days had simulated a number of likely terrorist threats such as stealing of high technology equipment from a major industrial city, bomb attacks and kidnapping of hostages in Baotou, Inner Mongolia's major township. The People's Liberation Army is also reported to have been involved in these exercises.[33] Location of the exercises in Inner Mongolia which is considered as a province with potential threat of dissension, second in priority after Xingjian is considered significant. The head of the Chinese anti-terrorism department under Public Security is reported to have said that the exercises indicate new progress in anti-terrorism in Inner Mongolia.[34]

The use of tanks and armored personnel carriers during the exercise is relevant, as anti-terrorism measures do not warrant such high caliber systems. This may either reflect Chinese thinking on counter terrorism operations which denotes dealing with a heavy hand or a reminder to the Inner Mongolian populace of the likely reaction in case of an uprising.

Joint Anti-Terrorism Exercises—China and Kazakhstan. China held joint anti-terrorism exercises with Kazakhstan during August, to enlarge the scope of political and military relations between the two countries, members of the Shanghai Cooperation Organization. These exercises were conducted in the Almaty region of Kazakhstan and Xingjian province of China from 24 to 27 August 2006.[35] The long frontier of over

1700 kms between Kazakhstan and China is riddled with insecurity of the Uighur militancy attempting to raise its head against reported authoritarian Chinese Communist policies in the area. Popularly known as the Eastern Turkistan Islamic Movement (ETIM), it is an amorphous movement which is seeking self-government for the Chinese Xingjian-Uygur Autonomous Region. The joint interests of the two countries are seen in security of the oil pipeline which is said to be pumping over 1 million barrels per day, likely to go up to 3.5 million barrels per day by 2015 as per a Reuters report published in www.defencetalk.com. The Chinese thrust in developing areas beyond the core Han territories is resulting in increased scope of engagement with peripheral states as Kazakhstan.

China also held joint exercises with Tajikistan, its Western neighbor at Kulyab in Tajikistan during the month. These comprised of counter terrorism drills, code named Coordination 2006 in September. These are reportedly held under a memorandum of understanding between the two countries within the overall framework of the Shanghai Cooperation Organization. The aim of the drills was to tackle the three evils of terrorism, separatism and extremism and saw participation of over 300 Tajik troops and 150 Chinese troops.

China is creatively employing the SCO to upgrade its counter terror profile in the region as the problem of Islamic separatists in its Western province of Xingjian is engaging attention of Chinese leaders over the years.

China's growing focus on joint military training with neighbors included a major anti-terrorism exercise with Pakistan in Abbottabad in December. Code named Friendship 2006 exercise extended over eight days and included a number of counter terrorist maneuvers.

China—Long Arms of the Dragon

1 July 2006 was a red letter day for the people of Tibet. 6 July, a red letter day for the people of Sikkim. On Saturday, 1 July, the first train from Golmud the gateway to Tibet from China's North Western Qinghai province chugged to Lhasa,

through one of the highest mountain systems in the World. Justly regarded as an engineering marvel, the railway line connected the fate of the people of Tibet interminably with China. It promises much progress and prosperity in its wake along with the bane of modernity, pollution and environmental degradation.

On 6 July the Nathu La, a pass on the Sino-Indian border in the Indian state of Sikkim, opened for trade between India and China after 44 years. Nathu La is a strategic outpost on the Silk Route which had been a prosperous pathway of commerce for the people of Sikkim as well as North Bengal before the 1962 Indo-China War. The new era of transparency in relations between New Delhi and Beijing was slated to restore primacy of this area in Sino Indian trade, with China likely to become India's largest trading partner in the coming years. This may take some years as presently the scope is restricted to border trade. The border trade marts on both sides will be open from Monday to Thursday every week between 0730-1530 hours Indian Standard Time. The trade mart shall remain open from June 1 to September 30 every year. However, the designated authorities of the two sides may extend or reduce the period of trade when considered necessary on account of exigencies like weather conditions.

Traders from both sides would use trade passes for the purpose of border trade. Trade passes would also be issued to drivers of vehicles. To start with, 60 four-wheeled vehicles including passenger buses, if any, would be issued border trade pass. This number could be increased or decreased based on mutual agreement. Border trade would be transacted for items contained in the agreed list of commodities between the two countries, which presently includes 29 items for exports from India to China and 15 items of import into India from China.

Perhaps with removal of insecurities, on either side, it is anticipated that Kolkata will be a favored destination for commerce to and from China's Western region, restoring the erstwhile capital of British India to its pristine glory. While there has been a longstanding demand from the people of Sikkim for opening of the Silk Route, there was obviously no such pressure on the Chinese side. The opportunity has been created as part of the central policy of the Chinese government of shifting focus of development to the Western province which had been comparatively neglected over the years, thus hoping to prevent internal fissures through a policy of proactive development of infrastructure and economy.

Sikkim and North Bengal as well as India will gain by these measures economically and hence Sikkim's Chief Minister Pawan Chamling had been lobbying hard for opening the Nathu La. The strategic gains made by China through these developments based on an agenda of economic engagement, however need some consideration, not with a view to create insecurities but only to provide a perspective of what lies ahead in the highly dynamic field of international and regional power relations.

Chinese economic engagement neatly fits in with the need for, "stabilizing the periphery" or what Deng Xiaoping has called, "Wendingz bhoubian" as Mahendra Lama has recently brought out. While the Indian military view of acceleration of force mobilization and build up for any Trans border aggression by the Chinese through Tibet due to the railway line coming to Lhasa are well founded, a more significant issue is the underlying Chinese intent of balancing power with economic engagement. The train to Lhasa has placed at rest dying hopes of greater autonomy to Tibet. The Chinese have also accepted India's sovereignty over Sikkim, which was never in doubt as Beijing had been using it merely as a leverage for negotiations. This *ipso facto* does not imply in any way Chinese accommodation in other sectors of the vexed Sino Indian border as the continued negotiations during the recently concluded Eighth Round of talks between the Special Representatives of India and China, M.K. Narayanan, the National Security Advisor and Dai Bingguo, Vice Foreign Minister concluded on 27 June 2006 and deliberations later in the year have indicated.

By externalizing its internal agenda, China is stabilizing possible restiveness in its Western region while extending the reach of its power beyond the national borders. Nathu La will lead to Kolkata, the closest warm water port to Lhasa. China has excellent relations with its South Eastern neighbors and is extending the Kunming Highway to Bangkok as well as developing road links to Yangon, following up on the Second World War vintage, Stilwell road.

In the West, China had invested many decades ago in the Karakoram Highway connecting Xingjian with Pakistan. Reports indicate that the width of this Highway is being extended three times from 10 to 30 meters for which an agreement has just been concluded between Pakistan and China. Chinese engineers are developing the Gwadar-Pasni port-cum-energy complex in Pakistan apace. This will provide it a new warm water link at the edge of the Arabian Sea for trade with the Gulf States. Simultaneously it is developing oil and gas pipelines to Central Asia. Some strategic analysts have likened Chinese policy to acquiring a "string of pearls". Thus what we have is a three pronged access to China's Western provinces, through Myanmar and Kolkata to the Bay of Bengal and through Gwadar to the Arabian Sea.

Chinese policy of assiduously cultivating Pakistan is well-known. Pakistani nuclear scientists are even presently reported to be training in China, while it is supplying Pakistan JF-17 aircraft and F-22P frigates, gratefully acknowledged by President Musharraf recently. Myanmar and Bangladesh have demonstrated healthy respect for Chinese sensitivities if not down right obeisance. While the present trajectory of China's rise is peaceful, by linking its economic engagement with carefully calibrated power calculus in the long-term, China is keeping its options open in the decades ahead. This is perhaps what is constantly rankling American leaders and analysts alike who tend to view China from a paranoid perspective. Given that China is USA's largest trading partner, China's policy of balancing power concomitant with economic engagement is substantiated.[36]

REFERENCES

1. Source Peoples Daily Online web edition.
2. Source. Peoplesdailyonline and Xinhua.
3. South Asia Security Trends December 2006. Published online by Security-risks.com.

4. South Asia Security Trends December 2006. Published online by Security-risks.com.
5. South Asia Security Trends October 2006. Published online by Security-risks.com
6. Source Xinhua.net.
7. Based on reports in http://english.people.com.cn//200610/24/eng20061024_314673.html.
8. With inputs from Xinhua.net.
9. South Asia Security Trends November 2006. Published online by Security-risks.com.
10. South Asia Security Trends January 2007. Published online by Security-risks.com.
11. South Asia Security Trends January 2007. Published online by Security-risks.com.
12. South Asia Security Trends January 2007. Published online by Security-risks.com.
13. South Asia Security Trends January 2007. Published online by Security-risks.com.
14. South Asia Security Trends January 2007. Published online by Security-risks.com.
15. Based on reports in scidev.net.
16. South Asia Security Trends November 2006. Published online by Security-risks.com.
17. South Asia Security Trends November 2006. Published online by Security-risks.com.
18. Based on reports in Xinhua.net.
19. Hindustan Times Report. *Hindustan Times*. 30 September 2006. p. 12.
20. South Asia Security Trends January 2007. Published online by Security-risks.com.
21. Based on White Paper downloaded from http://english.peopledaily.com.cn/whitepaper/defense2006/defense2006.html.
22. South Asia Security Trends August 2006. Published online by Security-risks.com.
23. Based on a report at http://www.defencetalk.com/news/publish/article_007191.php.
24. South Asia Security Trends July 2007. Published online by Security-risks.com.

25. Based on reports at www.defencetalk.com.
26. Based on report at http://www.defensetech.org/archives/002759.html.
27. South Asia Security Trends November 2007. Published online by Security-risks.com.
28. South Asia Security Trends October 2007. Published online by Security-risks.com.
29. South Asia Security Trends October 2007. Published online by Security-risks.com.
30. Based on reports in Xinhua.net and South Asia Security Trends November 2007. Published online by Security-risks.com.
31. Based on reports at http://www.defencetalk.com.
32. Based on reports at http://www.defencetalk.com.
33. Based on reports in Xinhua.net and South Asia Security Trends November 2007. Published online by Security-risks.com.
34. Based on reports in Xinhua.net and South Asia Security Trends November 2007. Published online by Security-risks.com.
35. South Asia Security Trends September 2007. Published online by Security-risks.com.
36. Based on MEA India Press Release—6 July 2006 and article published by the author at www.boloji.com.

Global Trends: A World in Conflict

8

KEY TRENDS

- Iran—Rise of Persian power in the Middle East. Intransigence over nuclear issue leading to confrontation.
- Iraq—Civil war and fratricide continues.
- Palestine—Internal Conflict—Hamas versus Fatah. No end in sight.
- Somalia—Consolidation of peace through multilateral intervention should be the path ahead.
- Lebanon—Overcoming the misery of a state at the crossroads of Middle East conflict remains a challenge.
- Thailand—Military assumes power as the militancy in the South raises an ugly head.
- Fiji—A coup shackles growth of democracy.
- Maldives—Rumblings of political dissent soil the shores of Male.
- North Korea—Courting global anger through nuclear profligacy, can it throw in the nuclear towel easily?
- Africa is emerging as the new frontier for the Great Game of the 21st Century.
- Oil and arms spending increases while piracy and maritime crime are controlled.

GENERAL

2006 remained perilous not just for South Asia but also for other parts of the World as people at large particularly in developing countries remained at the mercy of the bomb and the gun. Civilian deaths crossed the figure of 100,000 in Iraq which saw maximum violence during the year. Iraq is surely and steadily hurtling down the road of a full-fledged civil war and much ethnic bloodshed is expected, while in other regions of West Asia, continued strife wrecked homes of thousands. Lebanon was the hardest hit with the kidnapping of Israeli soldiers by the Hezbollah leading to retaliatory air strikes by Tel Aviv. For the first time, the Israeli population felt the heat of the war as Hezbollah rockets continued to rain on many vulnerable cities. The death count was supplemented by thousands who had to be evacuated including many from South Asia. The internecine conflict in Palestine continues unabated with President Jimmy Carter now calling it apartheid against the Palestinians. Lebanon and, Palestine are likely to see increased violence which again will be the result of internal rumblings rather than external threats. The various factions in Palestine need to negotiate a common ground which appears remote at present. The Hezbollah propped by Syria and Iran continues to be a spoiler in Beirut.

Further South, Sudan and Chad saw continued fighting between rival factions and even the United Nations logistics complex was looted by miscreants. Congo held elections but bloodshed continues. Somalia is another African country in the critical area of the Horn of Africa which saw the Islamic Courts battling with the United Nations backed regime in Baidoa, the, "notional capital" of the country supported by Ethiopia. The country is already a haven for pirates, with all ships warned to keep off the coastal areas notorious for waylading. Ethiopia has openly declared war against the Islamic Courts Union. Building an alliance which is favourable to the West appears to be the solution but with reported involvement of the Al Qaeda and the delicate religious and tribal balance in the state, the situation is likely to remain unstable. The Caucasus and Central Asian states are caught in an ideological cum religious and governance quagmire. Abject poverty in some states along with despotic regimes has created fertile ground for operations by terrorists as well as mercenaries of many hues who have a free access to and from Afghanistan.

In South East Asia, the growth of groups such as the Jemma Islamiya and the Abu Sayyaf whose influence remains relatively unchecked are signs of worry in a region which was otherwise peaceful despite the coup in Thailand, which saw some civil disturbances. Fiji and other small states of the Indian Ocean should also retain their calm albeit with some disorder given the intricate nature of relationship of the governance structure with a predominant role for the Armed Forces. North Korea having carried out its nuclear test was more amenable to restraint as sanctions seem to be having a salutary effect.

There were many discordant political issues which affected the developed World ranging from trouble on the US-Mexican border to the Quebecois in Canada, Russia's energy play and Nigeria's oil mafia. After reaching a record high of $ 78.40 per barrel, oil prices dropped during October by more than 20 per cent to 60.55 and are expected to retain this level.[1] As the UN Secretary General, Kofi Annan demits office after a decade's service to bring peace; the flash points in a volatile World continued to simmer. But none of these issues were as dangerous as those portrayed in the developing and the underdeveloped World. Sadly external influences howsoever attractive may not be able to create much impact as solutions will have to emerge from within.

Iran

Iran continued to place the World powers on the horns of a dilemma throughout the year, till exasperated, with Tehran's antics, the United Nations imposed sanctions on the Ahmadinejad regime. Iran did not agree to halt uranium enrichment and reprocessing and continued to play hot and cold. Options for controlling uranium reprocessing include providing it light water reactors and conduct of enrichment cycle in a third country, Russia also did not provide relief.[2] Nuclear weaponisation is a means of self-assertion of the conservative regime for which it appeared to be willing to confront international public opinion.

Iran is fast emerging as the key power in West Asia. Iraq stands undermined with prevalent anarchy; Egypt lacks the economic power while other Arab states as Saudi Arabia are politically weak. A Shia Iran is attempting to fill this vacuum. The deterring factor once again being religion, wherein the Sunni dominated Arab world will be loathe to accept Iran as a power undermining their influence. Thus ironically the US operations in Iraq of toppling the Saddam regime may end up benefiting its main adversary in the region, Iran. These are the unintended consequences of an interventionist policy.

Iran was also suspected to be playing a major role in the militancy and violence in Iraq as well as confrontation between Hezbollah and Israel which broke out in August. Militarization of the state continued with fears of Tehran seeking the role of the hegemon in the Middle East. The array of arms build up and training exercises also demonstrated a new found confidence in the regime. Large scale war games and exercises code named, "Zarbat Zolfaghar" or The Blow of Zolfaghar (the two headed scimitar of Imam Ali) were conducted in the south-eastern provinces of Sistan-Balochistan followed up in 15 other provinces. A number of missiles, fighter aircraft and mines were demonstrated during exercises and briefings. The range of missiles has improved considerably to cover Israel, the key target in the Middle East. The country also exhibited its military power during a major army parade on 22 September 2006. The Shahab 3 missile was displayed and it perhaps was a signal to the United States of America and Israel as it has a range of 2000 km covering the entire Middle East where considerable US assets have been located. The Saegheh missile with a range of 50 to 150 miles is also said to have been tested during this period. An airmine system was also demonstrated to deter hostile strikes.

The rise of Iran is likely to further complicate the already complex Middle East security situation and fragment the conflict into a Shia-Sunni plus Arab-Persian inter play. A Shia dominance of the Muslim Umma is not sustainable due to adverse overall demographic balance, with the Sunnis being in greater numbers. This raises greater scope for disharmony between Sunni and Shia block of nations in the forthcoming future.[3]

Iran's doctrine, however, as observed from the manoeuvres during August is essentially defensive. However, an increase in missile power provides it considerable potential for causing death and destruction in the Middle East as was seen in the recent Israel-Hezbollah stand off. Hezbollah rockets caused over 40 Israeli civilian casualties. By being able to target its missiles at counter value and counter force targets, Iran will continue to pose a threat to the inimical powers in the Middle East including Israel.

Thus, to shackle Tehran's nuclear enrichment programme, the UN Security Council unanimously imposed sanctions on Iran in December 2006. How far it will prevent Iran from pursuing its ambitions to acquire a Persian bomb is not yet clear. The immediate reaction from the leadership including President Ahmedinjnad has been strident. The possibility of Iran cowing down to the World body appear limited at present, given the aggressive posture adopted by the ruling hierarchy along with the recent advantages it has gained in Iraq and Lebanon through proxy forces and the oil kitty swelled due to high prices in global energy markets during 2006. The reactions will have to be watched as the implications of the decision sinks in the ruling hierarchy in Iran and domestic opinion veers towards greater responsibility. Domestic pressure may be the key factor as the ruling party has clearly lost in the local council elections held in the country during the month.

The critical facility in Iran is at Natanz which is reported to be planned for 54,000 Uranium enrichment centrifuges of which 164 centrifuges are operational. This is enough to supply 20 nuclear power units. The Bushehr nuclear power plant with Russian assistance will go critical in September 2007 providing electricity by November. On the other hand, the same experts say, given the political will, the 54,000 centrifuges can be used to create five to seven nuclear charges within two weeks once a decision is made, increasing the threat of nuclear proliferation from Iran. This will also enable Tehran to retain its nuclear capability without having to make a bomb.[4]

While domestic opinion in South Asia is in favour of enabling Iranian sovereignty in exercising nuclear choice, a wider consideration is needed to understand the broader implications of Iran's nuclearisation. Many analysts believe that this will be the tipping point for other West Asian states as Egypt, Saudi Arabia and Syria to go nuclear. The tensions in the region with particular reference to the growth of non-state actors in Iraq and Lebanon, particularly the Hezbollah and the presence of the Al Qaeda does not augur well in case of covert as well as overt nuclearisation of the area.[5]

Iraq

Iraq saw a new government taking up the gauntlet of running the country in the throes of a civil war in May.[6] The Prime Minister, Nurri Al Maliki is faced with imposing challenges with the countryside carved up by political parties based on sects and castes, running their own militias and criminal gangs filling the vacuum of policing. Basra is the flash point at present. The expectations from the government cannot be very high despite Americans pledging their support and neighbouring Iran promising aid. The key issue is revival of economy which in turn will come about only once the security situation stabilizes. This will necessitate the following actions:

(a) Establishment of an indigenous security grid based on Iraqi military and Para military personnel. Policing will not provide the solution in the circumstances in which the country is at present and a military grid is the answer.

(b) An Iraqi-American grid in the initial stages will be essential and as the capability of the Iraqi forces enhances an exclusive Iraqi grid can be established with American forces in the background.

(c) Local militias loyal to the government can be included in the grid, with a judicious intermix of coalition and Iraqi forces.

(d) Corruption needs to be strictly controlled so that is not seen as a means for aggrandizement by the anti government forces.

Abu Musab al Zarqawi was killed in a strike by the US Special Forces which had zeroed in on him through the spiritual leader, Sheikh Abdul al Rahman. This is the first major success against Al Qaeda for a long time. However, the likelihood of the US capitalizing on this is limited as it will only lead to emergence of a new leader both in the Al Qaeda command line up as well as in Iraq.[7]

The American forces in Iraq went through one of the fiercest campaigns in insurgency any time in the World. There were reports of 960 attacks every week on American and Iraqi troops in Iraq in December 2006. Civilian deaths are reported to have reached an average of 93 per day. The terrorists are noted to adapt their tactics to the deployment and tactics of the American forces limiting their own casualties. The death toll of US soldiers is said to have crossed 3000 during the month.[8]

A bottom up approach has to be adopted in Iraq, neutralizing the militias, starting with the smaller ones. The aim should be to reduce the number of parties to the dispute, which enables reasoned negotiations. For this purpose it may be better to actively seek merger, neutralization and pay offs to restrict the players. This approach also has the softer side of ensuring that the relief reaches the last man on the street.

Given the problems of physical deployment in Iraq in the face of local antagonism, the United States is evolving a strategy which will entail deployment of large presence of naval warships and air forces to neutralize adversary forces from afar. How far this strategy will enable controlling the activities in the hinterland remains to be seen; however the principal necessity of the US to maintain its presence in Gulf to ensure stability and support in oil rich area is underlined.

The solution in Iraq apparently is to empower the moderates on both sides of the spectrum. Thus, the focus should be to marginalize the powerful militias led by Moqtada Al Sadr's Shia, the Sunni militias and death squads. Involving regional groupings including Syria and Iraq and increasing security to the last man on the ground along with functional infrastructure appears to be the answer. The common Arab heritage of the

Shia and the Sunni of Iraq including their secular heritage of the recent past needs to be reemphasized and the militancy and political networks simultaneously reworked to enhance security while simultaneously undermining the influence of the militias. The surge in deployment of American forces in Iraq, indicated a new found determination to restore order amidst chaos engineered from beyond.

Palestine

The continued strife between Hamas and Fatah resulted in mindless violence in the crucial West Asian emerging state. Fatah and Hamas representing the political and militant arm of the Palestinian struggle finally buried their hatchet and agreed to form a national government. There were divergent reasons provided for this union. A joint bloc against a weakened Israel after the recent setbacks against the Hezbollah is stated to be one motive, while another is to avoid sanctions likely to be imposed in case a resolution of the internal power struggle within Palestine is not achieved. Possibly a combination of both could have forced the two groups into submission.

Lebanon

West Asia was once again witness to a major conflict, one that has been evaded the region for at least a decade since Israel withdrew from Southern Lebanon. As Israel bombed Beirut airport on 13 July 2006 and simultaneously blockaded the Lebanese ports, all indications are of an Israeli drive into Lebanon to take out the Hezbollah guerrillas ensconced in multiple lairs in and around Southern Beirut. The Israeli spokesman said so in as many words indicating that the blockade will last till the conflict goes on, implying until the Israeli soldiers were released by Hezbollah.[9] The stand off was apparently a part of the ongoing turf war within the Palestinian community, Iran's quest for dominance in the region, business interests of various players and the Sunni-Shia conflict within Islam. It is this vortex of multi pronged interests which has dangerous portends for the region. Its end would also denote a new balance of power in the Middle East, based on Iranian prominence, a tilt which may not favour America.

The above premise is based on a number of factors. The first and foremost is emergence of Iran as a primary force in the region based on the bellicose policy of its regime. The slow and steady rise of the Shia in West Asia for the first time in many decades and Iran's growing assertiveness in maintaining its nuclear sovereignty needs to be seen in this light. The significant factor relevant to the current crisis is Iranian support of the Hezbollah which has bolstered its strength as well as image. Hezbollah apart from its terror network has considerable rocket power to cause destruction on Israeli strategic targets and has seized the opportunity opened by the military wing of Hamas led by Khaled Meshaal in kidnapping an Israeli soldier, Corporal Gilad Shalit by going one up and capturing two Israeli soldiers in a fire fight.[10] This has had a, "strategic corporal" effect on the militarized Israeli society, which has been shocked into action as it views its military superiority and credibility in the region at stake.

In the continuing power struggle within ruling Hamas, an increase in influence of the militant Meshaal group will be a blow to the moderates in the ruling regime. Israeli capitulation over Corporal Shalit or the soldiers kidnapped by Hezbollah would provide these groups the impetus to capture the fundamentalist space within the current power struggle in the Islamic diaspora in the Middle East torn between a Shia-Sunni, Arab-non-Arab and a moderate-fundamentalist divide. The people of Lebanon are paying the price for the ineptitude of their government by being a sanctuary for fundamentalists as the Hezbollah despite considerable support from Western governments. This is indicated by the virtual go ahead for Israeli invasion of Lebanon by President Bush as far as it does not de-stabilize the government in Beirut.

The Middle East saw a new form of conflict which has emerged for the first time in modern military history where a non-state actor, the Hezbollah successfully took on a state, Israel. The crisis which has been the result of kidnapping of two Israeli soldiers by the Hezbollah has spun out of control with unrestricted bombing of Lebanon by Israel and a declared intent of eliminating the Hezbollah and establishing a buffer with international troop presence in Southern Lebanon. The going for Israel was not favourable. Its air strikes failed to make the desired impact in neutralizing the Hezbollah capability, as Hezbollah missiles continued to rain down on Israel, particularly the port city of Haifa. The air offensive on the other hand caused large number of civilian deaths in Lebanon which invited international approbation for Israel, as also enhanced the support for the Hezbollah in the Arab world and for the first time Shias and Sunnis are seen to be speaking in one voice. The ground offensive was also checked with heavily fortified positions of the Hezbollah in the south comprising of tunnelled defences in villages dominating the axis of movement providing ideal defensive country for the guerrilla group which is excelling in small unit action. Israeli tanks and fire power was less effective in this narrow, gullied country. International mediation has had limited impact as the United States backed Israel offensive, keen as it is to see the decimation of Hezbollah. Evacuation of thousands of foreigners from Beirut and other areas left the country ravaged and war torn.

The truce between Israel and the Hezbollah came into force on 14 August which saw return of the hapless refugees from Southern Lebanon to their homes. Meanwhile, a multinational force led by European Union nations was organized under leadership of France along with other European countries. India's troops in UNIFIL will continue to be deployed there and are likely to be integrated in the international force, despite reports of likelihood of withdrawal by India keeping in view sensitivities of the Muslim population in the country as well as relations with Iran. The wages of war for both sides were very high. Hezbollah lost its entire infrastructure in Southern Beirut and also a large quantum of its fire power. To what extent it can rebuild its military capacity with assistance from Iran needs to be seen. Lebanon lost 811 civilians in the conflict including 68 Hezbollah cadres, though Israel claims to have killed 530 guerrillas, 916,000 people are said to have been displaced with losses worth $ 9.4 billion.[11] Hezbollah's social and political capital in the Middle East remains high; its fate within Lebanon however is another issue as there appears to be increased resistance to it for causing avoidable destruction due to its policies of violence such as kidnappings. Israel on the other hand lost 120 soldiers and 41 civilians in a war that raged for 34 days with war waging costs ranging from $ 3 – 5.7 billion. There is increased pressure to set up a commission to investigate the circumstances that led to the war and its conduct which has certainly dented Israeli military confidence.

Some of the salient lessons which can be derived from the current conflict are summarized as follows:

- *Israel's Strategic Fatigue.* Long years of conflict with neighbours have led to strategic fatigue in Israel. Classic instances of strategic fatigue were evident such as, lack of timing, indecision, unclear political and military goals, and confused direction to the military and so on. This weariness given Israel's power strangulation was inevitable, that it has happened through a war rather than initiation of peace has unfortunate consequences for the nation.
- *Need for a Benign Strategy.* The war again highlights the need for Israel to adopt a benign strategy to assuage its neighbours, a two track hot and cold policy with the belligerent and cooperative interjections working simultaneously will pay rich dividends for Israel and increase stakes in the region. The reality for Israel is that it has to survive in the region, where the sum total of its power, including asymmetric will never equate that of its neighbours, particularly so since Iran is increasingly attempting to increase its role and stakes in the Middle East.
- *Emergence of Asymmetric Strategies.* The utility of asymmetric strategies has been amply proved by the Hezbollah. Israel needs to focus on the future to combat such techniques if not strategies *per se*.
- *Iran's Gambit.* Iran's gambit to have increased stake in the region appears to have paid off. It has achieved possible primacy in the area at a very low cost. This will considerably enhance its bargaining power inside

as well as outside the region. However, it has to consolidate its gains in a holistic manner without merely relying on belligerence as the sole element of its strategy.

The political crisis in Lebanon continued till the end of the year with the government considered anti Syrian locked in conflict against the opposition backed by the Shiite militant group Hezbollah. There appears to be no end in sight for the hapless people and migration of skilled labour to other gulf countries is reported to be continuing.

North Korea

A fresh crisis emerged in North Asia with North Korea belligerently firing six missiles including a long range one. The launch of the missiles was very appropriately timed with the American Independence Day 4 July. The long range Taepodong 2, however failed immediately after launch. The launch was expected, but the exact dates were not clearly designated. The failure of Taepodong 2 the ICBM led to great relief in the US leadership as was evident from a visibly relaxed US Secretary of Defence, Donald Rumsfield at the press briefing immediately thereafter.[12]

In October, however the situation worsened with Pyongyang ending much awaited suspense by conducting a nuclear test on 9 October. The Test was of less than one kiloton. The UN Security Council imposed Resolution 1718 on 14 October, five days after the tests which banned imports by North Korea of weapons and luxury goods and also stopped trade in missiles and weapons of mass destruction. The sanctions imposed by the United Nations are unlikely to have an immediate impact, especially since there are divergent voices being heard from Russia and China, some conciliatory towards North Korea. However, a firm signal from China has prevented North Korea from a second test which was expected by some analysts. China has also persuaded North Korea to return to the six nations (North and South Korea, China, USA, Japan and Russia) talks. North Korea has indicated its willingness to join the multi national disarmament talks after intense pressure by the Chinese.

The tests were declared as a protest against hard line US policy of sanctions including blocking routes of money laundering. Reports in www.defencetalk.com indicate that a group of three generals in the all powerful army had forced the leader Kim Jong-Il to conduct tests assuring him that World reaction would be muted. These generals were identified as Pak Jae-Gyong, Hyon Chol-Hae who are deputy chiefs of the politburo of the Korean People's Army and Lee Myong-Su, the deputy operations chief. The generals are reported to be a part of the inner coterie around Kim and influence all his decisions, frequently goading him towards brinkmanship. The initial statement pronouncing the test also indicated a role of the Korean People's Army (KPA) as it specifically stated that the tests would have pleased the KPA.

Nuclear Non-Proliferation Issues Raised by Crisis

Nuclear tests by North Korea increased concerns of the International Atomic Energy Agency (IAEA). There are approximately 20 to 30 nations awaiting development of nuclear weapons in addition to the nine nations already in possession of the same (Five permanent members of the UN Security Council, India, Pakistan, Israel and North Korea). International nuclear non-proliferation strategy had been to restrict the number of nations possessing nuclear weapons. However, El Baradei, the IAEA Chief admitted in Vienna that the policy had not succeeded in keeping more nations out of the nuclear weapons race.[13] While spread of nuclear energy was beneficial, it was highlighted that non-peaceful uses has been widespread. A new generation of states regarded as virtual nuclear weapon states were coming up which also increased the threat of nuclear trafficking and likelihood of these falling into the hands of non state actors as the Al Qaeda. The key issues highlighted by Baradei to promote non-proliferation by the IAEA are funding which should be independent, legal mechanisms which enhance powers of weapons inspectors and advanced technology such as satellite imagery and environmental sampling for detecting undeclared nuclear activities. This will also have to be supplemented by inspections of facilities on the ground.

A report in Stratfor.com, by Fred Burton indicated that there was a possibility of terrorists in Iraq manufacturing a dirty bomb which is said to be a radiological dispersion device which could be linked with an Indigenous Explosive Device (IED). This would raise the conflict to a new level. There are two possible implications of such a strike, retaliation by the US and increased pressure on US and other coalition members to withdraw from Iraq.

The report coming after the nuclear test by North Korea also raised the issue of effectiveness of the global nuclear non-proliferation regime. Evidence so far suggests that nations which are determined to acquire nuclear capability have invariably succeeded in the same. India, Pakistan, Israel and now North Korea are the most salient examples of this truism. South Africa is the only state which has abdicated the nuclear option voluntarily. This may be so as it is not facing a substantial threat. Libya did so after intense pressure by the USA. Iran is continuing with its programme of nuclear proliferation and as the trend goes a Persian bomb will be a reality within a decade. As the report by Fred Burton and other studies have revealed, terrorist organizations are gradually attaining the capability to strike with a dirty bomb. The key issue for terrorists is the extent of damage that such a device can cause, which will certainly exceed that of 9/11. For a nation state, nuclear capability implies power, prestige and realignment of relationships when accompanied by other political and economic developments. The key to non-proliferation thus is demoting the value of currency denoted by the atom bomb which can come about only if big powers make major demonstrative sacrifices in abdication of their options.

There is no doubt that the hands of the IAEA need to be strengthened. One option is to make it an independent regulatory authority which is not reliant on financial support by any nation. Establishing a global corpus will provide for such funds providing it greater independence in decision-making. On the other hand it is essential to enhance technology which can enable remote sensing to be followed by physical inspections. The key to the problem is, however, dissuasion of prospective nations starting with Iran, which is reportedly on the threshold of a nuclear test, though this brink, may be some years away. A political understanding between the three major powers, USA, Russia and China alone can bring about a change in the overall global nuclear power matrix.

Somalia

Somalia is a strategically placed state in the Horn of Africa overlooking the Gulf of Aden and the Red Sea. It controls the sea routes in the area and piracy is reportedly widespread. A large number of criminal gangs are also operating off the shores of Somalia. War lordism was the prevalent form of governance which was tantamount to anarchy. Sheik Sharif Ahmed, Chairman Islamic Courts Union, a group supported by Al Qaeda, gained control of the Capital Mogadishu in June and promptly proclaimed rule by Sharia.[14] The Sheik indicated that his party was a part of the Al Qaeda network but later backed out. The Islamic Courts Union has been fighting the Alliance backed by the United States. It is a conglomeration of 15 small clan based courts. The Islamic Courts Union is financed by a large number of donors from the Middle East. The battle between the two factions is said to have caused over 300 casualties. The warlords who have been holding sway in Mogadishu have been dislodged for the first time after 1991 when Mohamed Said Barre was ousted.

The interim prime minister, Mohamed Ali Gedi congratulated the Islamic Court for ridding the country of the menace of warlords. The interim government holds the southern city of Baidoa. This is also seen as a direct confrontation with the United Nations which had approved the interim administration in the country. The emergence of the Islamic Courts Union did not quell warlords as Bashir Rageh and Muse Sudi Yalahow who have vowed to fight back. Personnel loyal to the warlords, mainly of Abgal clan held a protest rally at a stadium to the north of the capital immediately after the takeover by the Islamic Courts.[15] The emergence of the Islamic Courts Union in Somalia was seen as a setback to the US in the region particularly since it has confirmed links with Al Qaeda.

Reports of the United States strengthening the security forces of Somalia's interim government as per a statement attributed to the Jendayi E. Frazer, the US State Departments' top Africa Official before the House Committee on International Terrorism and Non-Proliferation led to the spectre of raising the ante in the East African state.

Thus, Somalia saw full-fledged civil war erupting in December 2006 as Ethiopian forces combined with government troops prevented the Islamic Courts from capturing the capital Baidoa and then extended the hold of the government further inland. The United States reportedly supported Ethiopian moves as troops advanced towards Mogadishu to unseat the provisional alternate government established by the Islamic Courts Council. The Ethiopians used tanks as well as aircraft to overcome resistance. The United States was forced into action with reports of the Al Qaeda having made inroads in Mogadishu. Al Qaeda fighters withdrew towards the southern borders with Kenya and were engaged by American air strikes in an attempt to eliminate the menace forever.

Somalia—Case Study of A Failed State[16]

Somalia is a country which was at the mercy of the warlords till the Islamic Courts Union (ISC) took control of Mogadishu and other key locations six months ago. However, their writ did not run across the country. The Islamic Courts offered an alternate to warlordism as well as the Westphalian state. They supplanted these themes with control by political Islam which appeared a good alternative to the Somalis who were sick of the continued state of anarchy in the country. The people were soon disillusioned by the Islamic Courts as the country became a refuge for Islamic terrorists of all hues.

As per Shamso Omar, a Somali analyst, the ISC comprises of three groups. The first group led by Sheikh Sheriff is moderate but was undermined by the other two groups led by Sheikh Aweys and an Eritrean cluster. Sheikh Aweys leads the Al Itihad group which follows the Qutubi sub sect of the Salafist ideology. These proponents see Islam under siege and seek to destroy its opponents. Their aim was to adopt Islamist tenets of governance such as trading based on the Khat system, banning cinema and fostering a Taliban like ideology. They portray the purpose of the state as combating non-jihad elements. The third group comprises of Pan Islamists supported by Eritrea. The key aim of this group is to reduce Ethiopian influence in the region. The main impact of ISC has been increased Islamic influence in Somalia. The Islamic Courts attempted to win over the youth through their appeal to bring order into a society which prefers clan over other forms of loyalty. Another layer in the struggle is the battle between the Hawiye clan of Southern Somalia, with the Darod tribe led by the President of the Transitional Federal Government (TFG) Abidallhi Yusuf who has the support of Ethiopia.

The ICU developed a very deep network of business groups and through the influence of the religious leaders in their teachings in mosques attempted to undermine the TFG as well as the warlords. They used the combined ambitions of many elements inimical to the interests of Somalia as per Omar to create a critical situation combined with ideology to undermine the authority of the TFG. Islam has been used as an ideology rather than a religious tool.

The Al Qaeda was hoping to open a third front against the Western forces after engaging them in Iraq and Afghanistan for the past few years. Osama Bin Laden in a taped interview had indicated in June that Somalia should form another front in the Jihad. The extension of the jehadists into neighbouring Ethiopia, Kenya and Djibouti on the plea of uniting ethnic Somali population in these states is also said to be one of the reasons for Ethiopian intervention. The demonstrated interests of Iran in the region are also being viewed seriously by Western analysts as the extension of Iran into Djibouti would provide it a controlling influence in the crucial Red Sea port where the Red Sea forms an extremely narrow corridor. The Horn of Africa dominates the tri junction of the Indian Ocean, the Persian Gulf and the Red Sea with the Gulf of Aden and is thus critical from the maritime point of view. Somalia is also said to have substantial deposits of Uranium at 6600 tons.

The complexity is underlined by the fact that both Eritrea and Ethiopia are hostile neighbours with a Christian majority and substantial Muslim population. The Al Qaeda has been quick to give the fratricidal conflict in the region a religious colour, though there has been a legacy of hostilities between the states dating back to many decades. The availability of Uranium which provides options to countries as Iran facing UN sanctions provides another dimension to the conflict. The World cannot ignore warfare in this critical region which is also significant from the point of view of maritime trade and oceanic security.

Other Areas and Issues of Concern

Sudan—Darfur

Darfur, Sudan's Western province continued to remain unstable despite the peace deal which has been signed by one of the rebel groups, Minnawi's Sudan Liberation Army in May.[17] The other groups, Justice and Equality Movement of the Fur and Masalit tribes continue to be on the war path and the area is apparently neatly divided between the warring groups, with each foraying into the other's territory periodically, with a return to renewed civil war in the future a distinct possibility. The ethnic dissimilarity has raised the temper of the conflict as Sudanese rebels are attempting to overcome Arab domination. The rebels turned to launch direct attacks on government forces indicating a large build up of arms and training. It is reported that Chad and Eritrea have been supporting the Sudanese rebels. The predominantly Arab Janjaweed militia is accused of frequent raids and violations despite deployment of African Union and UN troops in the area. The Arab versus African struggle in Sudan will continue to plague this poverty stricken area where an estimated 200,000 to 400,000 deaths have occurred so far. The wide margin would indicate the magnitude of the problem as there are no correct estimates of the human tragedy available.

Fiji

Signs of the government in Fiji being replaced by a military coup were imminent in November as talks between the military and Prime Minister Laisenia Qarase arranged through the initiative of New Zealand failed to end on a positive note. The Fijian Army was set to take over parts of the capital and preceded the same by military exercises as the efforts by New Zealand to conclude peace between the Prime Minister and the Military Commander Frank Bainimarama failed in Wellington. The exercises were reportedly being held to prevent any foreign intervention with Australian troops on stand bye in case negotiations failed in the Island.

The crisis was precipitated due to legislation proposed by the Qarase government including amnesty for the coup leaders of 2000. Bainimarama is particularly unhappy with the proposal for amnesty to the coup leaders who had attempted to kill him in 2000. The Pacific Island Forum Foreign Ministers met in Sydney on 1st December to attempt a diplomatic solution to the crisis.

The coup in Fiji came about with Commodore Voreque Bainimarama taking over the presidency and dissolving the Parliament. This was the fourth coup in the fragile region with a retired army physician being sworn in as the interim Prime Minister. The administration is said to be firmly in control of the Army.

Instability in Thailand

Thailand saw return to military rule through a coup engineered on 19 September, supported by the Monarchy. General Sondhi Boonyaratkalin, an ethnic Muslim who headed the coup had been appointed as Chief of the Army as he represented the minority Muslim community waging a low intensity war against the state in southern Thailand in which over 1200 people are reported to have been killed so far. The dispute over tackling the insurgency with the Army proposing a softer approach and Thaksin a hard line one led to the final break up. The military coup has been welcomed in the urban areas, where the misrule of Thaksin Shinawatra, the deposed Prime Minister had led to large scale unrest.[18] His policies were seen to be overly populist and there were allegations of personal corruption particularly in profiting from the sale of Shin Corp to Singapore. On the other hand Thaksin's Thak Rak Thai party is extremely popular in rural areas, the key vote bank in the South East Asian state, with its policies of debt relief and subsidized health care.

The situation remains under control and the military is expected to provide some stability even leading to checking the growing Islamic militancy in the south. Politically though turbulence is likely to continue because of a large number of factors such as the rural-urban divide, divisions in the military and the overall experience of failure of military rule in bringing transformation in Thailand over the past many occasions.

South East Asia just as some parts of South Asia is afflicted by lack of growth of political institutions except for India. Political parties are devoid of committed leaders and there are poor oversight mechanisms for corruption at high places. Thus street protests and military take over form the norm in many of these states, Thailand being no exception.

Maldives Political Uncertainties

Maldives is a picturesque holiday resort with a number of beaches. The economy is dependent on tourism which to some extent has led to induction of outside culture and values. A large number of Indians from Kerala are reported to be working in the many resorts in Maldives. There was some rift seen between these workers and the locals. The work of Christian missionaries and aid organizations has also come in for criticism even by the government.[19]

Leaders of Maldives opposition parties were in Delhi a number of times during the year, blaming the Gayoom government for autocratic rule. The situation remained politically volatile and presented prospects of instability in the years ahead. Leaders of the Maldives Democratic Party claimed that the government's repressive policies against the opposition continued, though Mohammed Nasheed, its Chairman, was released last August. The political battle between the ruling and opposition parties in Maldives is generally played out in Sri Lanka and India, with the opposition hoping for greater support from its larger neighbours. India's reluctance to dabble in internal polity of SAARC countries is well-known, however, the situation needs a close watch to avoid armed intervention.

Reports from Maldives also indicated that there is a growing concern of Islamisation of the state with an increase in the number of fundamentalists persuading the people to adopt more radical policies. Social change instituted by the Islamists is already visible with enforcement of the Burqa, ban on Western music and radio stations airing Christian sermons. Reports indicate that these forces have government support. The opposition and the government are also said to be at loggerheads over democracy but are relatively complacent and conciliating over the spread of Islam. The predominantly Sunni Muslim society is easy to be influenced from outside given the general growth of the creed the world over. Tension was also seen amongst the Indian community in Maldives as there have been a number of attacks on Indian nationals in the island state. As a reaction some Maldivians were attacked in Thiruvananthapuram, Kerala in the second week of July. There have been some reports of antagonism against the workers from Kerala in the tourism and hotel industry in Maldives.[20]

The instability in Maldives is not a new phenomenon. India had to intervene in the 1980's to save the government being taken over by a group of militants who had even chartered a ship in the Indian Ocean for the purpose. It was an excellent operation by the Indian paratroop brigade which salvaged the government in the nick of time. The increased exposure to tourists from all parts of the World is having its backlash in the form of Muslim fundamentalism. This is a common feature in many parts of the world today. However, Maldives geographic isolation and remote location in the Indian Ocean makes its government especially vulnerable to such threats.

East Timor

East Timor saw violence erupt in May with 27 deaths and 40,000 displacements. A split in the government forces occurred due to allegations of discrimination by 600 soldiers from the western part of the country, who claimed that the leadership in the Armed forces dominated by eastern leaders was parochial in patronage.[21] The rift between the President and the Prime Minister seems to be root cause of the problem. Australian troops were also deployed to stem the violence. The problem of nation-building even in small and reasonably homogenous states as East Timor which has only recently been granted independence from Indonesia are thus underlined. It is a general truism that when larger groups are split on ethnic grounds they tend to divide further on differences as geography, religion, region or ethnicity. Creating small nations may not necessarily lead to permanent solutions. Fragility of newly independent small states on the fringes of nowhere falling prey to revolutions is thus very high. Redistribution of power within the existing system may be a better option and has invariably succeeded, the Indian example being the most obvious one.

Africa's Emerging Importance

The importance of Africa is being increasingly acknowledged. The Continent has been a treasure of resources of strategic minerals which have been milked over the years by unscrupulous rulers as Charles Taylor of Liberia in concert with some Western firms. The continued humanitarian crisis as well as growth of Islamic fundamentalism in states as Somalia which is critically located on the Horn of Africa astride the major sea lanes from the Gulf to East Asia has also been a matter of concern. Darfur has seen major humanitarian crisis over the years. It is perhaps against the backdrop of these significant issues that reports indicate that the US Armed Forces is setting up an Africa Command which will look after US interests in the Continent. This will also enable Central Command to focus on the vital areas of Middle East and Central Asia including Afghanistan where there are increasing signs of longer commitments for the United States. A new trend in US military thinking is to view Central and South Asia as one continuum. As the dominant global power, any US interests in an area indicates greater deployment of resources, aid, economic as well as military. China is also making increasing inroads in Africa and has developed considerable linkages with African states, details of which have been covered in the chapter on China.

Africa is likely to emerge as a principal area of interest only in the long term, say beyond 2025. South and Central Asia are already on the horizon. The New Great Game is in full swing. European powers have once again entered the fray in Afghanistan, and the USA is a new entrant, while Russia watches from the side lines.

WAR AGAINST AL QAEDA

Anti Al Qaeda Operations—Major Intelligence Success in London

10 August 2006 was a landmark in the battle against terror by the Al Qaeda, with a module of the terrorist organization exposed by the London police. In wide sweeping arrests, 24 people of a possible 50 were arrested while a large number were detained. In an operation which involved penetration of the Al Qaeda cell primarily drawn from immigrants to Britain from Pakistan, an eight-month vigil ended with exposure of the plot in London. The scale of the operation and the expanse of the network spread globally should be a cause for alarm and thus the reports of Al Qaeda having made inroads into Kashmir cannot be totally ignored. A combination of technology and human intelligence was skilfully used by the Scotland Yard to penetrate the communications network of the Cell which resulted in the interception. It was the biggest intelligence success against the Al Qaeda. The exposure of the plot came only when it was feared that the plotters were about to launch the strike. The discovery of liquid explosives being used in the attacks was also alarming, as it indicated the technological reach of the Al Qaeda which is forever seeking innovative means to cause mass casualties. The use of aircraft as a target and preference for a transportation system is another indicator that the attacks were directed by Al Qaeda's operatives.

Al Qaeda's Information War—Video Strategy

An Al Qaeda video released in August 2006 apart from a sermon by the principal, Ayman Al Zawahiri also included a call by a 28-year-old American Muslim, Adam Yehiyae Gadahn for all Americans to convert to Islam or face a threat of extermination.[22] It was a perfect copy to influence those in

America who were sitting on the fence to join the struggle. The importance of these videos cannot be undermined. These have great potential of motivating Muslim youth. These are also issued coinciding a major terrorist strike, a signal to the network, an indicator that something is in the offing. These seem to come as a message or an instruction to the plotters in particular, to carry out a strike and also indicate that the Al Qaeda is alive and kicking respectively.

The large number of videos released during 2006 is an indicator that the Al Qaeda continues to sustain itself as an organization as well a movement, primarily because its cadres seem to be swelling with disaffection of Muslim youth the world over.

GLOBAL ARMS PROLIFERATION

Global Arms Spending

An Oxfam report has indicated that global arms spending is set to rise to $ 1.06 trillion during 2006 thereby crossing even the record figures of the Cold War. This will only contribute to lengthening conflicts, though the correlation between arms spending and triggering conflicts is not fully established. During the Cold War global arms spending had reached $ 1.3 trillion in 1988 but had substantially tapered till 1999, a brief period of 11 years. The rise over the past seven years is likely to continue as global arms majors have spread their tentacles far and wide reaching the developing countries particularly in the Middle East and South Asia. Russia, Israel and former Soviet republics as Ukraine are in the forefront in enticing countries with reasonably fat purses, real or imaginary tensions and regional ambitions into buying arms and armaments. Thus, Saudi Arabia, India and Pakistan continue to be high value customers for military firms.[23]

A report in the news website, UPI.com indicated that eight nations were engaged in developing inter-continental ballistic missiles. This included the United States, Russia, North Korea, India and France. Twenty-six ballistic missiles of 23 different types were reported to have been launched on 24 occasions during the year. Russia launched six types of missiles, however its key program the sea launched, Bulava failed on two consecutive occasions. The Indian Agni III also failed after a successful launch. The United States successfully tested Minuteman III and Trident II missiles during the year and deployed the W 87 warhead on the Minuteman III system. China also test fired DF 31 ICBM. The report which had sourced information from Federation of American Scientists blog raised fears of a Sino-Indian missile stand off as a possibility in the future. There would thus be a need to propose a ballistic missile limitation treaty on the lines of US Russian arms limitation talks between India and China.

Small Arms Proliferation

The complexity of small arms proliferation in the World was highlighted by the limited consensus achieved during a global conference on controlling trade in small arms in New York from 26 June to 7 July 2006, which failed to reach a final agreement. The problem of gun trade will be evident when as stated by the UN General Secretary Kofi Annan, more than a quarter of the $ 4 billion trade is said to be illicit. The final agreement is said to have been blocked by countries as India, Cuba, Russia, Pakistan and Iran. Twenty states are said to account for 77 per cent of all the world's weapons with China, Russia and North Korea having some of the largest arsenals. United States with 3 million firearms was ranked twelfth. The only success story is said to have been in Cambodia where over 131,000 weapons were removed from circulation which included at least 60 per cent of the weapons circulating outside the official government stocks. A study in Brazil and Colombia showed that the cost of armed violence stood between $ 40 million and 90 million every year, with $ 10 million lost productivity due to death of working age men in Brazil and $ 4 million in Bogotá.[24]

Nuclear Issues

ITER (International thermo Nuclear Experimental Reactor)

The construction of a joint nuclear fusion plant in France was formalized with 30 states signing the ITER or International thermo Nuclear Experimental Reactor Agreement to develop cheap and clean energy from nuclear fusion in November 2006.[25] The reactor will be built at Cadarche near Marseilles in southern France. China, the European Union, United States, Japan, India, Russia and South Korea along with the host nation are joint partners in this agreement. The aim is to replicate the energy chain reaction in the sun by turning deuterium in water from the sea into energy. One litre of deuterium is said to produce energy worth 300 litres of petrol. The possibilities seem to be unlimited though scepticism in the scientific community is likely to mar its eventual fructification.

International Convention for Suppression of Acts of Nuclear Terrorism—2005

India became a signatory to the International Convention for Suppression of Acts of Nuclear Terrorism, 2005. This Convention is a part of the series of acts against terrorism and is designed specifically to target Nuclear Terrorism. State cooperation is sought in prevention, investigation and prosecution of offences through information sharing, extradition and mutual legal assistance. Numerous surveys including the influential Lugar Survey conducted under the aegis of US Senate Foreign Relations Committee Chairman, Richard Lugar, have indicated the likelihood of a terrorist attack using nuclear weapons at 79 per cent. Thus there is a greater sense of urgency to ratify this treaty.[26]

Maritime Security

On Board Piracy has been one of the major issues of concern over the past few years. There have been a large number of incidents of piracy which have occurred across the board, with the coast of Somalia, Chittagong in Bangladesh, Nigeria, Malaysia and Indonesian Islands emerging as the most vulnerable areas in 2006.[27] However, an overall decline is being reported in the last three years. Despite the increased threat of piracy International Maritime Organization (IMO) did not accede to permitting merchant ships carry firearms to fight off attacks on the plea that they will become targets for pirates attempting to seize weapons. Armed escorts are being provided by private security agencies especially in the Straits of Malacca.

With 50,000 ships transiting in the area each year, carrying 50 per cent of the trade and 80 per cent of the oil of China and Japan, shipping is highly vulnerable to maritime attacks. The threat of piracy and vulnerability of the ships did not persuade the officials at the IMO the need to arm the ship farers. The IMO has instead recommended an increase in preventive measures rather than arming the sailors.[28]

Cyber Security

Cyber Security is emerging as a major concern as the information technology network expands globally. The United States is leading in cyber security and the Department of Homeland Security has been at the forefront of enhancing awareness as well as suggestions for greater cyber security. Key findings of the U.S. Department of Homeland Security's (DHS) National Cyber Security Division (NCSD) after exercise Cyber Storm I held from Feb. 6 to Feb. 10, 2006 included the following issues which could be extrapolated by other countries, agencies and organisations:

- Interagency and cross-sector information sharing enhanced overall coordination, communication and response leading to improved information security.
- Contingency Planning, Risk Assessment and Roles and Responsibilities should be clearly defined across processes and procedures to increase overall ability to plan for and assess situations.
- Correlation of Multiple Incidents between Public and Private Sectors was difficult and the cyber community faced challenges in cross-sector situational awareness during a coordinated cyber attack campaign.
- Ongoing exercises will strengthen awareness of cyber incident response, roles, policies, and procedures.
- Establishing expectations, roles, processes and communications in advance will dramatically improve coordination and response.
- Early and ongoing information sharing across governments and sectors created a common framework

for response and strengthened relationships between domestic and international response partners.

- Public messaging is an important aspect of incident response and empowers individuals and industry to take appropriate action to protect themselves and the nation's critical infrastructure.
- Improved processes, tools and technology focused on the physical, economic and national security aspects of a cyber incident will benefit the quality, speed and coordination of a response.[29]

REFERENCES

1. South Asia Security Trends. November 2006. Published Online by Security-risks.com.
2. South Asia Security Trends. June 2006. Published Online by Security-risks.com.
3. South Asia Security Trends. June 2006. Published Online by Security-risks.com.
4. Based on inputs at http://www.defencetalk.com/news/publish/wmd/List_of_Iranian_entities_or_individuals_that_could_face_UN_sanctions17009442.php.
5. Based on inputs of analysis by David Eshel in www.defence-update.com
6. South Asia Security Trends. June 2006. Published Online by Security-risks.com.
7. Based on inputs from US Centcom Website.
8. South Asia Security Trends. January 2007. Published Online by Security-risks.com.
9. South Asia Security Trends. August 2006. Published Online by Security-risks.com.
10. South Asia Security Trends. June 2006. Published Online by Security-risks.com.
11. Hindustan Times Report. *Hindustan Times*. New Delhi. 21 August.
12. South Asia Security Trends. July 2006. Published Online by Security-risks.com.
13. South Asia Security Trends. November 2006. Published Online by Security-risks.com.
14. South Asia Security Trends. July 2006. Published Online by Security-risks.com.

15. Times of India Report. *The Times of India* 8 June 2006. p. 28. nd).
16. Based on inputs from Matt Bryden at_http://forums.csis.org/africa/.
17. South Asia Security Trends. October 2006. Published Online by Security-risks.com.
18. South Asia Security Trends. October 2006. Published Online by Security-risks.com.
19. With inputs from http://www.whatisindia.com.
20. South Asia Security Trends. August 2006. Published Online by Security-risks.com.
21. South Asia Security Trends. June 2006. Published Online by Security-risks.com.
22. South Asia Security Trends. October 2006. Published Online by Security-risks.com.
23. Based on reports in http://www.oxfam.org/en/programs/campaigns/controlarms/.
24. Based on reports in www.zenit.org.
25. South Asia Security Trends. December 2006. Published Online by Security-risks.com.
26. South Asia Security Trends. July 2006. Published Online by Security-risks.com.
27. Based on inputs at http://www.icc-ccs.org.uk/main/publication.php.
28. Based on inputs from www.defencetalk.com
29. Extracted from www.dhs.gov.